AF477875

St Antony's Series

General Editor: **Jan Zielonka** (2004–), Fellow of St Antony's College, Oxford

Recent titles include:

Stefania Bernini
FAMILY LIFE AND INDIVIDUAL WELFARE IN POST-WAR EUROPE
Britain and Italy Compared

Tomila V. Lankina, Anneke Hudalla and Helmut Wollman
LOCAL GOVERNANCE IN CENTRAL AND EASTERN EUROPE
Comparing Performance in the Czech Republic, Hungary, Poland and Russia

Cathy Gormley-Heenan
POLITICAL LEADERSHIP AND THE NORTHERN IRELAND PEACE PROCESS
Role, Capacity and Effect

Lori Plotkin Boghardt
KUWAIT AMID WAR, PEACE AND REVOLUTION

Paul Chaisty
LEGISLATIVE POLITICS AND ECONOMIC POWER IN RUSSIA

Valpy FitzGerald, Frances Stewart and Rajesh Venugopal (*editors*)
GLOBALIZATION, VIOLENT CONFLICT AND SELF-DETERMINATION

Miwao Matsumoto
TECHNOLOGY GATEKEEPERS FOR WAR AND PEACE
The British Ship Revolution and Japanese Industrialization

Håkan Thörn
ANTI-APARTHEID AND THE EMERGENCE OF A GLOBAL CIVIL SOCIETY

Lotte Hughes
MOVING THE MAASAI
A Colonial Misadventure

Fiona Macaulay
GENDER POLITICS IN BRAZIL AND CHILE
The Role of Parties in National and Local Policymaking

Stephen Whitefield (*editor*)
POLITICAL CULTURE AND POST-COMMUNISM

José Esteban Castro
WATER, POWER AND CITIZENSHIP
Social Struggle in the Basin of Mexico

Valpy FitzGerald and Rosemary Thorp (*editors*)
ECONOMIC DOCTRINES IN LATIN AMERICA
Origins, Embedding and Evolution

Victoria D. Alexander and Marilyn Rueschemeyer
ART AND THE STATE
The Visual Arts in Comparative Perspective

Ailish Johnson
EUROPEAN WELFARE STATES AND SUPRANATIONAL GOVERNANCE OF
SOCIAL POLICY

Archie Brown (*editor*)
THE DEMISE OF MARXISM-LENINISM IN RUSSIA

Thomas Boghardt
SPIES OF THE KAISER
German Covert Operations in Great Britain during the First World War Era

Ulf Schmidt
JUSTICE AT NUREMBERG
Leo Alexander and the Nazi Doctors' Trial

Steve Tsang (*editor*)
PEACE AND SECURITY ACROSS THE TAIWAN STRAIT

C. W. Braddick
JAPAN AND THE SINO-SOVIET ALLIANCE, 1950–1964
In the Shadow of the Monolith

Isao Miyaoka
LEGITIMACY IN INTERNATIONAL SOCIETY
Japan's Reaction to Global Wildlife Preservation

Neil J. Melvin
SOVIET POWER AND THE COUNTRYSIDE
Policy Innovation and Institutional Decay

Julie M. Newton
RUSSIA, FRANCE AND THE IDEA OF EUROPE

Juhana Aunesluoma
BRITAIN, SWEDEN AND THE COLD WAR, 1945–54
Understanding Neutrality

St Antony's Series
Series Standing Order ISBN 0–333–71109–2
(*outside North America only*)

You can receive future titles in this series as they are published by placing a standing order. Please contact your bookseller or, in case of difficulty, write to us at the address below with your name and address, the title of the series and the ISBN quoted above.

Customer Services Department, Macmillan Distribution Ltd, Houndmills, Basingstoke, Hampshire RG21 6XS, England

---

Family Life and Individual Welfare in Post-war Europe

Britain and Italy Compared

Stefania Bernini
European University Institute

In Association with
St Antony's College

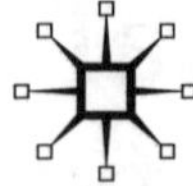

First published 2007 by
PALGRAVE MACMILLAN
Houndmills, Basingstoke, Hampshire RG21 6XS and
175 Fifth Avenue, New York, N.Y. 10010
Companies and representatives throughout the world

PALGRAVE MACMILLAN is the global academic imprint of the Palgrave Macmillan division of St. Martin's Press, LLC and of Palgrave Macmillan Ltd. Macmillan® is a registered trademark in the United States, United Kingdom and other countries. Palgrave is a registered trademark in the European Union and other countries.

ISBN-13: 978–1–4039–8795–2 hardback
ISBN-10: 1–4039–8795–5 hardback

This book is printed on paper suitable for recycling and made from fully managed and sustained forest sources. Logging, pulping and manufacturing processes are expected to conform to the environmental regulations of the country of origin.

A catalogue record for this book is available from the British Library.

Library of Congress Cataloging-in-Publication Data
Bernini, Stefania.
    Family life and individual welfare in postwar Europe:Britain and
    Italy compared/Stefania Bernini.
        p.   cm.
    Includes bibliographical references.
    ISBN 1–4039–8795–5 (alk. paper)
    1. Family—Great Britain—History—20th century.   2. Family policy—
    Great Britain—20th century.   3. Family—Italy—History—20th century.
    4. Family policy—Italy—History—20th century.   I. Title.
    HQ613.B47 2007
    306.85094—dc22   2007023077

10   9   8   7   6   5   4   3   2   1
16   15   14   13   12   11   10   09   08   07

Printed and bound in Great Britain by
Antony Rowe Ltd, Chippenham and Eastbourne

Contents

Acknowledgements

This book began with a course on the family in modern Europe taken many years ago at the University of Florence and developed through as a Ph.D. at Royal Holloway College.

Throughout the years, the ideas explored in the book have been reconsidered and refined following many valuable discussions with colleagues and friends, not all of whom I will be able to mention here. John Turner and Paul Ginsborg, who supervised my work in London and Florence, have provided criticisms, advice, and encouragement throughout the years. Martin Francis, Janet Finch and Jonathan Morris offered insightful critiques of my thesis, some of which I hope I was able to address in this book. Jürgen Kocka, Christina Hardyment, and Richenda Gambles all helped this book in different ways. Nora Fisher and Steven Mark edited the manuscript and provided much appreciated comments.

The research behind this book was possible thanks to the support of a number of institutions: particularly the Art and Humanities Research Board, Royal Holloway College, the British Council, the Institute of Historical Research and the British Federation of Women Graduate. A Monte dei Paschi Visiting Fellowship in Italian Studies allowed me to take this project to St Antony's European Studies Centre. That the book came to light owes much to the support (and welcomed criticisms) of Jan Zielonka, editor of St Antony's Palgrave series.

Families and friends have helped me through the years with their love and patience. Thanks in particular to Ombretta Ingrascì, Pietro Di Paola, Marta Bonsanti, Claudia Baldoli, and all the London companions for the many hours spent together; to Ruth, Paul, Anya and Nick for making me part of their family; to Francesca, Laura, Serena, Barbara and Marcella for proving over the years that distance is a relative concept.

Thanks to Daniela and Giorgio, for their love and trust; and to Dan, for sharing this project through the years and making it his own. The book is dedicated to Giovanna and Bruna, both of whom, I hope, would have enjoyed seeing it born.

Abbreviations

AAI	Amministrazione Aiuti Internazionali (International Aid Administration)
APC	Archivio Partito Comunista (Italian Communist Party Archive)
CCO	Conservative Central Office
CEA	Church of England Archive
CPA	Conservative Party Archive
CPC	Conservative Political Centre
CRD	Conservative Research Department
CUCO	Conservative and Unionist Central Office
DC	Democrazia Cristiana (Christian Democrat Party)
ECA	Enti Comunali di Assistenza (Council Bodies of Assistance)
FSU	Family Service Unit
INAM	Istituto Nazionale per l'Assistenza di Malattia ai Lavoratori (National Health Insurance Institution)
MH	Ministry of Health
MI	Ministero dell' Interno (Ministry of the Interior)
MWC	Moral Welfare Council (Church of England)
NHS	National Health Service
NSPCC	National Society for the Prevention of Cruelty to Children
ONARMO	Opera Nazionale per l'Assistenza Religiosa e Morale degli Operai (National Organisation for the Religious and Moral Assistance of the Workers)
ONMI	Opera Nazionale Maternità e Infanzia (National Organisation for Maternity and Child Welfare)
PCI	Partito Comunista Italiano (Italian Communist Party)
PRO	Public Record Office
UNRRA	United Nations Relief and Rehabilitation Administration
WNAC	Women's National Advisory Committee (Conservative Party)

Introduction

The regulation of family life and its implications at the social level are high on the political agenda of most European countries. Public order, social cohesion, even the ability of contemporary multicultural societies to integrate their citizens in a cohesive body have been variously linked to the ability of the family to perform its role. Most of the references to the role of the family in the political arena may have a tinge of populism, but this does not reduce the 'appeal' of the family in political debates. At the same time, a growing diversification of domestic arrangements has rendered increasingly problematic to talk about the family as a recognisable (and even less uniform) entity.

A significant part of current discussions focuses on the ability/inability of contemporary families to provide for their members' welfare. Much emphasis is put on the family as the primary locus of individual responsibility, particularly in relation to processes of welfare retrenchment and a rolling back of the state.[1] At the same time, there is much discussion concerning the consequences of the family's alleged 'crisis', whose manifestations would include wide divorce rates, lowering fertility rates (especially in Italy), growing rates of births outside marriage. Many current arguments 'in defence' of the family seem to imply that each of these symptoms is the result of lowering commitment to the responsibilities of family life.

Most of these discussions originate from a particular understanding of the family, its social role and the relationships between its members and by an enduring fear that changes in individual desires and expectations will result in undesirable social costs. Both recent political discourses and scholarly works have emphasised the transformation undergone by the family as an institution and have suggested various interpretations of their consequences. While some authors have given a relatively positive interpretation of changes taking place in family life, particularly linking them with growing individual freedom, others (arguably in greater number) have read changes as inevitably leading to problems and decay.[2] In Göran Therborn's words, 'the "Western family" is widely seen by writers with loud voices and strong opinions to be in "great disorder"'.[3] This book originates from a desire to understand how changes in family life have been perceived, conceptualised and discussed in two different political, social and cultural contexts throughout the post-war period.

A recurrent theme in studies of the family is the attempt to pin down 'moments of change' both in demographic and cultural terms. A vast consensus exists among historians of the modern and contemporary period that 'many of the most dramatic family changes … actually occurred after the early 1960s'.[4] Most of the original research upon which this book is based concentrates on the period between 1945 and the mid-1960s. However, the analysis of the immediate post-war period is set in a wider chronological context and an attempt is made throughout the book link with the narrative from the past to a number of contemporary developments. My aim in doing so is to trace the origin and consolidation of particular understandings of the family that have informed the regulation of individual behaviour throughout the post-war period.

The 1950s are often described as a period when traditional roles within the family were still largely unchallenged and the domestic realm was still unshaken.[5] Nonetheless, 1950s observers commented (and lamented) the transformation of the contemporary family with no less concern, urgency and sense of finality than later commentators. Then as now, discussions about the family went beyond patterns of cohabitation, marriage or reproduction. In discussing the destiny of the family, post-war observers discussed expectations and anxieties wider than the dynamics that were taking place within the household and yet inextricably linked to them.

Comparing the experiences of Italy and Britain demonstrates that the definition of what constitutes a family is both the result of social and cultural transformations and the outcome of specific political processes. It is the interplay of contingent political factors and long-term cultural legacies that determine different understandings of the nature and role of the family and that explain the origin of different approaches to the regulation of family life, the promotion of individual welfare and the legitimate spheres of state intervention.

The regulation of family life is considered within the book as a means of pursuing actual political interests as well as of fostering particular values or visions of society. In the post-war period as now, the family acted as a catalyst for a range of anxieties and was used as a privileged instrument of political propaganda. Real and perceived changes in the relationships taking place within the home attracted a disproportionate level of interest not because they threatened the existing social order, but because they provided a powerful means of expressing concerns related to changes in individual aspirations and lifestyles and the most effective way of capturing the interest of the public.

Family and social policy: The state of the debate

While references to the state of 'the family' in contemporary societies fill political rhetoric and public debates, what the term actually describes is at once ambiguous and taken for granted.[6] I come back to this discussion in Chapter 1, where I also explain how the concept of 'the family' is used within this book. Before doing so, however, it is useful to review briefly some of the current discussions dealing with family and social policy in contemporary Europe and to explain the contribution that this book brings to these ongoing debates.

Although a number of works exist that deal with different aspects of the history of the family in modern Europe, rather few of these have concentrated on the specific impact of state intervention and even fewer have done so combining a historical and a comparative perspective.[7] Moreover, the relationship between state and family has been largely neglected in 'classic' studies of the welfare state, and even the growing number of works dedicated to the relationship between gender and social policy has often overlooked the family as a concept.[8] Similarly, the influence exercised by the state upon the family through social policy has entered only sporadically into studies dealing with the 'theory of the family' and its relationship with the political sphere.[9]

This patchy situation is repeated in the case of studies specifically dedicated to the Italian and British cases. Although important works have centred on the development of family policy in Italy up to and including the fascist period, few authors have looked at the relation-ship between social policy and the family after 1945, especially from a historical perspective.[10]

Greater attention has received the history of the family in post-war Britain, with particular attention given in recent historical works to cultural transformations and their impact on the construction of the domestic sphere.[11] Moreover, historians of sexuality have drawn an increasingly accurate map of the complex transformations of intimacy in the modern period. However, most studies of sexuality have made little reference to the family as a concept, perhaps as an understandable reaction against a concept for long time synonymous with normalised (hetero)sexuality.[12]

To sum up, while a growing literature exists on particular aspects of the history of the family, with increasing attention given to a cultural historical perspective, and a consolidated tradition has explored the political history of social policy, these two levels have rarely met. This lack of dialogue between those who have concentrated on the changes taking place within the family and those who have concentrated on the transformation of the role of the state may contribute to explain the endurance of polarised interpretations of the position of the family in contemporary societies.[13]

This book is an attempt to consider some of these issues from a different perspective, looking at how the family has been understood and regulated in relation to care in two different historical contexts. The aim is to put forward a comprehensive interpretation of the ways in which normative definitions of the family came to be constructed throughout the post-war period (particularly through political, medical, religious and sociological discourses) and to confront these sets of ideas with the treatment applied to specific situations where the family appeared to be failing in its prescribed role.

Scope of the book

My main interest is the construction of the family in post-war public discourse and the interaction between dominant ideas about the nature and position of the family and state intervention in family life. Although differences in welfare policy in Italy and Britain are discussed at various points within the book, the book itself is not about models of welfare intervention or different models of family life.

Rather, the book is about the attempt made in different political contexts to regulate individual behaviour according to specific notions of family life. The main questions I seek to answer are: which were the main actors responsible for the creation of dominant definitions of what is a family in the post-war period? Which were the main interests according to which particular definitions of family life were upheld and challenged over time? How and why such actors and interests diverged in the Italian and British contexts?

On one side, I try to show how changes in individual behaviour and expectations in relation to family life reflected cultural transformations and influenced political choices. On the other, I suggest that political interests influenced the way in which family policy was conceived as a means of social intervention. In its essence, I seek to demonstrate that the treatment of the family should not be seen as a one-way route dominated by the state, but rather as a process of constant mediation taking place between contrasting interests at state, social and individual level. The outcome of such process was strongly influenced by specific national conditions.

In order to illustrate the different characteristics assumed by the treatment of the family in Italy and Britain, I seek to combine two levels of analysis. The first level concerns the construction of the family as an ideal in different (and sometimes conflicting) discourses, with particular attention given to the position expressed by political, religious and medical authorities. The second level of analysis looks at a specific case of policy intervention, namely the treatment of 'children in need'. I use the case of 'children in need' to show how social intervention represented not only a means of improving individual circumstances, but also a way of promoting particular types of family relationships, considered better able to cope with adverse circumstances better. The comparison between Britain and Italy highlights the cultural, political and social factors that contributed to shape attitudes towards the family and helps to review some lasting assumptions concerning the supposedly peculiarly 'familistic' nature of the Italian political culture.

Approaches to family and social policy differed in post-war Italy and Britain. This was the result of a number of different factors, including institutional circumstances, economic conditions, political dynamics and cultural legacies.[14] I will discuss the different weight exercised by these different elements throughout the book. Here, my only aim is to sketch some of the most apparent differences that characterise the approaches to social policy and the family in Britain and Italy at the aftermath of the war.

The post-war British welfare state established a system of benefits and services that seemed to provide the state with the means of integrating and if necessary even substituting the family in some of its core functions in relation to care. The modesty of Italian post-war welfare policies seemed to leave to the Catholic Church an unchallenged authority over the family and to the family an overwhelming responsibility for individual care.

Among the possible explanations that have been suggested in order to account for such differences in approaches an enduring assumption is that the family played a more important role in Italy than in Britain.

This is not without reason. Throughout the post-war period, Italians (although not Italians alone) have shown a greater tendency than their British counterparts to live with or in the proximity of their close relatives and to maintain intense daily exchanges with family members and close friends.[15] As it has been noted, however, the meaning of such enduring closeness in terms of individual investment in family life is in many respects ambiguous. As Paul Ginsborg has pointed out, the transformation undergone by the Italian family in the post-war period is significant from whichever point of view we decide to look at it. In the space of a few decades, Italy went from having one of the highest birth rates in Europe to one of the lowest birth rate in the world. Although the causes of such sharp decline were complex and multifaceted, the apparent lack of enthusiasm of Italian couples towards procreation must inevitably question the desire to invest in the family and perhaps the status of the family as such. The apparent closeness and reciprocal support suggested by the relative proximity in which different generations still tend to live in Italy cannot be read only as a sign of family solidarity. Financial pressures and lack of social policies providing alternative to the family as main provider of individual support need to be taken into account, together with the potential costs that such protracted dependence on the family may have at individual level.[16]

Equally ambiguous appears the relationship between the Italian family and other social institutions, a relationship that has been often portrayed in sharply contrasting terms.

On one hand, the Italian family has often been seen as a powerful institution, able to provide support to individuals in the face of a poor system of public welfare. (The definition of the Italian welfare state as *familista* has stressed the extent to which welfare policies have relied on the family as a provider of individual care and support.) On the other hand, the apparently exclusivist nature of Italian family life has been read as a factor antagonistic to the flourishing of civic engagement and to the emergence in Italy of a rich civil society. Of particular interest for this book are the analyses (mostly by English and American commentators) that have sought to describe the different role played by the family in the Italian and British political development. In many respects, these arguments represent the starting point of my research. Throughout the book, I try to discuss some of their origins and to reassess whether they can tell us something about the make up of the Italian and British society and more generally about the way in which the family has been seen and regulated throughout the post-war period.

Three main ideas are explored within the book. First, that both in Italy and in Britain the family was conceptualised and treated as mainly responsible for individual and collective welfare and as an instrument of political penetration. Second, that in neither country–state intervention was aimed at reducing the functions of the family; rather it aspired to increase the means of shaping family life in a direction considered suitable to the interest of society as a whole. Third, that both the conceptualisation and the treatment of the family varied between Italy and Britain, as a result of the two countries' social, cultural and political specificities.

Comparing Britain and Italy

Throughout the post-war period both Britain and Italy had to confront social, demographic and economic developments that modified individual needs and expectations and challenged the ability of existing social services to keep apace with fast-changing demands. Changes in households' composition, diminishing birth rates, population ageing and women's growing participation to the labour market transformed the scenario upon which post-war social policies were built and required the establishment of new paradigms for future reforms. So did changes in attitudes towards marriage, divorce and cohabitation.

However, Britain and Italy differed in the pace at which transformations took place and in the way in which social services and the state reacted to them. Focusing on the post-war years reveals differences in scope, sequence and logic in British and Italian approaches to social policy and the family, but also similarities in the way in which family life in post-war society was discussed and regulated.

Differences in family politics were the result of both long-standing cultural factors and specific post-war political and social conditions. It is useful to sketch here some of the factors at work in Britain and Italy since 1945.

In Britain, the Labour landslide in 1945 initiated a period of extensive social intervention and economic transformations. The widespread reforms introduced by the Labour government elected in 1945 were widely presented as a consequence of the experience of the war and followed, at least in part, plans developed by the wartime coalition government.[17] Nationalisation programs and the creation of the welfare state marked an unprecedented role of the state in economic management that could only be partially reverted to by Conservatives after their return to power in 1951. The 1950s represented a decade of rising living standards and increasing consumerism, consistently promoted by Conservatives.[18] During the same years the Labour Party suffered three electoral defeats and had to confront a growing Conservative appeal among the working classes and growing internal divisions before returning to government in 1964.

In Italy, the end of the war brought about a rapid but intense phase of political and institutional transition. The fall of the fascist regime in 1943 was followed by 2 years of virulent armed confrontation between nazi–fascist militias and anti-fascist organisations. The years between 1945 and 1948 were characterised by far reaching institutional transformations, culminating in the abolition of the monarchy and the creation of a new republican state. The same years saw rising expectations of social transformations, encouraged by the temporary alliance established between Christian Democrats, Communists and Socialists, following their common participation to the resistance struggle. However, the political and social climate changed appreciably after the electoral victory obtained by the Democrazia Cristiana (Christian Democrat Party) (DC) in the elections of the first-republican legislature held in April 1948. This marked the beginning of a long period of continuous Christian Democratic power, but also of uncertain political coalitions, frequent cabinet reshuffles and constant searches for more stable alliances. The political system created after the war aimed to guarantee plurality rather than effective government, by distributing power among a number of reciprocally controlling institutions. In the political polarisation that followed the war, it encouraged coalitions held together by a determination to keep the Communist Party in opposition rather than by common programs. This combined with the predominance gained within the DC by the socially conservative and economically liberal faction in frustrating expectations for extensive social reforms. The development of the Cold War strengthened the political polarisation between Catholics and Communists, and enhanced the importance for political parties for acquiring a strong social presence. The family became a central theme upon which they grounded their respective commitments to the country's values.

Equally relevant are some of the differences that characterised British and Italian social development. By 1945, Britain was a fully industrialised country, with the majority of its population employed in industry and a marginal agricultural sector. The social and political consequences of the industrial revolution had long been confronted and a consolidated tendency to low social conflict achieved. At the same time, the social costs of the mass unemployment of the 1920s and 1930s constituted a powerful reminder of the possible consequences of an unregulated economy, and contributed to make measures intended to sustain economic growth acceptable among traditional advocates of economic liberalism, including businessmen and 'progressive Conservatives'.[19]

As for Italy, in 1945 agriculture was still the largest economic sector and informed the social structure of most of the country, with the only noticeable exception of the main industrial cities of the North. The fast economic growth that took place from the late 1950s (in contrast with the economic slow down in Britain during the same years) promoted a process of urbanisation completed in Britain by the end of the 19th century and radically changed the country's social and demographic structure.[20] However, it did little to reduce the country's social inequalities, and particularly the distance that separated living conditions in the north and south of the country.[21]

Finally, something needs to be said about social policy in the two countries, in order to set the context in which debates concerning the role of the family took place.

Post-war British and Italian social policy differed in nature, style of implementation and scope. The British welfare state represented a comprehensive system of intervention, which aimed at providing universal protection in all situations of need, at least in the case of employed men. Social policy in Italy remained based on a corporatist system characterised by sharp contrasts in the protection available to different professional groups and by extremely modest social services delivered by the state.

Equally different was the implementation of reforms in the two countries. The British welfare system was built upon the detailed blueprint elaborated by William Beveridge in 1942. His *Report on Social Insurance and Allied Social Services* envisaged a package of reforms that were implemented in a relatively short period of time between 1944 and 1948. In Italy, an equivalent of the 'Beveridge's Plan' never emerged and fragmentary reforms spread over a long period of time without any wide-ranging project behind them.

Finally, policies differed sharply in their purpose in relation to the family. In Britain, reforms were guided by a largely accepted view of social policy as a means of fostering certain kind of social relationships in general and of family life in particular. In Italy, on the other hand, social policy was never conceived in such a coherent way because the very notion of state intervention in social life, and even more so in family life, remained a highly divisive issue.

British Post-War Governments implemented measures of social policy based on a coherent model of family life, which envisaged the male as the main, if not the only, breadwinner. Albeit modified in important respects, the defence of the main (male) wage earner model has remained a recognisable feature of the British welfare state since. Intervention in Italy reflected a much less clearly defined view of social relations. While strongly biased towards the protection of the male head of the family in areas such as employment legislation and pensions, Italian social policy never included measures explicitly supporting 'his' family in case of need. Rather, the family was implicitly treated as the main provider of individual support and collective welfare.[22]

Structure of the book

Chapter 1 describes the origin of the book by going back to some influential interpretations of the role played by the family in British and Italian political development and discusses how the terms 'state' and 'family' are employed in this book. Chapter 2 and 3 trace the main characters of the ideology of the family prevalent in Italy and Britain during the post-war period through the analysis of dominant political, religious and medico-scientific discourses. Chapter 4 and 5 look at provisions for children in need in the two countries. Chapter 4 looks at approaches towards 'children in care' in the two countries and the relationship established between the family and the state under such circumstances. Chapter 5 concentrates on the treatment of illegitimacy and maladjustment as 'pathologies of the family' and explores differences in attitudes towards adoption and fostering as means of recreating the family. In both chapters, the attention is on what children's treatment has to say concerning the family, rather than on the actual experiences of children themselves.

1
Family, State and Democratic Development in Britain and Italy

From fiction to scholarly works, the Italian family has exercised a powerful fascination over foreign observers. Popular representations have emphasised the ideal image of large rural families, characterised by strong ties of support between different generations, despite the fact that such a family hardly represents the situation of the majority of households in today's Italy. Academic analyses have looked at the interaction between the family and other social institutions. Attention has been drawn alternatively to the Italian family's authoritarian nature, resilience in adverse political circumstances and slow pace of transformation. Many of these descriptions have established implicit parallels with the position of the family in different social and cultural contexts. This chapter looks at how the role of the family has been analysed in relation to democratic development in Italy (drawing comparisons with approaches towards Britain) before moving on to introduce how the family is treated in the book.

The civic culture approach

Since the 1950s, Italy has represented a popular subject of study among (predominantly Anglo-American) scholars. This was at least in part because of the supposed 'peculiarities' of the Italian path to democratic development, which, in the words of the American scholar Joseph La Palombara, forced scholars 'to revise or expand' theories of the democratic state.[1]

Of particular interest for my argument are analyses of Italian political and civic culture that made explicit reference to the influence exercised by the family on the country's democratic development.

In a study published in 1973, the American political scientist Robert Putnam compared Britain's 'celebrated tradition of consensual evolution' with the Italian political history, characterised by 'disunity, instability, and authoritarian adventures'. Among the most relevant of the differences pointed out by Putman was the fact that the Italian government lacked the 'justified reputation for effectiveness, stability, and responsiveness' that characterised the British one.[2] At the same time, Italian politicians showed higher degrees of ideology, partisanship and hostility for the opponents than their English colleagues. The explanation, according to Putnam, laid partly in the greater ideological distance that separated Italian political parties, and partly in the two countries' different patterns of historical development. Politicians reflected the 'pervasive social distrust among Italians generally' and their 'greater sensitivity' to social conflict, encouraged by the fact that the Italian 'socio-economic pie' was 'smaller and less well distributed than in Britain'.[3]

Putnam's interpretation followed the analytical approach set forth in 1963 by Almond and Verba in *The Civic Culture*. In its classical formulation, the civic culture thesis defined democracy as a participatory political system, where (among other things) ordinary men acted as influential citizens. In other words, democracy required a consistent political culture, based upon citizens' participation in civic affairs, high level of information and widespread sense of civic responsibility. A civic culture was a 'pluralistic culture based on communication and persuasion', which integrated 'consensus and diversity' and therefore 'permitted change' while moderating it.[4]

Stable democratic processes, which allowed change while preventing disintegration and polarisation, were the result of the successful encounter of 'modernising tendencies' and 'traditional powers'. Such processes could be observed at their best in Britain and in the United States. In Italy, on the other side, the contrast between tradition and change had been too strong for a shared culture of political accommodation to emerge, determining the survival of a 'pre-modern social and political structure'. Almond and Verba found that the relationship between the family and the larger polity had played an important part in this process.[5]

Setting the paradigm: Families, morality and backwardness in Montegrano

According to Almond and Verba, the Italian family had played a role antagonistic to 'the bureaucratic authoritarian organs of the State' and the 'civic-political organs of party, interest group and local community'.[6]

Far from preparing individuals to enter civil society, the family had remained their unique sphere of interest and identification, preventing them from trusting and engaging with other areas of social life. Moreover, the family had acted as an instrument of political partisanship, contributing to the reinforcement of existing political and ideological divisions.

This reading of the Italian family as a powerful force antagonistic to political modernisation relied heavily upon the familistic paradigm, set in the mid-1950s by the American anthropologist E. C. Banfield. In *The Moral Basis of a Backward Society*, published in the United States in 1956 and in Italy in 1961, Banfield presented the outcome of observations conducted in the town of Chiaromonte (renamed Montegrano in the study), in the Southern province of Potenza. Banfield's own standpoint was declared from the outset.

The book opened with a quotation from de Tocqueville's *Democracy in America*: 'in democratic countries the science of association is the mother of science; the progress of all the rest depends upon the progress it has made'.[7] In sharp contrast with de Tocqueville's precept, Banfield found in Chiaromonte a society dominated by an 'amoral familistic ethos', summed up in a single principle:

> Maximise the material, short run advantage of the nuclear family; assume that all others will do likewise.[8]

In essence, a society of 'amoral familists' was one where 'no one will further the interest of the group or community except if it has private advantage to do so'. As a consequence, Montegrano lacked entirely the 'civic improvement associations, organized charities and leading citizens who take initiative in public service' which could be found in small American towns.[9] By contrast, the only two organisations operating in Montegrano were the church and the state, both of which existed because they were 'provided from the outside', but neither of which could prosper.[10] The inability to associate relegated Montegrano to the backward majority of the world, far away from the thriving American community life.

The definition of amoral familism introduced by Banfield constituted a modified version of a concept used by contemporary American sociologists to describe middle classes' 'investment in the familial system of the society'. In this context, 'familism' defined a lifestyle choice involving 'marriage at young ages, a short childless time-span after marriage', and a preference for large families and suburban living.[11] Moving to the suburbs represented a choice alternative to 'upward vertical mobility' and 'consumership', expressing the desire to live in a location suitable to family life. People who had moved to the suburbs stressed a 'quest-for-community' at the basis of their decision, including 'more friendly neighbours, greater community participation, and a sense of belonging'. The new ideal included the possibility of living among 'people like themselves' with regard to 'age, marital, family, financial, educational, occupational or ethnic status'. The sociologist Wendell Bell did not find anything amoral in this kind of familism, which on the contrary appeared to him to support community growth and to reflect America's democratic values.[12] Similarly free of moral connotations was Robert Winch's description of 'extended familism'. The notion was forged as a critique of the identification of the American family as a 'typically isolated nuclear family', and described a way of life in which individual households lived in the same local communities with their extended and supportive kinships.[13]

Despite the methodological problems of Banfield's study and the criticisms advanced by many against its determinism, the idea that a perverse form of 'familism' represented a particular feature of Italian culture has survived and informed a number of interpretations of Italian political development since.[14]

Among the most enduring aspects of Banfield's interpretation was the idea that traditional attitudes and acceptance of patriarchal norms had transformed the Italian family into an instrument of political fragment-ation. Such an interpretation reappeared in a number of later studies and informed, albeit variously modified, numerous theories of Italian political development.

In 1964, the American political scientist Joseph La Palombara drew extensively upon Banfield's study in support of his own thesis, namely that the primary socialisation imparted by family and school failed to 'provide tens of thousands of Italians with a coherent view of the *national* political system and with a sense of efficacious involvement concerning it'.[15] In rural Italy, not only in the south, but also in 'the poorer and more isolated regions' of the centre and north of the country, 'the most important claims to the loyalty and allegiance of the individual' remained 'the family, the kinship group, the neighbourhood, and the village'.[16] Such an exclusivist involvement prevented political organisa-tion and rendered the whole of the country vulnerable to widespread corruption and prone to authoritarian temptations.

La Palombara added to Banfield's analysis his own interpretations of the nature of family relations in Italy: rural and urban families alike were 'organized around the central idea of unquestioning respect for and obedience to parents and grandparents', a feature that determined their essential authoritarianism.[17] La Palombara observed that the extensive power exercised by mothers within the household (towards the education of children, their introduction to their 'first chores' and their supervision in their 'religious needs and attendance') rendered inaccurate definitions of the Italian family as 'essentially patriarchal'.[18] Both parents, it seemed, contributed to the creation of an authoritarian domestic environment that had pernicious consequences in terms of children upbringing. Growing up in a home where they were hardly ever allowed to participate in decisions concerning themselves, children tended to express their complaints 'in the form of emotional protest' or 'violent behaviour', rarely experiencing any 'training in the kind of pragmatic give and take that a democratic polity require[d]'. In other words, the political socialisation they received was not to 'a sense of effectual involvement' in democratic politics, but on the contrary, to an idea of power exercised 'physically and readily in order to exact obedience'.[19]

While Banfield's analysis had focused specifically (though not accurately) on the Italian south, interpretations based on his work were readily applied to the role of the family in the whole of Italy and became the basis for cross-national analyses. La Palombara discussed the question of the inadequate political socialisation provided by the Italian family again in his contribution to Pye and Verba's *Political Culture and Political Development*, published in 1965. La Palombara's analysis was in sharp contrast with the analysis of the role of the English family developed by Richard Rose.

Rose described the positive influence that the structure and culture of the family had had on England's civic and political development, arguing that the 'political influence of the family' in the country had been 'a stabilizing one'. Early industrialisation had consolidated the traditions 'of an urban, industrial society'; parents taught their children 'to take industrial society for granted' and helped them to forge 'strong face to face ties' in the communities to which they belonged.[20] Rose saw the family both as a product of social and economic conditions and as an agent of their transformation. In the English case, the strength and cohesion of the family had not prevented change, but had supported a peaceful transformation towards a democratic, stable and cohesive society, the ultimate outcome of which had been the post-war welfare state. The belief in 'mutual aid', which was necessary to support welfare values, originated in 'strong' families and was transmitted through the political education that took place within the household.[21]

A resilient concept

The question of the role played by a pervasive familistic culture in Italian political life is still debated among historians, anthropologists and sociologists. In 1971, Luca Pinna proposed an analysis of Sardinian social structure according to which the family represented the 'only social structure within which people [satisfied] all their social and existential expectations'. Although rejecting Banfield's definition of familism as an amoral ethos, Pinna found a direct relationship between the social role of kinship and phenomena such as patronage.[22] In the mid-1980s, Carlo Tullio-Altan re-launched the idea that Italian's excessive familism impinged negatively upon the country's political and economic development and Giorgio Campanini called familism the excessive privatism that threatened the family in contemporary industrial societies.[23] The relationship between 'collective action' and 'family and familism' has been proposed by Paul Ginsborg as one of the 'central themes in the history of Italian popular classes since 1943'.[24]

Equally strong have been the reactions against the use of the familist paradigm as a generalising representation of the Italian south.[25]

Despite the differences that characterise them, many of these discussions have taken the idea of familism out of the comparative framework where it originated and have used it as a concept specific to the Italian situation.[26] However, both Banfield's original definition and its successive use by other authors depended heavily on an implicit comparison with a positive model of interaction between individuals, families and other social institutions. The comparison with Britain and the United States in particular were essential to define the familistic paradigm as a key factor in Italian political development.[27]

From a different methodological perspective, the idea of familism has been usefully employed to describe a (negative) quality of residual welfare systems characterised by a large reliance on the family as a provider of care. In this context, the idea of familism describes a political 'strategy' whereby the rhetoric of investment in family values is used to justify inadequate levels of public intervention.[28] The comparative context is equally important here, since the relationship between state, family and individual is used to identify a specific 'type' of welfare regime found prevalently in southern Europe. Such an interpretation does not see familism as an unchanging ethical character associated to particular cultures. It nonetheless presupposes that the investment in the family is stronger in certain cultures than in others, often without providing an explanation of where such a different investment originates.

In all these different treatments, the concept of familism seems to run the risk of over-determinism, and therefore of being of little analytical use. Nonetheless, the idea has the merit of bringing the family (and its treatment) to the fore of political analysis as an important variable in processes of political and social change.

The issue is central to the questions this book tries to answer: how, why and to what extent has the investment in the family differed in Britain and Italy throughout the post-war period? Are there identifiable differences in the way in which family relationships were conceptualised? And, finally, were differences in family politics the result of cultural factors, socio-economic structures or political conditions?

States and families

States

Much of the discussion presented in this book makes reference to the state in institutional and administrative terms and to the welfare state as one of the most characteristic signs of the expansion of state activity during the twentieth century.[29] This is to say that I look at the welfare state as an entity with the power to provide services and organise institutions and policies within a definite territory. I also treat it as an event that has irrevocably modified the relationship between state and citizenry, creating a new crucial terrain for the formation of individual rights.

However, my discussion of the role of the state vis-à-vis the family is also influenced by the model of 'policing' set out by Jacques Donzelot and Christopher Lasch. Here the state is seen as acting not just as an organisation holding power and the means of coercion, but as a system of regulations, which apply to 'everything that relates to the present condition of society', with the end of ensuring 'the good fortune' of the state itself.[30] Greater attention is given in this perspective to 'controlling' powers supposedly associated with the growing presence of the state in individuals' lives. The tangible face of such powers being the work of those public officers 'who claim to come with the best intentions but come armed, all the same, with statutory powers and administrative instruments' and 'who claim to know best how to manage our private concerns'.[31] The model set by Donzelot and Lasch has important implications for the understanding of the regulation of the family in welfare societies. In particular, it allows questioning of the knowledge upon which social policy rested and how it contributed to the construction of dominant understandings of family relationships, gender roles and individual conduct. In other words, looking at the relationship between the state and the family in terms of power/knowledge provides a useful tool to question the 'naturalness' of specific forms of family life and the assumptions attached to them.

These two ways of looking at the state (in administrative terms and as policing) have their own different implications, weaknesses and strengths. However, they have been rarely used together, perhaps as a result of an enduring difficulty to communicate across different disciplines.

This work moves from the idea that understandings of the state in administrative/institutional terms are not antithetical to understanding it as policing, and that using a notion of power as diffused at a multiplicity of levels should not lead to ignoring actual political interests or specific dynamics at work in particular historical contexts. This is perhaps most clearly visible in a comparative perspective, since it is when we look at processes taking place in different political and social contexts that it becomes possible to connect the logic presiding over the working of actual political institutions in the creation and reproduction of knowledge. The analysis of Italy and Britain is set to point out the intersections that exist between specific political interests, the shape of welfare intervention and the creation of particular understandings of the family and its role. Looking at the family as a changing historical experience rather than as an abstract concept helps to uncover the distance between notions and representations of family life as an ideal (and a norm) and the almost endless variety of family life as an actual experience.

Families

Defining 'the family' is far from easy and attempts to do so requires some justification. In choosing this terminology, I take on board Janet Finch's warning that 'the family' constitutes an ideologically charged and analytically vague concept, which nonetheless is able to make sense of the social and political discourse.[32] The overlapping of notions such as family, household, kinship, marriage and parenthood generate almost inevitable ambiguities.[33] An even more insidious problem is presented by the fact that no definition of 'the family' can usefully represent the range of experiences covered by this term, and that simply speaking of 'the family' has the potential 'to concede the existence of an institution that [...] is essentially and naturally there'.[34] Dominant understandings of the family in current discussions continue to portray it as a unique institution, based on heterosexual marriage and aimed at reproduction. I am aware that acknowledging that such understanding is historically and culturally specific is not enough to avoid the risk of silencing those relationships that are still not recognised as family in public discourses and the danger of hiding the inequalities and asymmetries of power that lurk behind the image of the family unit.[35]

Nevertheless, I do use the term 'the family' in this book, not only for lack of a better word. In post-war public discourses 'the family' represented a narrowly defined and largely accepted concept. Throughout the book I discuss the normative attributions of the family in order to highlight the complexities and tensions that characterised an apparently established notion and to discuss its role as a locus of political relations.

A relevant part of the discussion of the attributes of the family concerns the question of which sphere does the family belong to. To which extent does the family coincide with the private sphere – as common language often suggests? What are its 'public' responsibilities for instance in terms of political socialisation? To what extent is it possible and legitimate for an external authority – the state in the first place – to act upon the family in order to transform or improve its performance? A useful suggestion is provided by Morgan's submission that the family can be understood not only 'as occupying an active space between the individual and society', but also as 'being both of these at the same time', that is, 'both societal and individual, both institutional and personal, both public and private'.[36]

My analysis moves from the premise that in order to capture the complexities associated with the family as a concept, it is necessary to acknowledge that the way in which the prerogatives of the family are understood is the product of a constant interaction taking place between public and private discourses. The idea that family life represents a major determinant in a number of social processes has informed mainstream economic and sociologic arguments and shaped rich debates on how to intervene in the life of those families considered less able to provide a desirable environment for the nurturing of young people. At the same time, the dominant representation of the family remains that of an institution devoted to the satisfaction of our most private and intimate needs. Such a representation is not only the result of discourses constructed outside the family, but also the outcome of our own investment in family life as a major source of satisfaction and protection.[37] In John Gillis' words, we do not only live *with* a family, we also live *by* a family through which we represent 'ourselves to ourselves as we would like to think we are'.[38] If the families we live with may be troublesome and conflict-ridden, the families we live by are harmonious, caring and protective. That they may not represent the actuality of family life does not reduce the family's symbolic importance and appeal.

Throughout the post-war period, public discourses promoted an image of the family compatible with the welfare of society at large, by appropriating and exploiting images of family life as a place of unfaltering co-operation, loyalty and support. Post-war welfare rhetoric upheld an image of the family as the place where primary obligations towards its members were naturally met unless unforeseeable events prevented it. Within this established paradigm the role assigned to the state was not that of interfering with families in the discharge of their daily duties, but rather that of fulfilling in lieu of the family in times of need. To use Janet Finch's expression that of the state was a 'reluctant but necessary intervention', justified with the failure of some families to fulfil their 'natural obligations' towards their members. The aim of such intervention could be conceived either as that of bringing families back to their responsibilities or of substituting them altogether.[39] In either of these situations, however, it was families' failure that upset the ideal relationship between family and state where the role of the first was that of providing for the welfare of its members and that of the latter to sustain it in its role.

The place of the modern family

In 1945, the American sociologists Burgess and Locke argued that the family was in the process of being transformed from an institution to a companionship. In this transition, the family would cease to respond uniquely to the demands of social pressure, and start to depend instead on the bonds of intimacy and affection that existed among its members.[40]

The primacy given to emotional bonds as the basis of family life in post-war discourses was closely related to the identification of romantic love as a prerequisite of marriage and of marriage as the only possible outcome of romantic love. The expectation that romantic love, marriage and family life should go together has been seen as a feature of the interwar period further reinforced in the post-war years 'to the extent that until the 1960s it was almost impossible to imagine love taking any other form'.[41]

Not all was positive, however, in this transition from institution to companionship. In post-war discourses, images of domestic life based on the romantic attachment of men and women went hand in hand with the impression that families acted increasingly as 'privatized' and isolated nuclei: (almost) self-sufficient units often outside the reach of influence and support of 'extended kin, friends, and neighbours'.[42] It went almost without saying that such a family was heterosexual, monogamous and organised around gender-specific roles.

In Ronald Fletcher's words, the characteristics of the family were universal in the sense that they responded to the 'same biological propensities and needs: mating, the begetting of children, and the rearing of children'.[43] However, post-war dominant sociological descriptions of the family stressed how the typical characters of the modern family had been acquired over time, as the result of a process of adaptation to social and economic changes. Classic functionalist theories of modernisation linked the emergence of the (supposedly) isolated nuclear family to processes of industrialisation, seen as the main cause of the displacement of people from their original communities and the disruption of their kinship networks.[44]

Such a thesis has been convincingly challenged by historical and demographic studies since the late 1960s. On one hand, the emergence of the nuclear household has been traced back to the pre-industrial period, at least for parts of western and northern Europe.[45] On the other, the importance of kinship ties has been suggested not only as a resilient element of industrial societies, but also as an important contributing factor to the success of early industrialisation.[46]

For post-war sociologists and social observers, however, the increasing isolation of the nuclear family did not represent an issue of historical interpretation, but a compelling social problem.[47] Although often portrayed as the outcome of a process of modernisation, post-war families showed tensions and contradictions that roused a number of different and sometimes contrasting worries.

Women's growing participation to the labour market seemed to bring about a blurring of gender roles that threatened the strength and cohesion of the domestic unit. The apparently increasingly privatised lifestyles of the nuclear household seemed to affect men's public role and political engagement, particularly in the workplace.[48] The supposed isolation of contemporary families seemed to undermine the care, protection and support associated to larger kinship ties.[49]

Although each of these issues played a part in both Italian and British debates, significant differences emerged in the way in which they were discussed and understood in the two countries, as I will show throughout the book.

Of particular importance for this analysis is the issue of the supposed isolation of the post-war family and the implications of such (real or perceived) isolation for policy making. The question of whether and how the support provided by an increasingly small family could be integrated through social policy interventions represented (and still represent) an integral part of discussions concerning the role of the state in modern society. The cases of Britain and Italy highlight that the pursuing of different approaches to state intervention in family life may represent the outcome of the combination of different conceptions of the family, different political conditions and different relationships between state and non-state sectors.

Despite such differences, however, there are some crucial similarities in the two countries' attitudes towards the family. Most striking of all was the reluctance with which Italian and British politicians alike looked at the extension of state services as a means of integrating or even substituting the family in the provision of individual care. Even when a certain consensus existed on the fact that widespread caring responsibilities put an unhealthy strain upon contemporary working families (although it was upon women that those responsibilities disproportionably fell), concerns with the preservation of the main prerogatives of family life (or of its ideal) proved stronger than the desire to find alternative forms of personal care. The primary and irreplaceable responsibility for the care of its members emerged as the most enduring and characterising feature of the way in which the family was conceptualised throughout the post-war period. What differed in the two countries examined here was the consideration of what type of intervention was best suited to improve the families' performances in the delivery of care.

2
The Family in the Political Debate

For the greater part of the post-war period an overall agreement seemed to exist on what the family is and how it differs from other forms of social arrangements. Recent political discourses and subsequent legislative changes throughout Europe, however, have appeared to have the potential to erode or even break this long-standing consensus.

A recent and controversial example of the transformation undergone by understandings of what constitute a family is perhaps the legal recognition of same sex unions. Legislation in this area has been introduced in the last fifteen years in Denmark (1987), Norway (1993), Sweden (1994), Iceland (1996), The Netherlands (1998/2001), France (1999), Belgium (2000), Germany (2001), Finland (2002), and most recently Spain, Luxemburg, Switzerland and Britain.[1] Each of these pieces of legislation is the outcome of different political and social circumstances and reflects different priorities and concerns. Nonetheless, the short time span in which legislation in this area has been passed in different countries – and by different governments and parties – testifies of a growing awareness and sensitivity towards the legal definition of family relations.

Moreover, (although this book does not deal specifically with the issue of homosexuality and family life), some elements of the debates surrounding the regulation of same sex partnerships point out enduring concerns related to the definition of what constitute a family and represent a useful starting point for the analysis presented in this chapter. In Britain and in Italy, changes have been campaigned for as a means of expanding individual entitlements and on occasions as a means of acknowledging and protecting family life in all its complexity. On the opposite front, such changes have been accused of devaluing and undermining the institution of marriage and the prerogatives of the family as a unique institution, based upon heterosexual marriage and procreation. Both critics and supporters of legislative measures aimed to recognise same sex unions seemed to agree that such measures render the position of married and unmarried same sex partners more equal, opening up the definition of what constitutes a family. A closer look at the legislation passed in recent months in Britain, however, suggests a more complex situation.

The Civil Partnership Act 2004 (active from December 2005) has been defined as a 'formal legal relationship akin to marriage', whose purpose is 'to remedy discrimination in existing legislation against gay and lesbian couples'.[2] The Act established rights and obligations for civil partnerships closely modelled on those attached to marriage. As in the case of marriage, civil partnerships must take place between two adults in an enduring relationship, and although a sexual relationship is not explicitly required, it is indirectly suggested by the exclusion of close relatives living together.[3] At the same time, however, the new institution is clearly not meant to provide an alternative to marriage, as proved by the exclusion of heterosexual cohabiting couple from this form of legal relationship.

In this respect, it could be argued that by creating a specific legal category for same sex unions while assuming heterosexual marriage as a model institution, civil partnerships have to some extent reinforced, rather than undermined the traditional values of marriage. Marriage remains an irreplaceable institution, which binds men and women for life and is geared towards procreation. Nonetheless, the acknowledgement in law of same sex partnerships represents a significant step towards the recognition of the existence of a multiplicity of (legitimate) living arrangements and lifestyles.

In Italy, measures aimed at recognising not only same sex partnerships but also not married heterosexual ones, the so-called *coppie di fatto*, have finally entered the political debate. The issue represented a contentious theme of political confrontation in the electoral campaign of 2006 and remains a difficult area of regulation for the centre-left coalition in power as this book goes to print. The formula agreed by the centre-left coalition during the electoral campaign advocated the legal recognition of the rights and prerogatives of those living in stable cohabitations, independently from their gender and sexual orientation. According to this definition, legal recognitions should be based on the 'stability and self-willingness' of the relationship, and on the links of 'love, care and solidarity' that exist between the partners.[4]

The lengthy discussions and negotiations that preceded the agreement underlined not only the political challenge of reaching a common understanding of family relationship between ideologically diverse parties, but also the challenge presented by the effort of singling out the prerogatives according to which a partnership freely entered by two adults should gain public recognition and legal sanction.[5]

In general, these debates show the extent to which the definition of 'the family' and its regulation is indeed contingent and susceptible to change. They also show the scale of resistance that any of those changes are bound to encounter.

One of the main questions underlying this book is how the construction of the family in political discourses influenced the making of social policy and impacted on the actual experiences of men and women of different ages and in different socio-economic circumstances. The book also tries to explore how the transformation of individual behaviour has indeed forced social policy to adapt to respond to new and in certain cases unexpected circumstances.

Chapters 2 and 3 try to shed some light on these questions by looking at interpretations of the family, its nature and social and political role in political, religious and medical discourses popular in Britain and Italy since the end of the Second World War. Chapter 2 analyses the positions expressed by the main political parties in relation to family life and its regulation by the state. Chapter 3 looks at the role of religious authorities and medical experts in influencing interpretations of the family and approaches to state intervention. In these chapters, my aim is to discuss similarities and differences in the way the family is constructed in British and Italian political, religious and medical discourses and to analyse how the historical transformations of the family since the end of the war (starting from demographic changes) have affected political interpretations of the family and its role.

Both chapters rely on the assumption that political parties, institutionalised religious organisations and state agencies represented influential authorities, which shaped and divulged the language according to which the family was discussed and regulated.[6] I argue that their respective influence was and still is very much different in Britain and Italy, and I try to show how and why.

Political parties and the family

What follows describes mainstream attitudes towards the family in the main political parties operating in post-war Italy and Britain and suggests some possible legacies for contemporary debates. Christian Democrat and Communist Parties in Italy and the Conservative and Labour Parties in Britain have been chosen because they constituted the political forces with the largest social penetration, as well as because they represented alternative approaches to society and (at least to some extent) the family.[7] In my analysis, I try to consider the impact that the different political frameworks within which the four parties operated had on their ideological stands. I give particular attention to the absence of confessional parties and socialist anti-clericalism in Britain, a factor that, according to Donald Sassoon, deprived the Conservatives of 'one of the traditional weapons' of the continental European right, that is, the use of religion, 'to divide the potential supporters of the left' and the fear 'that an incoming "red" government would desecrate all that was hallowed'.[8]

A number of authors have commented on the greater role supposedly played by ideology in Italian politics compared to the greater 'pragmatism' of political confrontation in Britain. To some extent this seems to fit debates about the family. Throughout the post-war period, both Communists and Christian Democrats made strong reference to long-established doctrines formulated outside the parties themselves to justify specific positions on the family (for instance in relation to divorce), while Conservatives and Labour tended to present their decisions as being inspired by specific concerns rather than ideology. I argue, however, that for all the parties considered, the family represented an area where deeply set values could not be easily ignored, and where matching them with a pragmatic attitude and comparable values often appeared a challenging task.

The family as natural and immutable society[9]

Many of the positions endorsed by the Christian Democratic Party (DC) represented not the result of the party's original theorisation, but rather the translation in the political sphere of traditional Catholic values. In the words of Tupini, the party's religious inspiration provided a 'safe and solid ideology: Christianity understood as moral norm and realisation of justice'.[10] Throughout the years, the defence of a particular idea of family offered a means of showing loyalty to the church and of forging alliances with catholic powers.[11]

The first occasion offered to the DC to prove its commitment to the defence of a Christian family was the work of the Constitutional Assembly, between June 1946 and December 1947.[12]

The spokesperson on the family in the Assembly was Giorgio La Pira, one of the leading representative of the faction of the party committed to a political agenda directly inspired by the social teaching of the church. La Pira spoke of the family as society's funding institution and asked that the new Constitution acknowledged it as a 'natural unity' (*unità naturale*), preceding the state in time and based upon immutable principles.[13] Marriage itself should be regarded primarily as a sacrament, the authority over which belonged to the church. While the state was responsible for guaranteeing married couples' rights, it should not interfere with the church's overwhelming moral authority. Accordingly, the DC defended staunchly the introduction of the principle of the indissolubility of marriage within the constitutional text and opposed statements aimed to affirm the equality of the spouses and of legitimate and illegitimate children.[14] The elimination of differential treatment for children born inside and outside marriage in particular was refused as a measure bound to endanger the family 'as a moral and juridical institution'.[15]

Although the inclusion of the principle of the indissolubility of marriage within the Constitution was eventually rejected, thanks to a last minute political manoeuvre, Articles 29, 30 and 31 sanctioned the subordination of the 'legal and moral equality' of the spouses to 'the unity of the family' and the distinction between legitimate and illegitimate children. Both principles found direct application in the Italian civil code. Until the reform of family law in 1975, husbands retained the right to choose their family's place of residence, a different legal treatment was applied to male and female adultery, and unequal parental rights were guaranteed to men and women.

The Catholic jurist Domenico Barbero expressed in 1955 his satisfaction with the Catholic mark left on the Constitution. According to Barbero, the Union of the Italian Catholic Jurists itself could not have adopted 'a judgement more consistent with the dogmatic principles and the aspirations of Catholics in relation to the family'. Reading the constitutional text was like 'reading a passage from the social doctrine of the church translated in founding norm of the state'.[16]

The question was: did those principles reflect the values of the majority of post-war Italians?

A speech by the MP Franca Falcucci at a symposium organised in 1963 on the family and the transformations of Italian society gives us a glimpse of the challenges confronted by the DC. Falcucci challenged the idea that social changes should result in 'a radical transformation' of the family, arguing that Christians should not view the human conscience as a result of social and economic conditions, but according to 'objective values'. Neither nature nor the scope of the family changed over time: the family was an institution of natural law, whose origin coincided with the development of human life.[17] The indissolubility of marriage represented one of its fundamental characteristics and could not be questioned by the mood of the day. The 'increasingly popular' idea that 'absence of love' could legitimise ending a marriage lowered the status of marriage, made birth control acceptable and reduced parental responsibility.[18] In their different versions, all positions favourable to divorce overlooked the necessary link that existed between freedom, true love and sacrifice.

Falcucci ended her speech by reassuring her audience that the future belonged to the family values of which her party was the only champion and defender.[19] Forthcoming developments showed that the future may have indeed belonged to the family, but to a type of family rather different from that hoped for by the DC.

The Catholic sociologist Achille Ardigò offered in the same year an even more pessimistic account of the consequences of social trans-formations. Italy's 'exceptional industrial development' and the rapid urbanisation of the country had irremediably separated the 'artificial life of industrial and urban society' from the life of the family.[20] Mass media's exaltation of 'economic success' and 'the beauty of the woman-lover' eroded traditional values and endangered the most vulnerable families, such as those of the industrial working class. For Ardigò, this was partly the result of the government's failure to govern social and economic transformations and the inability of Christian Democratic policies to promote the integration of the family in modern society.[21]

A crucial element of the analyses lamenting the loss of a traditional way of life associated with the patriarchal household and rural life was related to the changing position of women.[22] In 1951, for instance, the Fronte della Famiglia, an association formed within the Catholic Action in May 1946, described the declining status of the father as an unfortunate by-product of the democratic reaction against the principle of authority which had followed the end of the fascist regime. The Fronte urged the DC to take up measures to safeguard the male breadwinner role as the first essential step towards the restoration of his authority. The introduction of a family wage was indicated as the first step in this direction and discussed at length within the catholic trade union.

Although the introduction of a family wage was never implemented, social policies favoured by the DC reflected its main tenets in relation to the family by presuming and occasionally supporting the family as main provider of individual welfare and women's domestic role. Explicit policies included the introduction in the mid-1950s of family allowances payable to employed capifamiglia (heads of families) not only for co-resident children (up to 18 years of age in the case of white-collar workers and 14 in the case of manual workers), but also for unemployed wives and co-resident parents unable to work. However, women's domestic responsibilities were rewarded not through a direct payment, but through benefits destined to the whole family and paid to the male worker on a means testing basis. Indirectly, women's 'domestic choice' was encouraged by the low investment in social services able to integrate the care provided within the family.

At the same time, the DC did not ignore that women represented a crucial part of their electorate and made at least formal attempts at recognising the expectations of the growing proportion of women who sought paid employment outside the home. Standards of protective legislation for working mothers were set in Italy at acceptable levels and the country was the first in Europe to ratify the ILO convention on equal pay in 1954. However, the sensitivity of the party to women's issues was limited in practice by the inefficient implementation of the norms and by the fact that only a minority of women was employed in regular occupations.[23] Overall, the support for a far-reaching transformation of women's treatment in relation to work was hampered by the commitment to an image of traditional family life, which required the presence of the mother at home.

In their different aspects, Christian Democratic attitudes towards the family reflected the party's commitment to act as the political representative of the Catholic Church. Catholic teaching provided the main text to Christian Democratic discourses; the interests of the church inspired its politics in relation to the family. While the church looked favourably to the creation of a legal framework based on its teaching in matters of morality and family life, it considered with anxiety an extended presence of the state in areas traditionally of its concern. The DC seemed to accept the idea (reaffirmed on many occasions by Pius XII) that it was only through the church that family and state could fulfil safely and perfectly their respective duties: the family as the first source of Christian education and the state as the guarantor of law. The DC proved successful in promoting the values of the church in the legal framework according to which family life was regulated. At the same time, the party defended a limited involvement of the state in the provision of services crucial to the family, whose organisation and management were left predominantly to the church.

Communist homes[24]

The family constituted a largely new territory for the Italian Communist Party (PCI) at the end of the Second World War. Formed in 1919 as a revolutionary party and made illegal in 1925, the party had spent the following 18 years with a minimal agenda beyond the fight against Fascism. Moreover, in the party's rigid Marxist reading of society, the family did not represent a question to be confronted on its own terms, but rather an issue that would have solved itself once the present bourgeois order was transformed in a socialist society.[25]

The situation changed dramatically at the end of the war when, after the popular insurrection of April 1945, the PCI became 'the hegemonic centre of the Resistance' and a mass movement directly involved in the running of the country.[26] This new context required the formulation of a new political agenda, able to confront the main issues of the moment. Tackling the condition of the family in post-war Italy was all the more important given the necessity of confronting the DC on one of its privileged grounds.[27]

Using a language familiar to catholic sensitivities, the communist leader, Palmiro Togliatti, spoke of the disruption of the family as 'the most dramatic aspect of the ruin brought to Italy by Fascism' and called 'the people willing to save the sources themselves of national life to mobilise for its recovery'.[28] Women in particular, should contribute to creating families free from 'corruption and hypocrisy', starting from which new and stronger solidarities could be built within the country.[29] Only cohesive and solid families could combat 'the disgraceful plague' of prostitution and save children from 'the moral and material hell' many of them inhabited.

As well as defending the family as an institution, Togliatti took a critical stance in relation to the inequalities and oppression that characterised contemporary family life, criticising in 1945 the 'feudal character' that the Italian family still held.[30] The double commitment to the defence of the family and to its reform in a more egalitarian and democratic direction informed the PCI's appeal to women both as voters and as possible members of the party.[31]

However, the message sent was not free from ambiguities. Togliatti avoided a confrontation on the most sensitive issues and disengaged his party from pursuing 'any measure likely to break or weaken the family unit', starting with question of divorce.[32] Moreover, despite the commitment of the PCI to women's legal equality both inside and outside the family, women were targeted primarily on the basis of their domestic role. Togliatti emphasised that to be a Communist did not require to abandon one's womanly duties, nor 'to lose in any way the attributes and graces of femininity'. What the party asked of the 'great mass of women' was to look for a collective way to solve 'the difficulties they experienced in their daily lives'.[33]

As Luciana Castellina pointed out, the main weakness of Togliatti's strategy was the failure to link the request for women's legal equality with a critique of traditional family roles.[34] The ambiguity of the communist position became obvious during the deliberations of the Constitutional Assembly.

The discussions taking place in the two preparatory Central Committees held by the PCI in July and September 1946 left little doubt that avoiding irreparable ruptures with the DC was a much greater concern than taking a stand on the regulation of the family.[35] Within the assembly, the spokeswoman on the family Nilde Iotti (one of the 11 Communist women elected in 1946) tried to reconcile the issue of reform of the family with catholic concerns. Jotti argued in favour of the rights of illegitimate children not only as a matter of justice but as a deterrent against adultery and presented spouses' legal equality as an aspect of the party's more general commitment to women's emancipation. Ultimately, the party remained faithful to its orthodoxy, according to which only economic independence could change women's position in relation to marriage. Only by ceasing to be seen as an economic expedient, marriage could become a means of satisfying natural, moral and social needs, and a freely taken step towards the development of women's personalities.[36] Conviction and political convenience combined in the decision to avoid an uncompromising stand on the question of the indissolubility of marriage. In February 1947, Togliatti explained that priority had to be given to the approval of the Constitutional text, avoiding the prospect that a discontented DC could decide to call a referendum against it.[37] He added that the principle of the indissolubility of marriage could be accepted, at least until the state was able to guarantee the economic self-sufficiency of those women for whom marriage constituted 'not a state but a profession'.[38]

Eventually, when the full assembly finally voted on this issue, on 23 April 1947, the PCI was able to oppose the original formulation proposed by La Pira thanks to an amendment presented by the Socialist Umberto Grilli. The inclusion of the principle of the indissolubility of marriage in the new Constitution was rejected by a majority of three votes.[39] The PCI's change of mind, however, did not change the general feeling that the DC maintained the lead on the question of the family.

In announcing the Communists' vote, Gullo felt the need of reassuring its audience about their attitudes towards divorce:

> We think that in the present moment, when so many needs are urging and so many problems wait for a solution, the question of divorce should not be raised. We may add that the classes we mainly represent do not feel this as a problem.[40]

The emphasis put by the PCI on the necessity of protecting the family was not only instrumental to reassure Italian Catholics. In Giovanni Gozzini's words, between 1949 and the mid-1950s, the PCI was transformed 'from the party of the proletariat into the party of proletarian families, represented by its deep rooting in the sharecropping culture of central Italy'.[41] Togliatti's new party accepted the idea that the family was central to Italian society and endorsed a view of its internal relationships only partially dissimilar from their catholic version. The Communist militant should prove within his family his sense of responsibility, morality and endeavour, avoiding frivolous attitudes likely to damage his personal life and political commitment. Not even the highest leadership of the party could escape these expectations. In 1946, Togliatti (who was already married to Rita Montagnana, leader of the party's women's organisation) and Jotti began a relationship that lasted until the death of the communist leader in 1964. The relationship met with the discreet but persistent opposition of the party's leadership and was conducted in near invisibility for a number of years, conforming to the idea that politics should have priority over the personal and to the determination to present an image of unfaltering morality for the PCI.

Reflecting on his experience in the Resistance movement, another Communist leader, Gian Carlo Pajetta wrote,

> I often wondered then, whether there were cases when the 'private' should be given priority over the 'public'. And I have wondered about it later in life. The answer has always been the same: never.[42]

Within the home, the political ideal of communist men and women should support their commitment to the success of the family as a whole. Reciprocal solidarity substituted patriarchal values without calling into question the importance of the family as a social institution.

> The family is no longer patriarchal. Our women have equal rights
> with our men and our mothers are equals to our fathers. Our
> families do not submit themselves to patriarchal authority but instead
> represent the Soviet collective.[43]

The definition was of the Soviet educationalist Anton Makarenko.
Originally published in the 1930s, Makarenko's work was translated and
published in Italy in the mid-1950s.

Individual sacrifice was as central to the message of Makarenko and
the Communist leadership as it was to their Catholic opponents. The
strength of the 'domestic collective' rested on the willingness of sacrifi-
cing individual desires for the good of the family and the welfare of the
new generations.[44] Makarenko's position on divorce was unambiguous:

> If you have two children and you have fallen out of love with
> your wife and you are in love with another, extinguish your new
> feeling ... [...]. You are duty-bound to do so, because in your child
> you are raising a future citizen, and you are obligated to sacrifice to
> a certain extent your own happiness in love.[45]

Although motivated by radically different considerations and grounded
in different ethics, Makarenko's answer led to the same conclusion
advocated by Falcucci three decades later. Individual desires, including
love, should not guide decisions in family life. The freedom of the individual should never prevail over his or her duties and responsibilities
towards others. However, if in the catholic discourse the family was
often presented as the ultimate sphere of individual realisation, the
communist family's private interests should be subordinated to those of
the social and political sphere.[46]

Communist households' participation to the anti-fascist struggle
constituted the most recent example of the willingness to sacrifice
private interests for a greater cause. Throughout the 1950s, the Resistance provided the PCI with a model of militancy for individuals and
families alike.

The story of the Cervi family, published in 1954 by Editori Riuniti,
provided a perfect synthesis of individual sacrifice, communist ethics
and familial bond. The Cervi were a family of farmers from Emilia whose
seven sons had been killed in a Nazi retaliation for the help given by
the family to escaped allied soldiers.[47] For Piero Calamandrei, one of the
most respected representatives of Italian liberal socialism and one of the
most prestigious figures to emerge from the Resistance, the Cervi offered

a civic model that unified cultures and traditions and exemplified the virtues of the patriarchal household:

> The father, the grandfather, the patriarch, the stock, is here among us. [...] If he is here, then the whole family is present. ... The assassins might have killed the seven brothers, but they could not destroy the family: the stock was solid, the root deep in the soil, the family was stronger than they were.[48]

To increase the appeal of the Cervi was the fact that, as in many other households, the catholic faith of the mother coexisted with the communist militancy of the sons.

> If it were true that different progressive faiths cannot get on together, then the history of my family would be destroyed, because if we have done something good, we have done it because we have the strength of these different faiths.[49]

No better metaphor could be found for a party engaged in forging an identity as a national political organisation committed to democratic style of political confrontation in a country increasingly exacerbated by the tensions of the Cold War.

However, the political commitment expected of the communist household was not limited to times of emergency. In 'normal times', its duty was to promote 'the renewal and progress of society' through its active participation in the life of the party. The PCI promised a type of sociality open to the whole family and reminded its (usually male) members that the recruitment of family members constituted a precise duty of any communist.[50]

The reality of militancy was however often different from what the party reassuringly promised, and tensions between political and domestic demands were accounted by many party activists.[51] In a study of communist militancy conducted in 1954, Gabriel Almond found that pressure on personal relationships had constituted a reason for leaving the party among a large section of his respondents. Tensions were particularly painful for militants living in catholic households:

> My mother appealed to my Catholic sentiments, asking me how I could deny the religious principles in which I had been raised. She saw in the party a movement which would destroy the family and

society, and was heartbroken when my young brother followed my example and joined the party.[52]

This was the other side of the coexistence model symbolised by the Cervi's family; it was also an equally symbolic reminder that the relative unity of aims experienced by Communists and Catholics immediately after the war was by the mid-1950s an experience of the past.

Finally, tensions between political and personal life pointed out the different meaning of political militancy for men and women. The construction of the party as a family-friendly organisation underplayed this difference. The rhetoric of the resistant family ignored the fact that for many women taking part in the resistance movement had meant a welcome rupture from traditional family life.[53] The encouragement to the whole family to participate in party's activities ignored the fact that the demands of political life made it practically impossible for a couple to participate equally while bringing up a family. It was men's political commitment that usually proved predominant, leaving women the greater burdens of family life. Moreover, while men's political commitments took them outside the home, sometimes with an underestimation of their own need for family time, in the case of women it was their domestic role that acquired political significance for the party.

The whole fabric of civilised society

Rodney Barker has seen in the conception of the family a unifying element between the distinct and sometimes contrasting positions expressed by the New Right thinking.[54] Among the distinctive characters of such understanding he has mentioned the private nature of the family and the rigid boundaries of possible state intervention. I would add that the family represented also one of the unifying threads between conservatism and New Right.

Despite the popularity of interpretations of the Tory tradition primarily in terms of political practice, the family represented not only a fruitful theme of political propaganda for the Conservative party, but also a constitutive element of its theoretical baggage. There is a substantial continuity between the emphasis put by the New Right on privacy and morality and the conception of the family expressed by the Conservative party since the Second World War, and significant similarities between Conservatives and Christian Democrats' approach to the family.

Despite the scant attention given by scholars to the importance of religion in Conservative thought during the second half of the 20th century, the reference to Christianity played a significant part in the effort to present a recognisable identity for the party at the end of the war.[55] Together with the acceptance of the inevitable imperfection of human nature, an organic interpretation of society and the importance of historical tradition, Christianity represented one of the characterising elements of what it meant to be a Conservative in modern society.[56] Conservatives' adherence to Christian teaching enabled them to see 'that a theory of progress [was] a delusion unless it [was] accompanied by a proper awareness of the ever-present forces of degeneration which afflict man's imperfect will'.[57] It also supported 'the attachment to the moral free agency of the individual' which justified Conservatives' resistance against the intrusion of the state into the private life of its citizens. A free society was based on the rule of law and the interaction of the spontaneous communities to which individuals naturally belonged.[58] The family represented the first and highest of such communities.[59] Within the family, individuals learnt their first lessons of duty and the fundamental principles of social interaction as well as having their freedom defended from the intrusion of an over-mighty state.[60] The family was 'prior to the state' and had 'rights which [did] not derive' from its fiat.[61]

In Quintin Hogg's words, the family represented a 'natural unit' and 'the foundation of the whole fabric of civilised society'.[62] It gave support and affection to the individual and transmitted the sense of tradition upon which society was based. Moreover, the experience of the family allowed appreciating social order and transmitted a will to preserve the present against the fear of sudden changes and their unpredictable results. The family was the citadel of individual freedom and its preservation equalled the defence of liberty within society.[63] The possibility for every household to enjoy the larger possible material autonomy, based first of all on a fair share of private property, was essential to this end.

> Above all they [the Conservatives] want to see property in the family, and the family itself an independent centre of power enjoying its own franchises and prerogatives and occupying its true position as the foundation of civilised society.[64]

The idea that private property and the family represented the principal means of defending individual rights and a free society informed Eden's political formula of a 'property owning democracy'. Throughout the 1950s, Eden's definition encapsulated the essence of a stable society in political allegiance with the Conservatives. Only self-reliant families forged independent individuals, able to act responsibly towards their own and their family needs. State intervention could support families but a clear distinction had to be maintained between their respective spheres of competence.

Setting the boundaries between family and state's responsibilities was all the more important in the new welfare society. While family and private property constituted the main 'safeguards against the over-mighty state', families themselves had to be protected from the dangers of welfare agencies' excessive intrusion. The spectrum of the socialist state lurked behind the new welfare society. In the words of Bernard Braine, 'today it is an official coming in to search your larder; tomorrow it may well be an official coming in to inspect your books and private papers'.[65] Social services could 'strengthen family life' only if firm limits were set against the risk of them becoming 'a substitute for it'.[66] As well as posing a potential threat to individual freedom, the expansion of social services posed a more immediate danger. They minimised parents' 'sense of responsibility ... for their family' and were therefore responsible for a growing lack of parental control.[67]

In the second half of the 1950s, the issue of lowering parental authority was directly related to the supposed rise in juvenile delinquency.[68] According to the Working Party on Parental Responsibility and Juvenile Delinquency, set up by the Conservative Party's Women National Advisory Committee (WNAC) in 1959, unstable home life represented the main cause of delinquency among young people. 'Adopted children', 'children of divorced parents' and those 'whose mothers go out to work' constituted the categories most at risk.

> The child who on return from school faces an empty house, sometimes even a locked door, is more likely to get into mischief than one who finds mother at home and ready with tea – an unconscious symbol of security in the child mind.[69]

Broken homes, shifting moral standards, feckless or selfish parents and lacking religious teaching and discipline in the home were the other most likely responsible factors for a child's little sense of security and purpose. Recovering families' sense of responsibility was essential to maintaining a cohesive society held together by religious and moral principles.

> Religious and secular life, originally united in the nation, remain united in the institution of the family, the foundation alike of secular and religious life. It is the business of the state to foster and support family life, but the core and centre of family life is religious consciousness.[70]

The question remained open of how to support family life, avoiding interfering with individual freedom. The Conservatives' recipe suggested support for traditional institutions such as marriage and a moderate use of social services likely to take responsibilities away from the family. Particularly crucial was, of course, the role of women within the family and within society.

In 1954, the WNAC wondered whether women having 'won most of their civil liberties' had now 'lost a sense of direction' and needed to be reminded of 'their natural responsibilities as parents and home-makers':

> There seems to be a danger that the woman's influence in the home is being forgotten, and for some there appears to be little aim in life other than money and amusement.[71]

Women were 'often anxious to earn' even when there was 'no financial need to do so', partly as a reaction to the fact that in many cases they were now for the first time getting 'money which they [were] free to spend as they choose'.[72] A similar consideration could hardly apply to the majority of women and indeed to the struggling housewife who had been at the centre of Conservative propaganda only a few years earlier. What the WNAC's observation suggested was rather a concern for a deterioration of middle-class family life, assumed as the model by the party. If women's domestic role started to crumble within households enjoying enough material, educational and moral resources, the situation could only be worse for those women forced to take up a job, or whose families had to rely upon state assistance.

Nevertheless, the WNAC considered that family welfare and women's aspirations could be combined, if mothers were given the possibility of flexible participation in the labour force. Ideally, women could take up a profession before marriage, interrupt it to look after the children and resume it when they had reached the school age, in a form allowing the satisfactory combination of domestic and professional responsibilities.[73] The proposal resembled closely those advanced by Myrdal and Klein in their *Women's Two Roles*, published in 1956, and supported what Martin Pugh has indicated as 'an understated defence of the working mother' 'calculated to lend her respectability in a conservative era'.[74] However, this formula could do little in the case of working-class women and seemed specifically devised to answer the complaints of middle-class-married women, whom the party saw as natural Conservative voters.[75] The party remained wary of social services enabling women to stay in full employment while their children were still young.

Conservatives' suspicion towards too extensive welfare services was accompanied by an unrelenting support for spontaneous initiative in the sector of care, particularly in the form of voluntary associations. Once again, the family offered the model for social relations based upon the offer of spontaneous help to those in need, rather than upon formalised obligations.

As the 1949 manifesto *The Right Road for Britain* explained, the future British society should have constituted

> [A] Family of free and energetic individuals helping one another in misfortune, spiritually alive, rich in the infinite variety of social organisms and communities.[76]

While socialist planning menaced the autonomy and stability of society by discouraging the sense of individual responsibility towards others, Conservatives promoted individual voluntary action through the defence of families' independence.[77]

It remained an unfaltering assumption that the welfare of the family should inform the social strategy of the party. As Macmillan explained at the Women Conservatives' Conference in 1961, 'the partnership of marriage and the family' constituted 'the purpose of most or our personal endeavours', 'the basis of all our institutions and the foundations of all Christian – and all civilised – life'. It was in order 'to foster and strengthen family life' that the Tories had embarked on their building plans, encouraged owner-occupation and promoted a society of affluence and choice.[78]

The dilemma presented to the Conservative party by the welfare state was apparently solved only with the election of Margaret Thatcher in 1979. Thatcher's government sanctioned the end of consensual politics and a return to a liberal approach to the economy. The market rather than the state was once again conceptualised as the best guarantor of economic efficiency, social welfare, political stability and freedom. Throughout the 1980s, New Right exponents criticised the social consequences of welfare systems treating citizens as passive recipients of benefits. The notion of 'active citizenship' emphasised competitiveness, self-interest and personal responsibilities and obligations. The idea of the 'citizen consumer', able to make rational decisions on the basis of expected benefits and costs and to treat social services as standard goods, informed documents such as the *Citizen's Charter* and the *Parents' Charter*, both published in 1991. The family was once again emphasised as the first place where individuals should show their sense of responsibility and find their first network of support.

The main texture of working-class society

An examination of Labour attitudes towards the family cannot ignore the familial relationships prefigured by the welfare policies realised by the Labour Government between 1945 and 1951, and based upon the male breadwinner model envisaged by the Beveridge Report.

The 'equal partnership' upon which marriage relied according to the Report implied diverse functions for women and men and acknowledged female dependency as a necessary aspect of an efficient household and welfare system.[79] The insistence on the partnership-like nature of sexual relationships sanctioned by marriage stressed the importance of marital harmony for national well-being. As in the post–First World War period, having 'peace and order on the private sphere of sexual relations' was necessary to create 'peace and order in the public sphere of social, economic, and political relations'.[80] The relationship between family and social welfare remained crucial to labour analysis while in government and throughout the 1950s, when the party had to confront the fact that inequalities and social distress had not disappeared in the new welfare system.[81] In the midst of the strategic and ideological disputes that divided the labour movement during the 1950s, the family emerged as one of the most important aspects of an endangered working-class ethos.[82] In Richard Hoggart's words:

> The more we try to reach the core of working class attitudes, the more surely does it appear that the core is a sense of the personal, the concrete, the local: it is embodied in the idea of, first, the family and, second, the neighbourhood. This remains, though much works against it, and partly because so much works against it.[83]

In his *Democratic Socialism*, published in 1940, Evan Durbin had given great attention to the idea that a direct relationship linked family and social relations. The study was concerned with what Durbin defined as 'certain psychological and anthropological problems', and focused upon a psychoanalytical interpretation of co-operation and conflict.[84]

Durbin paid tribute to psychoanalysis as the 'greatest single achievement of science in the twentieth century', and acknowledged John Bowlby's work as a 'strong' influence over his own understanding of familial and social relationships.[85]

Durbin saw in the 'democratic method' (the 'attitude to each other of people who disagree with one another') the only way of solving conflicts through compromise, and the only solution compatible with social peace.[86] The achievement of a democratic method was a necessary component of any struggle for socialism but did not represent the inevitable result of economic and political change. Democratic attitudes were the outcome of the emotional balance achieved by the individual during childhood.

> Revolutionaries who hate ordered government; nationalists who hate foreign peoples, individuals who hate bankers, Jews, or other opponents, may be exhibiting characteristics that have been formed by the suppression of simple aggression in their childhood education.[87]

Durbin related the frustration experienced in childhood to the restraining of impulses imposed by parents 'out of principle' and 'as a desirable form of discipline', and suggested that letting the child express his anger would have contributed to improve his social and affectionate impulses. The reward for this new parental attitude was a family life that was

> Not a nightmare of disorder, or the false calm of strong discipline, but a moderate, peaceful and very lively society of free, equal and willing co-operation.[88]

Durbin's analysis concentrated on the treatment of children, with little space given to the analysis of the relationship between the parents. His call for greater democracy within the family did not question the existence of normative and unequal gender roles within the household.

The treatment given to this subject by other Labour members and the model of family prefigured by the newly created welfare state suggested ideal-typical households based on clearly defined roles, willingly assumed for the sake of the family as a whole. The co-operation of the spouses allowed the family to provide material care and emotional satisfaction to the individual.

Authors such as Peter Townsend and Richard Titmuss, among the main experts in social policy and supporters of Labour's democratic socialism, explained that family ties provided a kind of solidarity and support which could never be completely replaced by the state. The existence of a strong family network represented not only an essential source of help at times of need, but also a condition of individual fulfilment and happiness all throughout one's life:

> The chief means of fulfilment in life is to be a member of, and reproduce, a family... the really great moments of life come not only in falling in love but in marrying, in having children and in maintaining one's love for one's parents.[89]

Marriage, procreation and intergenerational solidarity represented the three main features of family life. Their importance was proved by the fact that 'extreme attempts to create societies on a basis other than the family [had] failed dismally'.[90]

All these three aspects of family life, however, appeared under increasing strain during the 1950s. Although recognising the benefits brought by a certain democratisation of marriage, Richard Titmuss worried about the pressures put upon this institution by growing individual expectations – particularly among women. Titmuss acknowledged that new types of social policies were necessary to confront the 'apparent conflict between motherhood and wage earning'. Longer life expectations meant that women could look forward to a time in their life when the responsibility for child upbringing was 'nearly fulfilled' and they could dedicate themselves to new and different endeavours:

> With so many more alternative ways of spending money, with new opportunities and outlets in the field of leisure, the question of the rights of women to an emotionally satisfying and independent life appears in a new guise.[91]

Titmuss' awareness was not shared by the whole party and was not sufficient to question consolidated assumptions about gender roles within the family. Richard Crossman remarked in his *Plato Today*, originally published in 1937, but reprinted unchanged in 1963:

> [Marriage and the family] engage our attention for more hours a day than anything, except perhaps our work: they are the cause of more happiness and misery than any other single factor and lastly, they are the thread upon which the future race depends.[92]

The family satisfied three fundamental social functions: the regulation of 'the deep seated instincts of sexual life', the education and upbringing of children and the freeing of men from the burden of domestic activity, allowing them to dedicate the whole of their time to their work. This, however, required accepting clear roles within the household.

> If woman, like man is to put her profession first and her home second, can it still be asserted that the home is the best place for the upbringing of children at all? The justification for the home as the educational centre disappears when woman regards it as the place of relaxation from her daily work.[93]

The institution of the family could not be modified without grave prejudice to the whole of society, and a 'tragic dilemma' was posed between women's aspirations and the need to preserve family's traditional structure. Crossman quoted the reform of the family code introduced in 1920s Russia as a proof of the need for a strong regulation of men and women's sexuality. Only 'a few idealists in Russia did not abuse their own freedom: the common man either abused it or disliked it'. Stalin's family code reintroduced a 'new code of social morality' where 'wanton promiscuity and frequent divorce [were] now frowned upon'[94] Crossman had little doubt that if

> We value the institution of the family and doubt our powers to change the deep seated instinct of sexual life, then woman must renounce the status of man and retain the marriage partnership as the chief function in her life.[95]

Gender and family relationships found little space in the discussion of how to achieve a more equal society, which engaged the Labour Party during the 1950s. In the ideal society where 'no exploitation of man over man takes place', citizens were treated as a universal and sexless subject and the family depicted as a place of co-operation and reciprocal support. Equally modest was the engagement of the party with issues such as divorce, birth control and abortion. These were not only politically controversial or individualistic themes, antagonistic to the Labour preoccupation with the long-term construction of a cohesive society, as Martin Francis had pointed out.[96] They represented also potential threats to a definition of the family as the highest expression of individuals' aspirations.

The main theme of Labour's reflection on the family in relation to society and state was the capacity of the traditional working-class extended family to prevent hardship and promote social cohesion and community identity.

In 1956, Anthony Crosland pointed out that in a welfare society where primary poverty had been virtually eliminated, unwise spending, maldistribution of income within the household, and the decline in size and cohesion of the family group represented the most likely cause of any remaining hardship.[97] Changes in family life resulted in a 'steady contraction in the possibilities of mutual family aid at times of crisis or difficulties: during confinement, the illness of a young mother, chronic sickness, and above all old age'.[98] In asking for more extended social services, Crosland acknowledged that the welfare state created at the aftermath of the war was unable to substitute the family in providing individual support, and regretted the loss of an idealised extended family. A similar regret was expressed by Peter Townsend, who saw in the extended family 'the main texture of working class society' and by the sociologists Michael Young and Peter Willmott, in their studies of the effects of re-housing plans, which scattered around old and irreplaceable communities.[99] Young and Willmott described large family networks kept together by blood ties, geographical proximity and participation in the same kind of social life. The family did not constitute a secluded entity, concentrated in the defence of its own interests and in competition with the outside world, but an institution in constant interaction with the surrounding community. Working-class communities were kept together by their 'identification with a particular neighbourhood or street, a sense of shared perspectives, and reciprocal dependency'.[100] It was the awareness of 'distant connections to other extended families in the same block and nearby', which forged solidarities and 'neighbourly restraint'.[101]

Moreover, family relations informed the system of social mobility and permeated impersonal and bureaucratic transactions. Local residents knew that 'Mrs Brown, say, wants a place for her daughter' and believed that she should have precedence over 'any outsider'. Rent collectors or superintendents 'protect[ed] themselves from criticism by conforming to the unwritten code'.[102] The mixture of old residence and family ties gave traditional working-class communities a peculiar character that social and economic changes would inevitably consign to the past.

The definition of the family as best provider of care tended to treat it as a unity of undifferentiated interests and responsibilities; the idealised picture of working-class community life (a 'retrospective construction', in the definition of Joanna Bourke) ignored the potential for oppression and control with which it was associated.[103] In both cases, the Labour Party struggled to account for contrasting aspirations at the level of the individual. A partial departure from this attitude was represented by Crosland's plea to the party to embrace 'new spheres', such as 'personal freedom, happiness and cultural endeavour'. Crosland's re-evaluation of themes such as higher personal consumption, a rise in material standards of living and individual freedom and his opening to issues such as divorce and sexual freedom, implicitly questioned the representation of traditional Labour families and communities as the ideal place for individual fulfilment and social cohesion. His analysis, however, failed to suggest alternatives to the idealised view of traditional working-class households as well as to the model offered by middle-class, potentially individualistic, nuclear families. In this sense, the 'permissive' legislation passed by the Labour Government during the 1960s introduced significant innovations in matters of sexual morality and the family, but represented an acknowledgement of changes that had already taken place rather than an original reflection on the nature of family relations.[104] Evan Durbin's suggestion that only changes in family relations based on greater equality and psychological understanding would have promoted a radical transformation of society might have offered a point of departure in this direction, but found only a modest following within the party.

Political parties and the family: A comparative consideration

Little disagreement seemed to arise among the political discourses analysed here with respect to the idea of the family as a social institution based upon marriage and having its first end in the provision of emotional and physical care for its members, the children in particular. Nevertheless, different emphases characterised this general agreement.

The DC and the Conservative Party shared a view of society as based on religion, and a conception of the family as responsible for the preservation of moral values. They saw the family as a natural unit temporarily preceding the state and with natural rights independent from it; both identified religion as the first source of familial morality and recognised the state as having limited powers of intervention in family life. In Italy, Christian Democrats relied strongly upon conceptualisations formed outside the party, and explicitly endorsed the position of the Catholic Church on themes such as marriage, procreation and authority within the family. Despite references to a religious view of society and human nature, no similar identification with the Church of England characterised the Conservative Party during the post-war period. Christian Democrats and Conservatives shared the emphasis on the mother as the centre of the family, but not the Catholic emphasis on the authority of the father and the divine origin of the sexual hierarchy within the home. This is not to say that the man-father did not have an important role within the ideal Conservative household, but that this was conceived of more in terms of his responsibility towards the family (as breadwinner and status-giver) than in religious terms. Moreover, although maintaining marriage as the only basis of legitimate family life, Conservatives seemed to lack Christian Democrats' commitment (and unity) in matters directly related to individual behaviour such as contraception.

Communists and Labour shared a greater attention to the question of equality within the family than their Conservative counterparts, and a similar emphasis on families as active members of communities based on class and political militancy. In the case of the PCI, the society to which the militant and his family were called to participate coincided largely with the party. Within the Labour discourse, the social sphere was represented by the working-class community, kept together by long-term loyalties and a mixture of political and familial networks.

National contexts appeared as important as ideological factors in explaining attitudes and commitments towards the family. In Italy, the presence of the Pope influenced the political debate and the language adopted by both DC and PCI. The inability of the PCI to propose an alternative model of family was motivated by the political necessity of refuting Catholic accusations of promoting an agenda hostile to the family and its interests, as well as by the fact that an endorsement of marriage, parental responsibility and different gender roles suited the party's own strict moral code. The situation was different in the British context, first of all in the lower degree of ideological conflict between Labour and the Conservatives. The two parties recognised each other's political legitimacy and shared links with religious institutions, which exercised a very different role within the national political system. In the Italian situation, characterised by strong ideological conflict and the exclusion of the PCI from the possibility of governing, both PCI and DC tried to control growing sectors of society and used the family as an instrument of social penetration. The assimilation of the family to the sphere of political confrontation represented a vital step in the search for political control over society. In Britain, where larger spaces of society remained free from political competition, the family remained an important element of political appeal, but lost part of its relevance as instrument of political penetration. Differences in the character of political competition contributed as much as ideological differences to set the framework within which the family was understood and regulated in the two countries.

3
Moral and Scientific Discussions

At a conference on 'Freedom and secularism' held in Italy in October 2005, Pope Benedict XVI reminded his audience that fundamental rights are not created by human laws, but are inherent in the very nature of the human person and have their ultimate source in God. Although the Pope had simply re-asserted a long-standing Catholic principle, his statement made newspapers' headlines. The Pope chose to make his re-assertion at a conference organised by the then President of the Italian Senate, which had brought together a number of representatives of the centre-right coalition government in power at the time. Moreover, Benedict XVI's pronouncement fell in the middle of a heated public debate regarding the extent to which it was legitimate for the Italian Catholic Church to intervene in the country's political life. A national referendum on assisted reproductive technologies held a few months earlier had already raised angry voices about the church's open advocacy of the restrictive legislation recently adopted by the government. After the Pope's new declaration, liberal newspapers speculated whether the church was not trying to make sure that 'Italian laws were compatible with divine projects'.[1] The issue was not new to a country where the church had exercised a powerful and long-lasting influence over the regulation of issues connected with family life, sexuality and reproduction.

According to the American theologian Mark D. Jordan marriage 'remains the great testimony to the inseparability of church and state' and 'a topic uniquely suited to disrupt any distinction between secular and sacred'.[2] In the Italian context this represented more than a theoretical point. The bitter political battles that accompanied legislative reforms such as abortion and divorce left little doubt regarding the importance maintained by the alliance between political and religious powers in the country and had far reaching implications in terms of individual rights. The way in which transformations in the spheres of sexuality, marriage and reproduction have been dealt with at policy level represent perhaps the best way of testing the endurance of the convergence of interests between political and religious powers.

The question of what influence religious institutions are likely to exercise over the regulation of family life, reproduction and sexuality may be particularly obvious in countries characterised by strong catholic traditions such as Italy, but it is not exclusive to them. Post-war Britain and Italy offer good contrasting examples of how differences in the relationship between secular and religious authorities have influenced the way in which the family is understood and regulated. Their comparison shows that a number of political and social factors besides the presence of the church are important in shaping attitudes towards the family, but also that the family continues to provide a crucial area of mediation and convergence for religious and secular interests.

The aim of this chapter is to discuss the role played in post-war Britain and Italy by religious institutions and medical and social practitioners in shaping approaches to family life.[3] It suggests that while medical and psychological understandings of family relationships became predominant in Britain, the Catholic Church remained the main authority in matters of family and sexuality in Italy throughout the post-war period. The new social services created in Britain since the end of the war increasingly justified their intervention in family life on the basis of their scientific knowledge. This was not the case in Italy where the limited role of the state in providing services for the family left the dominant position of the church unchallenged.

The first part of the chapter analyses the respective roles of the Catholic and Anglican Churches and shows how differences in approaches to changing family life and individual behaviour resulted from the different social and political roles of the two churches. Particularly relevant to my analysis is the fact that while in Italy religious affiliation maintained a strong political significance throughout the post-war period, belonging to the Anglican Church was of little relevance for one's political affiliation in modern Britain, partly as a result of the absence of explicitly confessional parties. The Catholic Church remained a crucial element of post-war Italian politics and a major actor in the country's social transformation despite the continued decline in religious attendance. Although the institutional role of the Anglican Church was never challenged in Britain, its political relevance was modest compared to its Italian (Catholic) counterpart.

The second part of the chapter concentrates on the role played by the so-called 'helping professions' in setting standards of family life: doctors, psychologists, social workers and the like. The chapter will show their different kind and degree of involvement in the establishment and running of social services in the two countries and it will discuss the implications of this contrasting involvement for the treatment of the family.

Families, churches and state in the new welfare society

The experience of war and the post-war transformations in social and family life constituted an important source of concern for the main institutionalised churches throughout Europe.

In its 1949 Interim Report, the Anglican Church Moral Welfare Council (the main body dealing with 'all that concerns sex, marriage and the family') explained that 'the inauguration of the new state services' and 'the growth in number of voluntary bodies' concerned with family matters constituted a radical departure from the past, which questioned the usefulness itself of the Council's existence.[4] The ensuing discussion, however, concluded that the state was 'not going to take over moral welfare work', and that the Council maintained an important role of direction and inspiration.[5] In the case of the Italian Catholic Church, the minimum social services created by the state, the endorsement by the DC of Catholic positions on the family, and the scarcity of secular voluntary associations dealing with family welfare left the church in an apparently much stronger position. Such different perceptions of their respective role contribute to an explanation of British and Italian religious authorities' different attitudes towards the regulation of family life, and towards issues such as the nature of marriage, and the definition of roles and authority within the family.

Pius XII and the centrality of family life

Throughout his pontificate, Pius XII offered detailed teachings on family life, the meaning of marriage, and the relationship between the spouses, addressing in particular, although not exclusively, Italian Catholics.[6]

The audiences given to newly married couples, the seminars on family life and the many speeches delivered to associations and professional organisations became a trademark of Pacelli's papacy (particularly during its early years) and formed an extensive corpus on matters of familial and individual morality and behaviour.[7]

The addresses delivered to young couples in the midst of the war offered a complete handbook for Catholic family life, and a constant invitation to retain Catholic values as the centre of family life during a period of social and individual crisis. The seminars, run from 1941 onwards, examined themes such as the authority in the family, the respective roles of men and women, and the moral function of the family within society, and issues such as medically assisted reproduction, contraception and therapeutic abortion, which until that point hardly had been confronted publicly by the Catholic Church. The dialogue established by the Pope with professional organisations and associations was central to Pacelli's project of a Christian re-conquest of society, requiring not only individual adherence to religious principles, but also the creation of suitable catholic structures within society and state.

In fact, Pius XII's original contribution to the doctrine of the family remained rather marginal. Pacelli endorsed the most conservative positions established within the Catholic pastorate, and opposed innovations in matters of individual and family morality.[8] The great innovation of Pacelli's era was the ability to establish more direct communication with Catholic masses through audiences, an extended use of speeches *urbis et orbis*, and a radically new use of the radio.[9] Pacelli defined the family according to the most traditional teaching of the church; he strove to make such definition powerful and pervasive in Italian society through an unprecedented style of communication.[10]

'Founded upon love and for love', the family represented 'the first and essential cell of society and the safest shelter for its members'.[11] The basis of the family was marriage, a divine institution whose sacramental nature was based on the perfect and holy love that linked Christ to the church. As a sacrament, marriage was necessarily indissoluble:

> On the single bond of matrimony is stamped the seal of indissolubility. [Matrimony] is [...] the result of free will. However, though the mere will of the contracting parties can tie the knot, they cannot untie it. [...] [The consent] is perpetual because is a consent to the perpetuity of the bond [...]. There is no real marriage without indissolubility, and no indissolubility without a true marriage.[12]

Conjugal love was qualitatively different from the ephemeral sensuality experienced by the lovers and the enthusiasm of the *blind love* at the beginning of a relationship. It was true and faithful love, aware of the defects of the other and able to accept them with loving tolerance. Pacelli gave great attention to the question of the ends of marriage in order to reaffirm the primacy of procreation. Reciprocal support (*mutum auditorium*) and remedy against lust (*remedium concupiscientiae*) were also acknowledged as important but only in a subordinate fashion.[13]

> Marriage [...] has not as primary and intimate end the personal perfecting of the couple but the procreation and education of a new life. The other ends [...] are essentially subordinate to it.[14]

The emphasis on procreation implied the prohibition of any form of contraception, with the only partial exception of the so-called 'natural rhythm method' (largely known in Italy as *Ogino-Knaus method*).[15] Pius XII's prescription concerned not only the behaviour of the faithful, but also the conduct of professionals involved in administering services related to sexuality and reproduction. The Pope's overall aim was that of creating a social environment informed by Catholic principles, which automatically limited the choice available to Italian couples, independently from their own moral and religious views.

Catholic couples committed to the teaching of the church had to mediate between many contrasting messages. Whilst doctors and social observers pointed out the comparatively greater poverty of larger families, the Catholic Church forbade the use of 'scientific contraception'. The church showed little sympathy for fertility treatments, but the emphasis it put on procreation implicitly questioned the fullness of childless marriages. In his guide to a successful marriage Antonio Bianchi explained that the word *matrimonio* (matrimony) itself implied procreation. Only through marriage women could fully realise their nature, *quia prolem concipere, parere, educare, matris munus est.*[16]

> As of every eye it can be said that it is intended and formed to see, even if, in abnormal cases, owing to special internal and external conditions, it will never be in a position to lead to visual perception.[17]

The presence of the Pope and his regular interventions on social and political matters sustained the influence exercised by the Italian Church and supported its image as a cohesive organisation under the guide of Pius XII. Nevertheless, the slow pace at which the Roman Catholic hierarchy modified its positions on matters of marriage and procreation stood in sharp contrast to the transformations taking place in the attitudes of a growing part of the Italian people during the post-war years.[18]

According to polls conducted between 1951 and 1952, the majority of Italian women indicated as either two or three the ideal number of children (the number had fallen to two by 1965) and 63 per cent of Italians thought that either 'all' or 'most couples' used some method of birth control. The proportion of those who thought that all couples 'did something' to avoid undesirable pregnancies rose to two-thirds in the north of the country. The main reasons for not using any kind of contraception were indicated as religious motives, ignorance and 'no need' for such measures.[19] Even more revealing was the fact that, contrary to Catholic propaganda, many women described marriage and family life not as a source of fulfilment but as a major reason of unhappiness and disappointment in life.[20] Although the majority of people continued to declare themselves against divorce during the 1940s and 1950s, their number fell from 71 per cent in 1947 to 62 per cent in 1955. Although more women than men remained opposed to divorce, the number of those in favour grew steadily (and faster than in the case of men) during these years.[21]

Roman Catholic and Anglican precepts concurred in seeing the family as an original element of society, and an institution based upon marriage, informed by the teaching of the Gospel, committed to the education of new generations of Christians. For Anglicans and Catholics alike, family relationships were established 'in the natural order to provide a given status and place for children as they begin their earthly course'.[22]

Both churches endorsed monogamy and faithfulness as primary characteristics of a marriage. They diverged, however, in relation to the place assigned to procreation. Unlike Pius XII, the Anglican hierarchy maintained that procreation and companionship stood up as the two independent pillars upon which marriage relied. 'The need of man and woman for each other, to complement and fulfil each other and to establish a durable partnership against the loneliness and rigour of life', was as 'equally deep-rooted in Genesis' as the commandment to procreation. There was no relation of subordination to one another and they came together in 'giving responsible security to the children born of the love of husband and wife'.[23] The document *The Family Today* criticised the Catholic obsession with procreation as the result of a reproachable idea of sexuality as intrinsically evil, which Anglicans did not share.[24]

The distance was even greater in relation to the possibility of using birth control, following the Anglican Church's endorsement of 'responsible procreation' as a parental obligation:

The questions, How many children? At what intervals? Are matters on which no general counsel can be given. The choice must be made by parents together, in prayerful consideration of their resources, the society in which they live, and the problems they face.[25]

The report on *The Church of England and Family Planning*, published in 1949, referred to the question of which form of birth control could be used as a 'clinical and aesthetic choice' that should be left to the parents. Abstinence and natural method were however discouraged in favour of more reliable scientific means. In contrast with the Catholic positions, Anglican authorities indicated 'greater medical knowledge' as the source of the placement of greater responsibility placed upon married couples. Scientific advances confronted

Men and women with the need to make moral choices not previously asked of them, but which demand no less obedience and consecration than abstinence and self denial.[26]

Sexual intercourse was necessary to express and deepen the union of the spouses, and became immoral only when deliberately performed against its essential meaning, including the betterment of the relationship between the spouses. Nevertheless, contraception could become fatal to the marriage if used to the extent of eliminating the fundamental link between sexual intercourse and procreation. It was left to the responsibility of the spouses guided by the church to find the right balance between competing needs, starting from the solemn duty that husbands and wives owed to their family, first of all in the name of their children. Both churches agreed that the responsibility towards the children came before claims of 'personal liberty' and that there was no 'God-given "right to happiness"' that was able to 'over-ride the profound claims of children to a stable and dependable home'.[27] Even in this area, however, agreement was broken soon. In *The Family Today*, the Anglican Church accepted that breaking a marriage could be allowed if it became obvious that 'the continuation of the family and home will work greater harm than will a separation'.[28] Although practically administering annulments and accepting *de facto* separations, the Catholic Church mounted a fierce opposition to divorce, justified with the emphasis put by the church on the sacramental nature of the union.

Differences in attitude between the two churches were marked by differences in the language used to describe family relationships. Roman

Catholic discourses emphasised ideas of individual sacrifice and abnegation, especially regarding women. Greater emphasis was put by the Anglican Church on forgiveness as the main character of a Christian union, shared equally by both spouses. The authority of the Pope dominated discussions within the Catholic Church. Anglicans emphasised the church's counselling nature, which accepted different positions among its faithful and representatives and governed 'by love and not by fear', making 'every effort to understand' and laying down 'principles rather than rules'.[29]

Gender and authority within the family

Gender relationships within the Catholic household defined a patriarchal institution, based on incontestable hierarchies justified by theological interpretations. The exercise of male power within the family was not only a right but also a duty derived from God and representing the divine authority within the home. As any other 'well-ordered society', the family required 'a head' whose authority derived directly from God. The authority of the husband was exercised.

> First over the woman who has given herself to him as his companion... and then over the children who, with God's blessing will come to enlarge and gladden it.[30]

In many different speeches Pius XII reaffirmed the concept that husbands had the primacy of authority within the home, women the primacy of love. It fell upon women the responsibility of taking care of the 'innumerable little tasks' and 'imponderable and daily attentions' that made up the 'atmosphere' of a family. When these tasks were lovingly and carefully attended the atmosphere in a home was healthy, fresh and comfortable. When they were neglected the atmosphere became 'heavy and mephitic'.[31]

Men and women had different and complementary roles. Men had the duty of providing for the material necessities of the family; women that of providing for individual physical, emotional and moral needs through domestic work, emotional care and moral teaching. The whole 'make-up of woman, her organic construction, but even more her spirit, and above all her delicate sensitiveness' had maternity as its main purpose.[32] Women's most noticeable virtues were endurance, selflessness, comprehension, predisposition to pain, 'tolerant patience' and the willingness to 'complete[ly] sacrifice themselves' for the greater good of the family.[33] The Catholic magazine *Famiglia Cristiana* exhorted a woman abandoned by her husband to stand by her man, 'because you are not only his wife but also the honour of his name', and because of this 'one day, he will come back and bless you'.[34]

Maternity and family life counterbalanced women's inclination to superficiality and vanity and protected them from the danger of letting 'the unruly movements' of their spirit taking over their 'discretion and self-restraint'.[35] Women's overwhelming maternal nature should guide also their political attitudes and ideas. In Pius XII's words,

> A woman who is real woman can see all the problems of human life only in the perspective of the family. That is why her delicate sense of dignity puts her on guard any time that a social or political order threatens to prejudice her mission as a mother or the good of the family.[36]

The war had shown that when women left 'the safe sanctuary of the family' to enter 'the vastness and agitation of public life', both their morality and the cohesion of their families were put in danger, and they themselves risked being 'dethroned from their maternal mission'. Women employed in factory jobs easily lost 'any true concept of life and sense of sacrifice', becoming 'greedy only for luxuries, conveniences, amusements and material pleasures'. They created 'fictitious needs' that their modest salaries were not enough to pay for'.[37] Extra-domestic work was safer for single women, especially when it allowed them to put to use their maternal qualities such as was the case with teaching and care work.

The situation was radically different for men whose duty consisted primarily in providing for the material needs of the family by working and participating in what Pacelli called the 'external society'. In all their different roles, men acted as heads of the family, holders of its identity and symbols of continuity between generations.[38] A man could spend limited time with his family, without prejudicing his authority over his wife and children. Such an authority extended to 'moderately chastening his wife with words, or even discreetly striking her', if a grave cause existed.[39]

The family and the Anglican Church

Within the Anglican Church we find a similar image of the family as an ordered society based upon different roles for men and women and similar concerns for the consequences of changing moral standards upon family life.

Significant differences existed, however, in the understanding of the changes taking place in women's positions, towards which the Anglican hierarchy seemed to show a greater acceptance than the Catholic Church. Although working mothers were still considered with a certain apprehension, the apocalyptic language of Pius XII was substituted in Britain by a more pragmatic understanding of the transformations underway. In 1958, the Lambeth Conference expressed concern for the consequence of the work of the mothers of children under school age, especially when no substitute figure was available to 'mother the child and win its trust and affection'. Women's work, however, was given a positive consideration once children had started school, in the light of the fact that 'family life as well as the mothers' might gain from her work, especially if this was limited to the children's school hours. The Conference noticed that particularly 'in the homes of manual workers', mothers' work could result 'in shared interests' between parents and children, thereby 'reducing the educational gap' between them. Moreover, women's work could increase the couple's 'partnership in the running of the home', favouring 'joint-planning, budgeting, and spending – a happy expansion in the area in which married love operates'.[40] In the wording chosen by the Anglican hierarchy, women maintained an overwhelming responsibility for combining domestic and extra-domestic work; however, the domestic realm was not presented as the only possible sphere of their activity and their participation in society inevitably was not considered as necessarily leading to moral danger. Conversely, less emphasis was put on men's role as representatives of the family within society and as exclusive holders of economic power.

Differences in tone suggested not so much a different approach to the family in terms of doctrine as a greater acceptation among the Anglican Church of the social changes already under way, accompanied by an attempt to create a role for itself compatible with the characteristics and needs of contemporary society.

The role of the family in Christian societies

Both Anglicans and Catholics saw the family as the essential unit or cell of society, and considered it as the first agent responsible for social cohesion or decay.

Healthy families guaranteed the value and prosperity of a nation while disorder in family life harmed both individual consciences and society as a whole. At the same time, social changes affected the family, its values and its capacity to remain a solid foundation of the human community. It fell upon the church to oppose the progressive weakening of religious and moral values, brought about first of all by insensitive processes of modernisation. Roman Catholics and Anglicans also shared a similar conception of the family as the first place of education for the individual, where new generations of Christians were formed and society's most fundamental values preserved.[41] Social stability and welfare depended directly on the performance of the family because 'no society will be stronger than the family life which prepares its citizens for their part in it'.[42] *The Family Today*, stressed that for Church of England loving family relations should not be exclusive but expand to the rest of society, creating welcoming homes, open to 'near and distant' 'friends and neighbours'. The duty of the church was to be vigilant and receptive to society's changes, always placing itself at 'the creative end of social processes'.[43]

The claim to represent the highest authority on matters of morality highlighted the challenges that modern society presented to the church. Their reactions, however, differed. Pius XII launched his 'battle for civility' against the sinful character of the modern world while building a lasting alliance with Italian political powers in order to protect its institutional interests. The Church of England expressed a more resigned concern for its loss of centrality in British society, while trying to respond to the challenges presented by an unprecedented expansion of the role of the state in welfare work. In a report published in 1955, the Moral Welfare Council indicated in its programme for the training of welfare workers the promotion of research and the fostering of co-operation and understanding between church and state as its main duties.[44] The report emphasised the importance for the church to affirm a 'professional' presence within society, through the employment of specialised welfare workers able to act in constant interaction with the state and voluntary agencies. The profile of the Moral Welfare Worker resembled that of a trained social worker. Unlike the latter, however, the Moral Welfare Worker had an explicit commitment to Christian values and to the interest of the church. One essential means of serving Christian purposes was the voluntary worker's freedom from the concerns and regulations that 'hampered' the activities of the 'statutory worker'. In virtue of this freedom, the voluntary worker could champion 'questions of conscience' (such as the matching of a homeless child with Christian foster parents) with 'a freedom of speech and action of which her opposite number in the State service may often be envious'.[45]

Anglican and Catholic Churches shared not only the idea that they had a special authority over family matters, but also a view of state's responsibilities as necessarily limited and largely excluded from the private sphere. While the government's duties included the promotion of a social order supportive of family life and the pursuit of 'the good life', the state should not intrude in the domestic sphere, nor limit 'personal freedom and family integrity'.[46]

Different attitudes towards the relationship between family and state reflected differences in the relationship between state and church that took place in Britain and Italy. In Italy, where the secular state represented an historical enemy with whom only a recent and partial reconciliation had been achieved, affirming the Catholic Church's exclusive authority over the family constituted a political issue as much as a question of values. For the Anglican Church, on the other hand, the link with the British state was institutional, inscribed in its creation, and consolidated by tradition and social cleavages.[47] Crucially, the Anglican Church had welcomed the creation of the welfare state as 'more Christian both in spirit and in actual practice' than a state that 'did nothing to feed the hungry, to clothe the naked, or to restore those who had fallen by the way'.[48] Leading Anglican personalities such as William Temple had championed the cause of social reforms since the interwar years, making it possible for the Anglican Church to assert its own influence over the transformation of the role of the state and its specific competence. It was the church that inspired 'with the right spirit those who administer relief of every kind'.[49] Furthermore, carrying on a tradition inscribed in the British relief system since the New Poor Law, the Anglican Church was able to identify in those left out by the welfare system the privileged province of its intervention. It remained nonetheless crucial for the Church of England to be able to carve a role for itself, distinguished from that of the state. The good wishes expressed in 1956 by the Archdeacon of Oakham for a lasting partnership between state and church revealed both the potentialities and the ambiguities that characterised the role of the church in the new welfare society:

> If only we could understand, and make other people understand, that all that has happened is that the State has come in with its immense financial resources, not to supersede our work, but to add to it its potentialities and its scope and usefulness, we should see the present situation not as an invitation to sit back and fold our arms, but as what it really is, - an opportunity and a challenge to greater activity and better work.[50]

On the whole, Anglicans and Roman Catholics endorsed a similar definition of the family in terms of its responsibilities and functions. They differed, however, in relation to the regulation of individual conduct and with regard to the role of the church in a changing society.

The greater acceptance by the Church of England of issues such as birth control, women's work and marriage separation testified to an acceptance of those changes in social and individual attitudes which Pius XII strenuously opposed. The different nature of the two churches contributes to explain such differences. The Catholic Church's greater veneration for dogma, its stronger attention to the post-apostolic tradition and its centralised nature, brought to extremes by Pius XII, contribute to an explanation of the slow pace at which its position on the family changed during the 15 years following the end of the war. On the other side, the Church of England's greater tolerance for theological differentiation supported a more flexible attitude on matters of individual choice. As Wand noticed in 1951, while the Roman Catholic Church claimed 'an absolute authority over every detail of the life of its members', the Anglican Church asserted 'no infallible authority' allowing a wide range of differences 'even in matters of worship'. The question was, 'how far such freedom is compatible with clear and authoritative direction' expected from the Church.[51] The fact that the Church of England was confronted with rapidly decaying religious attendance may explain its more pragmatic attitude towards the role of the minister. The consciousness that morals had 'departed a long way from the old received standards' and that 'conventional church going' was no longer considered necessary by growing sectors of the population, encouraged the search for different forms of presence and the attempt at conjugating new moral standards with the fundamentals of Christian ethics.

In Italy, on the other hand, where church attendance was higher and the parish remained at the core of many communities, the fight against changing moral customs appeared to be one that could still be won, at least until the late 1950s. Furthermore, while the Anglican Church could feel safe that 'laws and politics still consciously referred back to religious sanctions', the militancy of the Italian Church was strengthened by the identification of the PCI as a natural enemy, representing everything that had to be rejected.

The importance of the traditional form of family based upon marriage, procreation and the education of children was strongly defended by both Catholics and Anglicans. However, in the British context, this did not result in an uncompromising battle against social and legislative change, but in an attempt to adapt and incorporate new positions. The opposition to an increasingly dangerous and pervasive external world, on the other hand, was never abandoned by the Italian Catholic Church and was effectively sustained by the effort of social penetration endorsed by Pius XII.

The professionals' point of view

No one more than doctors and welfare practitioners seemed apt to substitute priests and ministers in providing individual help and advice. Social workers, doctors and psychologists were often directly involved in their clients' family life and therefore apparently best suited to advice on family problems.[52] In Britain, the extensive emergency plans adopted during the war and the development of social services afterwards were accompanied by a flourishing of interpretations concerning family dynamics and behaviour which encouraged their use in the shaping of policies of social intervention. In Italy, the absence of a similar public involvement limited the possibility of experimenting with family life and relegated to a more theoretical sphere the influence exercised by welfare practitioners. Nevertheless, Catholic doctors offered a good example of the attempt to combine physical care and moral advice, incorporating scientific findings and established interpretations of family life. In the words of the Italian doctor and writer Cherubino Trabucchi, medicine had 'the right and the duty of enquiring and intervening in everything that could cause problems and illnesses', including patients' family life.[53]

The war and the disruption of the family

Among the various aspects of the disruption brought to civilian life by the war, nothing more than the suffering endured by children showed 'the undesirable effects of the disruption of family life' caused by the material and moral consequences of the conflict.[54] In Britain, the evacuation program was widely described as 'the most crucial life event experienced by the civilian population' after bombing, and for many children, a more traumatising one.[55]

However, evacuation programs and residential nurseries constituted not only an unprecedented effort to provide for children by agents other than their own families, but provided a fruitful means of sociological and psychological investigation, often informing theories which were more fully developed in the ensuing decades.[56] John Bowlby's studies of maternal deprivation relied mostly on data collected during the war in England as well as in other European countries and the United States.[57] Anna Freud and Dorothy Burlingham's observations at the Hampstead Residential Nursery pointed out the extraordinary opportunity of conducting research provided by wartime nurseries. The suitability of residential care for young children, the effect of 'lack of continuous emotional contact between the infant and his parents' and 'the consequent absence of the specific formative influence inherent in the family tie' remained crucial topics of post-war childhood studies.[58]

Finally, observations conducted on evacuated children contributed to emergent notions such as 'maladjustment' and 'neglect', both of which were to play an important part in post-war debates over child care.[59] Both of these constructs are discussed at length later in the book.[60]

Post-war champions of the welfare state, Titmuss among them, indicated wartime evacuation as one of the main causes of the novel inter-class solidarity upon which the new welfare state rested. Such an interpretation has been criticised by more recent analyses stressing the 'patronising attitudes', 'subtle disapproval' 'or outright dislike' encountered by many evacuees.[61] As Macnicol noticed, the reaction of Whitehall officials and middle-class opinion to the revelation of 'inner-city poverty' was 'to seek their cause in working-class *mores*' rather than to support the use of greater 'state intervention to raise living standards'. Encounters of the middle class with the offspring of the urban working class encouraged an enduring view of a (problem) child's condition as the direct result of family failure.[62]

More generally, wartime observations informed post-war debates on the role of the family in child development and fostered a growing confidence that the causes of inadequate parenting could be understood and treated through a combination of medical and social intervention. In turn, this strengthened the idea that the protection of the child justified entering the private world of the family when circumstances required to do so.

Educating mothers: natural roles and social expectations in Italy

While in Britain the war had encouraged the adoption of large-scale emergency intervention, in Italy, it had eroded the already minimal services available, leaving to the voluntary initiative of the Catholic Church and international agencies the almost complete responsibility for the organisation of assistance.[63]

Nonetheless, expectations for a stronger role for welfare professionals were expressed in Italy as well after the war, to which a number of publications and conferences testify. An interesting case study is provided by *Maternità e Infanzia*, the journal of the *Opera Nazionale Maternità e Infanzia* (from now on ONMI), whose publication was resumed in 1947. The National Organisation for Maternity and Child Welfare

(ONMI) was created in 1925 and maintained largely untouched after the war. Throughout the 1950s and 1960s, the ONMI represented the main national organisation responsible for providing maternity and child welfare services for women and children outside the insurance system.[64] Although the role of the ONMI in the post-war period has been largely overlooked in existing historiography, the organisation played an important role in the promotion of particular ideas of family and social relations, both through its activities and its publications. In its opening issue, *Maternità e Infanzia* promised to provide a 'free and democratic space' where concepts and ideas 'concerning assistance to mother and child' could be discussed.[65] This should provide the theoretical basis for the activities of the Opera and diffuse information and practical advice on child care among the general public. The journal's opening statement stressed the newly found freedom after the tight control of the fascist years. Throughout the 1950s, however, *Maternità e Infanzia* showed a strong continuity with the past at least in three respects: the adherence to Catholic values, the careful avoidance of criticism of governing powers and a strong moral approach to medical and social questions.

Rising illegitimacy, high infant mortality rates and high levels of child morbidity dominated the interest of the journal and were interpreted as the signs of weakening maternal ability and spreading moral decay. According to Franco Godano, a regular contributor to *Maternità e Infanzia*, only an inadequate moral attitude could explain the fact that infant mortality remained high among peasants, blue-collar workers and craftsmen despite their improved economic and social conditions and an extensive use of breastfeeding.

> Those who have never been close to rural people cannot imagine how often children are neglected. This is because, until the age when they become useful in the house or in the fields, they are not considered more than a cow or a pig, or a donkey, which cost money, and produce money with their work.[66]

Godano's comment echoed a judgement by the paediatrician L. D. Veronese, who in 1942 had affirmed that it was because of people's carelessness and laziness that ignorance and prejudices survived even where ONMI's clinics operated under the direction of 'renowned paediatricians who devoted so much of their activity to the teaching of child care', particularly in the south of the country.[67]

Ignorance brought to underestimate childhood illnesses and to give preference to superstitious practices over doctors' prescriptions; infant mortality was higher where 'illiteracy, and with it prejudice, superstition, false traditions and moral misery' were greater.[68] The course of action suggested by *Maternità e Infanzia* relied (at least formally) on the promotion of mothers' material and moral education.

The relationship between physical and moral health represented a recurrent topic of discussion on *Maternità e Infanzia* throughout the 1950s, establishing a powerful paradigm that helped to take the attention away from the shortage of specialised medical personnel employed by the ONMI and the inadequacy of existing maternal and paediatric clinics to answer the country's needs.[69]

A changing institution

Both in Britain and in Italy the consequences of the war catalysed the concerns of sociologists, social policy experts, psychologists and doctors. What Zweig called 'the forces tending towards disintegration, disruption and decay in personal, family and social life' included demographic, social and economic transformations.

The consequences of falling birth rates had represented a major concern both in Britain and in Italy during the interwar period and after the war. In the British case, early signs of a baby boom were overshadowed by the worrying conclusions reached by the Royal Commission on Population that in 1949 warned that the average number of children born per married couple was no longer sufficient to guarantee the continued replacement of the population. Although the Commission's conclusion were soon contradicted by a rise in birth rates that lasted for two decades, its message remained important in shaping ideas about the changing character of the family in post-war Britain, including the condemnation of 'the cult of childlessness and the vogue of the one child family'.

In Italy, rapid urbanisation during the second half of the 1950s produced strong fears of isolation and social anomie as traditional communities and extended families broke up.[70] Similar worries were attached in Britain to the apparent increasing isolation of the nuclear family, and its implications at social and individual level. In his studies of child development, Bowlby emphasised the negative consequences that the absence of a 'greater family' had on children 'deprived of a normal home life'. He stressed the sense of insecurity that derived from the awareness that 'should death suddenly overtake them', they could not count on the presence of 'relatives willing to care for their children', as it happened to those belonging to 'large and united families'.[71] Not even extended structures of public assistance could replace the 'insurance system' provided by large family groups. Bowlby suggested that even distant or unknown relatives could offer to a child a better reception and a greater integration than a foster family or, worse, an institution.[72] Bowlby shared Crosland's conclusion that family life constituted the main cause of hardship and deprivation in welfare societies. This was the result both of the structural transformation of family life and of parents' inadequate emotional and psychological skills.

> In a society where death rates are low, the rate of employment high, and social welfare scheme adequate, it is emotional instability and the inability of the parents to make effective family relationships which are the outstanding causes of children becoming deprived of a normal home life.[73]

A third set of anxieties concerned, both in Italy and in Britain, the transformation of women's role. Italian and British social observers agreed that most of the responsibility for good parenting rested upon the mother and that a specific link existed between women's participation to the labour market and the decline in birth rates.

In the occasion of the convocation lectureship of the National Children's Homes Association, held in 1946, the public health expert James Spence explained that motherhood remained 'the most rewarding occupation in the world', and the preservation of motherhood against growing social and political obstacles one of the purposes of the family. Men's contribution should consist in 'courteously and chivalrously [providing] both shelter and protection', as well as 'sustenance' for mothers' 'mind and spirit'.[74] A similar conclusion had been reached by Bowlby, who indicated the role of the father during the first years of a child in the provision of the economic and emotional support that could allow the mother to fully dedicate herself to the care of the infant in an 'harmonious' and 'contented' atmosphere.[75]

In Italy, doctors writing in *Maternità e Infanzia* saw in the strengthening of a 'cult of maternity' and the education of mothers 'to the meticulous observance of their duties' the main means of fighting infant morbidity.[76] The idea that increasingly young women had expectations other than the domestic role for their future raised concerns for the future of the family that lasted throughout the post-war decades. In 1959, Pugliaro lamented that the idea of womanhood no longer recalled 'the image of the mother', but rather that of 'a changing creature, in search of definition'. Contemporary women wanted 'to find and express' themselves according to their 'individual interests', in relation to which they 'did not allow other judgement' outside their own. Such independence and determination were the result of 'feminist thought'; to this, Pugliaro noticed, 'we owe a just and rightful revolution of the feminine personality, just and rightful, and yet dangerous'.[77]

Women's 'search for definition' threatened the stability and cohesion of the couple and the sense of security generated within the family by the union and agreement of the parents. The 'nervous' child, who had problems with eating and sleeping, typified the outcome of the parents' lack of unity and the consequence of a type of love that remained 'isolated and competing' and failed to make the child feel 'like the king of the home'.[78] British and Italian doctors and psychologists agreed that no material comfort could substitute for parental unity and unconditional love, and that emotional deprivation was likely to start self-perpetuating cycles of neglect and trouble in the family.

The definition of the model

The quality of family life was of immediate relevance for the welfare state. In the words of the report on *The Neglected Child and His Family*, published in 1948, the creation of new health and social services amounted to no more than 'locking stable doors after vanished horses', as long as there were 'neglected children, who [might] easily grow up to hate society'. Only by rescuing 'the child from his feeling of isolation and despair' it was possible.

> To free the community from the strain of trying to turn into good citizens great number of men and women who are thoroughly warped long ago in infancy. We can in fact begin at the beginning.[79]

The beginning was, of course, family life.

For the public health expert James Spence, the main purpose of the family was to guarantee the physical and psychological welfare of the children.

The main responsibility of the family was towards procreation and child rearing. Spence suggested that 'a family at its best would have in it five or more children', and would be at the centre of a large system of kinship. This kind of household was ideal because it provided the 'necessary range of characters' and a 'constant interchanging of relationships up and down the scale of the ages'.

Spence admitted that three conditions were important in guaranteeing the successful rearing of a relatively large number of children, namely the presence of a good mother, a certain degree of economic stability and a decent habitation. The observation seemed to take into account evidence showing that larger families experienced greater poverty and social distress. No degree of material comfort, however, could substitute mothers' ability. The mother was at the centre of the family thread, the preservation of the 'craft of living' being 'a woman's function as much as the preservation of the germ plasm within her ovaries'.[80] As Moscucci has observed, social roles were set in nature and 'a necessary relationship' linked 'women's biology and their social activities'.[81]

Italian doctors showed to be equally concerned with the issue of the size of the family. Too small a number of children encouraged a wrong relationship with the parents, required praxes of birth control unacceptable from a Catholic point of view and suggested egotistic reasons for the limitation of births. The Catholic commentator Antonio Boschi commented that 'where economic prosperity grows, the number of children diminishes', while 'poorer families' showed 'less fear of having children' than the better off.[82]

Italian and British observers seemed to agree on the fact that families' destiny was shaped more by parental individual abilities than by structural conditions. The abilities of men and women had a very different impact on family life. In 1947, the report on *The Neglected Child* commented that while 'many mothers in unpropitious surroundings' managed 'not only to rear a family but to make a real home', households living in acceptable social conditions could be ruined by parental foolishness.[83] In 1952 the sociologist Zweig observed that wives' 'qualities and abilities' contributed greatly to workers' status. A 'happily married man' had the necessary motivation to be 'careful to keep his job', and to make efforts 'to raise the standards of comfort in his family'.[84] An 'unsuitable' wife, however, had disastrous effects on any man's spirit and possibility to succeed.

The conclusion gained scientific corroboration from James Spence's observation that 'the capacity of the mother' represented the dominant factor in the correlation between environment and child health. If the mother 'failed her children suffered. If she coped with life skilfully and pluckily, she was a safeguard for their health'. The mother stood out 'as the cornerstone of the family structure' and 'the chief guardian of child's welfare': 'a family with a good mother [could] withstand a feckless or even a vicious father, but rarely [could] a family survive if the mother [failed]'.[85]

According to *The Neglected Child*, while both parents could be ruined by conditions such as 'ill health', 'mental problems', 'ignorance', 'marital conflict', 'apathy', 'irresponsibility', 'laziness' and 'alcoholism', consequences for the family were far worse when the mother was affected. The report commented that a man who drank did not necessarily neglect or ill treat his children and suggested that chances were that he drank 'to escape from squalling, dirty children, a slatternly wife and an unkempt home'.[86]

At the same time, the report recognised that mothers' more open behaviour during the war (particularly among middle-class women) could be read as a manifestation of 'the discovery that life need not forever be bounded by the walls of one's own home and the care of one's children'. This did not represent necessarily a sign of moral decay, but was instead 'an understandable' feeling, which should not be condemned and which explained how the 'total absence of fun' could indeed be detrimental to women's performances as mothers.[87]

The 1950s have been widely represented as a period of traditional domesticity, still far away from the sexual revolution that would have taken place in the following decade.[88] There is little doubt that maternity and home making remained the dominant images associated with women's role throughout the post-war years, although – as I try to show later in the chapter – the investment in motherhood rendered the male role, within society as well as within the home, more ambiguous than it is often suggested.

The emphasis put on the domestic environment as a cause of fathers' reproachable behaviour and women's overwhelming responsibility towards the preservation of appropriate mores became a further means of reinforcing prescribed domestic roles. At the same time, the normative definition of women as the sole responsible for the success of the family sent contradictory messages regarding the role of the father within the household.

Psychological, medical and social discourses sustained the identification between family welfare and satisfactory motherhood. In Italy, Bianchi postulated that 'seven times out of ten' women's 'laziness, negligence and extravagance' caused their men's 'misery, ruin and dejection'.

> We do not pretend that all wives should be expert dressmakers or cooks, but active and ingenious, it is reasonable to demand. What use is to the family the capacity of the father of earning an income, if the mother does not know the equally important art of saving and spending?[89]

Because of this, it was all the more important to choose a spouse not on the basis of a 'blind passion', but of a careful evaluation of those qualities necessary to the future success of the family.[90] Both men and women should be aware that the 'flaws of the parents' were a curse for the children, representing 'a second original sin ... cause of incalculable consequences'.[91]

Bianchi stressed the importance to make sure that there were no hereditary defects in the family of the prospective spouse, as well as to look for positive qualities in the chosen person. The most important qualities in a man were his religious principles, a faultless moral conduct and a willingness to work. For a woman, the list included all the prerogatives of a hard working housewife and mother. Not only she should have solid religious principles, but also the capacity of teaching them to her children. Piety, virtuousness and modesty were a wife's most important qualities; they were only occasionally found in beautiful women, since 'beauty and honesty rarely [went] together'. A badly managed home was bound to become 'hell after the first child is born' and increasingly intolerable as the family grew. A woman's good character, manners and health, together with proved domestic abilities, were essential to keep the family together, so that the husband was not 'pushed away from his home by the carelessness of his wife' whereupon he would begin to spend time in places of ill repute, drink and become brutal.[92]

Physical versus psychological welfare

One of the most important novelties of post-war developments in relation to child care concerned the increasing attention given to children's psychological as well as material welfare. This included the 'discovery' that lack of emotional care could be found among middle-class children as well as among those from lower social backgrounds. The former, however, were unlikely to be noticed, because of the predominant role assigned to material circumstances by child care agencies.[93]

The observation was indirectly confirmed by Bowlby's findings, according to which many children who had been ' "neglected" in the sense of their being dirty and ill-nourished' were however 'in excellent mental health' and without having 'suffered from the deprivation of love'. The preoccupation with physical health and physical appearance had sometimes produced 'the paradox',

> Of expensive social action being taken to convert a physically neglected but psychologically well-provided child into a physically well provided but emotionally starved one.[94]

The emotional needs of the child should also be treated as a complex phenomenon, which defeated common sense expectations. According to *The Neglected Child*, even a 'high grade' mentally defective woman, given appropriate training, could 'show at least a normal affection for and consideration for [her] children', and this constituted sometimes a better alternative to the removal of the child.[95] Bowlby found that children maintained a strong attachment even to those 'parents who, by all ordinary standards, are very bad'. Starting a new process of attachment required time and conditions of stability that were rarely achieved both in institutions and in fostering. Although admitting that more evidence was needed to evaluate the impact of institutional life on children's development, Bowlby stressed that it was important to remember that 'there may be something worse than bad home, and that is no home'.[96]

Italian commentators stretched the point to suit Catholic interests. For Trabucchi, by recognising that 'the worst home is preferable to the best institution', Bowlby's theory implicitly confirmed 'the irreplaceable role of the monogamous, exclusivist family', and therefore 'the natural law and the fundamental law ruling Christian marriage'.[97] The fundamental role of the family in the development of a child was jeopardised not so much by economic difficulties, as by parents' weak moral values and growing egoism.[98] Against this tendency, it was necessary to reaffirm what marriage and responsible parenthood entailed. The teaching of the church offered to Italian parents a safe and reliable guide, based on the affirmation of the centrality of the maternal role. The clarity with which women's role as mothers was affirmed and defined emphasised the ambiguity and contradictory expectations posed upon men.

Mothers and fathers: Towards a new definition of maternal and paternal roles?

In a brief but vivid portrayal of his father, Peter Lewis, has offered an effective synthesis of the characteristics most commonly associated to middle-class educated 'pre-war fathers'. He was 'strict and, though concerned about his children...not able to give, any more than he received as a child himself, affection of a close physical and emotional kind. Playing a correct stroke at cricket pleased him best: he was a brilliant club batsman and coached us from our earlier years'.[99] The description is episodic, but it conveys an image of fatherhood dominant since the Victorian period. The emphasis put during the post-war period on the importance of emotions in family relationships rendered such an image hardly satisfactory. Few scholars, however, have tried to map the transformation underwent by the representation of fathers during the post-war period.[100]

This is perhaps partly the result of post-war public discourses' overwhelming preoccupation with the maternal role, which overshadowed both women's changing expectations and the relevance of the father in the domestic scene. The war had proved that women were able to run their families (and provide for them) in the absence of their husbands; post-war psychoanalytical theories suggested to an increasingly large audience that children thrived through an emotional relationship with their mothers from which the father was largely excluded.

In 1944, with many men far away from home and family, D.W. Winnicott stressed the self-sufficiency of the emotional relationship between mother and child in his BBC radio broadcast. The father was important, but almost exclusively as an authority figure.[101] The centrality of the maternal role was even stronger in Bowlby's theory of maternal deprivation.Becoming a mother represented a process of fundamental transformation centred on the creation of an exclusive relationship with the new born, from which the father was largely excluded. Only in this way, mother and child could establish the 'close identification' upon which the healthy emotional development of the new born depended.

> The provision of constant attention night and day, seven days a week and 365 days in the year, is possible only for a woman who derives profound satisfaction from seeing her child grow from babyhood, through the many phases of childhood, to become an independent man or woman, and knows that it is her care which has made this possible.[102]

Bowlby acknowledged that the father was largely neglected within his study, and explained that 'the child's relation to his mother' constituted 'by far his most important relationship during these years'. In the eyes of the young child, 'father [played] second fiddle'.[103]

The emphasis on the importance of the relationship between mother and child inherently questioned whether any space could be left for women to cultivate identities other than as mothers. In the second edition of *Child Care*, published in 1961, two new chapters by Mary Salter Ainsworth dealt with a number of controversial issues that stemmed from Bowlby's theory. Among these was the question of 'supplementary care' (which is care from someone other than the mother) available to children in western society and, related to this, the question of the effect of mothers' work on children. Salter Ainsworth criticised 'the general finding that the children of working mothers and the children of non working mothers do not differ significantly'.[104] However, 'pressing mothers to delay resuming their careers' until children reached school age did not represent an adequate answer for those mothers 'unable to provide sufficient maternal care'. In these cases, 'both infant and mother might well thrive better with the mother working and with adequate and continuous care provided for the child'.[105] While apparently opening to women's work, Salter Ainsworth's argument implicitly suggested that the desire to go back to work could represent itself a sign of insufficient maternal capacity. Moreover, her conclusion implied that a working mother could be substituted, but she could not combine different roles.

Spence attributed the dilemma faced by many women to the pressure exercised by current social values, which encouraged women to take up a job 'when they should be paid to make a home'. Women would have had little reason to search for fulfilment outside maternity, Spence argued, if not for the negative attitude of present society towards the family, and the 'tendency [...] to exaggerate the economic difficulties of motherhood, to depict its tribulations and to belittle its compensations and rewards'.[106] Such attitudes had two major negative consequences. First, it caused women to marry later 'postponing the age of child bearing beyond the point of greatest fertility' and 'beyond the age of woman's greatest sensitivity to the lessons of marriage'. Second, it increased the number of single women seeking 'outlets' in professions substituting a 'mother's work'. Spence suggested that a more satisfactory solution would have been that of providing mothers 'with greater facilities, and more ample means of home making', therefore reducing the need for women employed in social services and guaranteeing better care to the children.[107]

The opposition to women's work was even more uncompromising in Italy. Women's maternal mission had been affirmed by the Pope, endorsed by Catholic doctors and social observers and implied by the absence of child care services.

More strongly than in Britain, Italian social observers emphasised that women did not choose to work, but were forced to do so by the 'political, economic, moral, cultural and social revolution' that had taken place in recent times. The worst scenario was that of mothers forced into factory work by economic need. In these cases, the home became little more than a hostel, where the spouses met only at meal times, tired and irritable after a day of hard work, and unable to give attention to their children, who ended up spending most of their time outside the home and on the streets.[108]

The situation could be less dramatic for those women (often in better social positions) who decided to gain a professional qualification, preferably as teachers or nurses. Even this solution, however, remained only acceptable if it did not question the assumption that a woman's 'best form of independence' remained 'depending from a loving husband who will make of her a happy mother'.[109] As Pugliaro wrote in 1959, women's aspirations outside the home might be 'rightful', but they inevitably endangered social stability.

Perhaps paradoxically, both in Britain and in Italy, the group of working mothers looked upon with greater suspicion were women from lower income groups, whose absence from home was deemed the inevitable source of endless damage. In the case of professional women, the more expressive nature of their work and their greater ability to provide good child care for their children tended to receive more sympathetic consideration, even from Catholic positions. However, not even these more favourable evaluations of women's work questioned the predominance and exclusivity of the mother–child relationship. The father, excluded to a large extent from this developing emotional bonding, was relegated to his breadwinner role.[110] Talcott Parsons' functionalist paradigm of the modern family placed great emphasis on the differentiation between the 'instrumental' role of men and the 'expressive' role of women, which involved changes in the social role of both parents. In particular, he suggested that the growing role of psychological interpretations of the mother–child relationship promoted a growing professionalisation of the maternal role, where the mother attempted 'to understand rationally the nature, conditions and limitations' of her love for her child.[111] In Ann Oakley's terms, 'capturing and intensifying the social reality of female domesticity', sociologists of the family promoted their 'most influential paradigm of women', 'a particularly precise reflection of prevailing cultural values'.[112] They also created a powerful paradigm of men, which limited their emotional relevance within the home at the moment when emotional and psychological well-being were becoming the main measure of the success of family life. Men remained the representatives of authority within the household, its main link with the outside world and the family's irreplaceable source of legitimacy. They maintained a position of power within the family, but the role they were expected to perform became increasingly unclear and the stage upon which they acted showed signs of crumbling beneath them. Women's growing access to paid employment and the critique of the family's oppressive nature by the social movements of the late 1960s questioned both men's economic role and their embodiment of authority. The question, which remains to some extent open, was, was it possible to create a new paradigm able to include men in the emotional bonds that constituted the essence of the modern family?[113]

Conclusions

Significant similarities emerged in the definition of nature and social role of the family offered by British and Italian welfare professionals and social observers.

In both countries, the definition of the family implied marriage and procreation and the family was recognised as the social institution best suited for the nurturing and education of children and in general for the provision of individual care. The family was seen as natural, necessary and irreplaceable. It rested upon a clear distinction of gender roles, and the recognition that the bulk of responsibility for the family belonged to women. In all these aspects, the post-war family fit the paradigm of the 'specialised agency' created by Talcott Parsons and characterised by two 'basic and irreducible functions': 'the primary socialisation of children' and 'the stabilisation of the adult personalities'.[114]

Despite the similarities that characterise the way in which the family was understood in post-war Britain and Italy, significant differences existed in the role played by medical and psychological professionals in the two countries.

A 'British school' of psychoanalytical interpretation, existed since the 1920s, centred around Melanie Klein's work on the child in psychoanalysis. Controversial discussions around the legacy of Freudian analysis resulted in a rift between Melanie Klein, Anna Freud and their followers, which informed the post-war psychoanalytical debate within and outside the country.[115] After the war, practitioners such as D. W. Winnicott and John Bowlby contributed greatly to the penetration of psychoanalytical approaches in current medical and sociological language. In Italy, the Catholic Church remained by far the most powerful authority in matters of family and sexuality, and moral rather than psychological concerns informed the language with which the family was discussed. Although references to Bowlby's work started to appear in Italy since the mid-1950s, the psychoanalytical foundations of his approach were largely left aside. Rather, Italian readings of Bowlby's theory emphasised the points of convergence with Catholic values in relation to the family and the maternal role. By referring to Bowlby,

Catholic doctors tried to support religious truths with scientific findings, although largely ignoring the conceptions of human nature upon which Bowlby's work relied.

In both countries, the family was discussed in the 20 years following the end of the war as the main determinant of social stability and individual adjustment. Such a paradigm was challenged from the late 1960s by radical anti-authoritarian political and social movements. Women's and students' movement denounced the inherently oppressive nature of family life. Critical practitioners argued that individual alienation and mental illness were not the result of deviant family life, but rather of the daily interactions that took place within the apparently 'normal' household. The result was an inverted image of the interpretations of the role of the family as provider of individual welfare and stability that had dominated the 1950s. In Laing's words, what psychiatrists diagnosed as illness became a 'socially intelligible manifestation' when placed within the context of the family's oppressive and mystifying relationships.[116]

4

The Edges of the Family: State, Citizens and the 'Children deprived of a normal home life'

In January 2006, Tony Blair promised to step up his government's plan to tackle antisocial behaviour through the so-called 'Respect Action Plan'. The plan promised to increase measures available to deal with 'low level crime' and to provide greater means of treating 'problem families', identified as the main cause of disorder in under-privileged areas. Parenting programmes represented a crucial aspect of the plan. They foresaw compulsory education schemes for parents of 'out of control' children, including residential parenting centres. Experimental residential centres are already run in a few areas of the country, targeting families already homeless or about to lose their home. Their main aims are to teach parents how to manage their home, maintain a routine and keep control of their children. Stress is put on families' commitment to pay bills and maintenance costs, as well as to attend courses in good parenting, including healthy eating, housework and literacy. Most importantly, parents are 'observed' in the daily domestic activities carried out within their flats. In presenting the new scheme, Blair described it as an attempt to respond to a new emergency, characterised by a lack of respect in every day interactions. This was not, Blair claimed, an attempt to go back in time, but rather a way of facing a new challenge with innovative instruments of intervention.

The Respect Plan could be read as the latest example of what Frank Furedi has called 'one of the defining features of New Labour social policy', namely the use of 'therapeutic intervention in family life in order to alter parenting practices and to curb antisocial behaviour'.[1] According to Furedi, parenting orders (through which the parents may be forced to attend 'counselling or guidance sessions') and residential centres for problem families represent examples of a system of 'therapeutic governance' in which emotions (and their control) have become of primary political interest.[2] Furedi locates the take off of the therapeutic culture in the 1980s, following a 'century long expansion of the influence of psychology', and identifies one of its distinctive features in 'a deep-seated aversion towards family and informal relations', identified as the prominent source of individual emotional pathologies.[3]

From a historical point of view, one of the most striking aspects of New Labour's approach is what appears as the deployment of traditional forms of intervention in the context of a new rhetoric. There is a striking resemblance between the new 'experimental' residential centres opened in Britain and Octavia Hill's late 19th century training tenements. The way "problem families" are currently being identified as the source of social disorder is also not new. In presenting the new scheme, Blair talked about the greater respect that characterised social relations in the past, and he remarked in a nostalgic way: 'as we get more prosperous and as deference declines, respect for authority is bound to fall away'.[4] Historians can easily cite similar rhetoric used by successive generations of politicians throughout the post-war period. Emphasis on moral responsibility may have been partially substituted by a call to the management of emotions, but the new Respect Plan brings back issues and dilemmas confronted by welfare societies at least since the end of the war. These include the limits of legitimate state intervention in family life and the extent to which it is possible as well as advisable to intervene in the family in the name of the interests of society at large.

In the previous two chapters I have discussed sets of ideas regarding the nature and function of the family, arguing that a coherent notion of the family existed in post-war Britain and Italy, based on the nurturing and rearing of children. The prominence given by New Labour to the possibility of tackling of anti-social behaviour through parental control, however, marks a significant difference with the Italian situation and suggests a different understanding of the relationship between the state and the family in the two countries.

Chapters 4 and 5 explore this issue by considering the type of intervention adopted in post-war Italy and Britain towards families who were seen as having failed their primary role as providers of a stable and secure environment for young people to grow up.

The analysis focuses on situations where young people were either considered victims of their domestic environment or identified as a threat to the rest of the community. As we shall see, the distinction between these two groups was (and still is) hardly clear-cut and a constant tension between care and control informed interventions towards young people throughout the post-war period.[5] Moreover, the treatment of young people has brought under scrutiny some of the fundamental prerogatives of family and state. The limits of parental responsibilities and powers, the definition of justified state intervention and the form and scope of 'substitutive families' emerged as controversial topics in successive reforms of child care system throughout Europe.

My analysis begins at the end of Second World War, when children seemed to gain a new visibility and political relevance, partly as a result of the legacy left by the war. Children were widely identified as the main victims of the conflict and the creation of new welfare states by democratic regimes seemed to imply an urgent necessity to create solid networks of support for the young victims of atrocities committed by the older generation. Moreover, the war had stretched beyond repair the already inadequate provisions available for the care of children in need. As I show, however, the actual implementation of reforms was far from straightforward.

Before discussing further the factors that brought young people to the fore of the political agenda, an important qualification has to be made. The focus of this book is the family and not children per se. This means that there is little space here for a very rich and important debate about the definition of child and the treatment of children in social policy.

A growing body of literature, both in history and social policy, adopts children as the focus of its analysis, with the aim of ending what has been described as young people's enduring invisibility. Historians have suggested different theories of the 'origin' of the child as a historical category and different chronologies of how changes in attitudes towards children have taken place in the Western world.[6] Scholars of social policy have tried to adopt a 'child centred' outlook when evaluating the impact of different areas of social policy on younger people.[7] The question of how childhood can be understood and defined, however, remains open. A general consensus seems to exist among scholars concerning the fact that childhood should be treated as a socially constructed notion, which cannot be defined purely on the basis of biology. To take the discussion of children away from age, however, remains a challenging task. It is even more difficult to find ways of representing children's experiences without falling into normative notions of what is expected of a child. As I said, the focus of my argument is what the treatment of children has to tell us about the family and its definition. These ongoing debates on the place of children in academic research remain in the background of my analysis and I try to make reference to them whenever necessary.

Parents and children in the new welfare society

The end of the Second World War represented a watershed in the treatment of children both in Italy and in Britain. In Italy, the collapse of fascism ended the regime's effort to garner young people's support through a pervasive network of youth organisations and its upholding of procreation as a civic duty. The new republican constitution recognised that parents held a unique responsibility towards their children's physical, moral and educational needs, limiting the intervention of the state to cases of parental incapacity.[8] In Britain, no written constitution defined the duties of the state towards children. The creation of the welfare state, however, created a new framework for the treatment of children and encouraged a wide discussion of existing provisions.

Towards a new equilibrium? State and voluntary sector in the post-war period

A widespread argument in post-war discourses suggested that the war had accelerated a transformation of individual values already under way while worsening the material conditions experienced by many families. The combination of these two phenomena had grave implications for children. In the words of Leila Rendell, Honorary President of the Caldecott Community, one of Britain's leading children charities, family life had begun 'to show signs of "dry rot"' since the interwar period, and by 1939 'this disintegration was having a repercussion on the lives of thousands of children'. The war had worsened the situation, bringing to a 'breaking point' the 'frail resources' available for dealing with children deprived of a 'normal home life'.[9]

Among the novelties of post-war approaches to child welfare was a growing confidence that it was 'both possible and necessary to uncover the needs of the child'.[10] In a positive light, such a confidence suggested the coming to an end of paternalistic patterns of relief and the beginning of an approach to child care more explicitly focused on the family.[11] In a more critical reading, this could be seen as the sign of a normative approach to the regulation of family life, justified by children's psychological and social needs.[12] My suggestion is that while socio-medical discourses increasingly informed the identification of children's needs and parental (particularly maternal) responsibilities, social stereotypes and moral judgements continued to inform the attitudes maintained towards children in care and their families, both in Britain and in Italy, well after 1945.

State and church in Italy

According to Article 30 of the Italian Constitution, the state had the duty to provide for children's maintenance and education in case of permanent or temporary parental incapacity. As the family law expert Lancellotti Mari explained in 1955, the state's duties towards children were part of the 'social function', which constituted a necessary aspect of any modern state.[13] Such duties included taking up parental rights in case of parental 'idleness, ineptitude, amorality and physical inability' to provide for the children's physical, moral and educational needs.[14]

As in other sectors of assistance, most of the post-war legislation was based on 19th century measures, systematised during the 1920s. The state was only obliged to intervene (through the so-called 'assistenza legale') when no voluntary provision (assistenza istituzionale) was available.[15] The statutory responsibility for the under 18 who found themselves in a state of 'material and moral abandonment' fell upon the Opera Nazionale Maternità e Infanzia (from now on ONMI), a fascist organisation left largely unreformed after the war. The duties of the Opera included the supervision of young people's institutions, although not the actual provision of institutional care. Abandoned illegitimate children, children with 'mental deficiencies' and the 'blind, deaf, and mute' also remained outside the responsibility of the ONMI, and under the care of provincial administrations, operating through the Enti Comunali di Assistenza (Local Boards of Assistance, from now on, ECA). These had the duty to promote legislation in support of orphans and abandoned children, and to assume their temporary care in case of emergency. A number of educational and judicial authorities dealt with specific categories of need, providing assistance to groups such as the orphans of parents killed in work accidents or during the war.

Institutional care remained the most common form of intervention throughout the 1940s and 1950s. Most children's institutions were run by voluntary (often religious) organisations and operated without the state's economic support and outside its controls.[16] At the end of the Second World War, the increasing economic difficulties experienced by voluntary organisations and their frequently inadequate performances brought into question the responsibilities of the state and the adequacy of a system relying mostly upon the voluntary sector.

In 1944, the United Nations Relief and Rehabilitation Administration (UNRRA) launched its first plan specifically addressed to children. The management of the operation fell in Italy upon the Amministrazione Aiuti Internazionali (International Aids Administration, from now on

AAI) under the leadership of the Christian Democrat Ludovico Montini, brother of the future Pope Paul VI. The AAI's functions included the distribution of food and clothes, and the financing of refurbishment works.

While providing precious material support in the aftermath of the war, international help highlighted the weakness of Italy's own system of assistance. In 1948, a series of interventions in *Maternità e Infanzia* sparkled a debate on how to improve the country's relief system. A possible solution was identified in the unification of existing major charitable works under the guidance of the ONMI, with the aim of increasing economic efficiency and service delivery.[17] The proposal, however, was criticised as being likely to put excessive burdens on public expenditure and to go against those charitable organisations that for centuries had constituted the core of Italian assistance.[18] In support of the maintenance of the existing system, it was argued that the 'constant flux' of international aid to Italy was not a sign of weakness, but rather the proof that the country was able to provide standards of care accepted at international level.

The shortcomings of this interpretation became increasingly clear in the early 1950s. Long-term economic difficulties and the slowing down of immediate post-war assistance imposed painful economic constraints on charitable organisations in general, and hit children's institutions particularly hard. Many of those involved in the running of voluntary homes commented bitterly against the 'feverish (and mortifying) searches for money' from the general public. Fund-raising strategies were largely based on the attempt to inspire pity in order to win the attention of the general public and wealthy benefactors. Common praxes included sending children 'in sad processions to the funerals of the various benefactors' of a home, printing 'calendars and magazines full of children's photographs and their most pitiful stories', and placing almsboxes near the door of orphanages, to remind passers-by of homes' dependence upon private generosity.[19] In 1952, the AAI itself expressed concern for the diminishing availability of nutritional food following the reduction in international aid. The attempt by the Amministrazione to substitute the goods previously imported by national products proved impracticable in large areas of the country.[20]

In many cases, homes' economic stringency was aggravated by the unreliability of public entities responsible for the payment of charges. In 1951, a leading figure in the debate, Ivo Pini, wondered whether the time had come for orphanages to 'resort to coarse forms of protest, reclaiming help from the state and at least the payment of charges in time'. He concluded, however, that this was against the character and nature of charitable work:

> None of us could think of taking children in the streets like workers on strike, protesting under the windows of ministries, prefects and those that should remember their commitments towards us. You must forgive us then, if we have to appeal again and again to the heart of our private benefactors for the good of our children.[21]

The few available studies confirmed that the system in place was both inefficient and largely unaccountable. An enquiry conducted in 1951, by the Istituto Centrale di Statistica (Central Institute of Statistical Analysis) and the AAI, admitted the difficulty of categorising institutions and obtaining reliable data. The study estimated the existence of 'at least three thousand institutions', providing assistance to 'around 200,000 children'. Most institutions had been created for 'specific categories of children', following the isolated initiatives of individuals and local associations.[22]

Ivo Pini summed up in an article published in *Maternità e Infanzia* the dilemma faced by practitioners favourable to a system of assistance largely independent of the state and yet confronted on a daily basis with the shortcomings of the present situation. Pini defended the 'richness' and 'variety' of the Italian voluntary sector, the result of the liberal and Christian tradition upon which Italian culture was based. Only a totalitarian state, he argued, could attempt to assume directly the responsibility of a function assigned to the family by nature, such as the education of young children. Nonetheless, it was the duty of the state to create a framework through which the 'solidarity of the nation' could be expressed. In this duty, the Italian state had been gravely lacking.

An even more critical position was taken in 1953 by the *Commissione Parlamentare d'Inchiesta sulla Miseria*. The committee (unique in post-war Italy) concluded that the minimal social presence of the Italian state was incompatible with the principles of social solidarity affirmed by the 1948 Constitution.[23] Their report criticised fragmented and uncoordinated responsibilities, which duplicated costs without providing satisfactory care. A range of semi-public bodies, often created by the fascist government and maintained after the war, held specific responsibilities for different groups of children in need. Different administrations were responsible for legitimate and illegitimate children, war orphans, young people who had lost their parents in work accidents and so on. Their oversized and expensive bureaucracies were rarely justified in terms of the services provided. Lack of coordination between different organisations or different sectors of the same one rendered it impossible to provide continual care and efficient follow-up of individual cases, often frustrating any possibility of restoring children to their families.[24] Outdated and overcrowded premises and lack of qualified personnel and training facilities made institutional care deeply unsatisfactory.

According to the *Guida Nazionale agli Istituti di Assistenza e di Ricovero*, a census of children's institutions published in 1954, 3200 institutions provided in Italy a total of 216 540 residential places for 'normal children'.[25] These included residential schools taking in quotas of non-paying children and represented by far the most common type of child assistance. The number of institutions diminished steadily as one travelled south: northern Italy accounted for 37 per cent, the centre for 27 per cent, the South for 22 per cent, and Sicily and Sardinia for just 14 per cent. More than one-third of the institutions were located in the chief towns of province. Although a similar number of beds was available for boys and girls, the number of girls' homes was more than double that of the boys', thereby allowing for smaller size and better accommodation. The imbalance was particularly noticeable in the south. Institutions admitting both sexes were rare, mostly due to the resistances of religiously run organisations. The length of care was also different for boys and girls, with the first being generally discharged shortly after the end of elementary school (at 10 years of age), and girls retained until they were 18. The vast majority of institutions (2809 out of 3200) provided schooling up to elementary level; only 938 of these, mostly in the centre and north of the country went on sending children to the media unica (unified secondary school) or to vocational schools. The enquiry found little comfort as far as professional training was concerned: girls seemed to be 'invariably trained in needle work, sewing, knitting, darning and tailoring', and although more alternatives were apparently open to boys (including mechanics, woodwork and agriculture), only 'few institutions' offered any training at all.[26]

Although the report did not provide exact figures for institutions dealing with 'young children, single mothers, homeless families and so on', organisations for young children were said to constitute the most significant presence within this group (106 homes dealing with 12 574 children).[27] These same bodies were often responsible for fostering on behalf of provincial administrations.

In the introduction to the census, Ludovico Montini argued that no improvement of the situation could take place within the present legislative framework. The presence of so many different private and public bodies represented 'a deterrent to any attempt to improve and modernise'; the Ministry of the Interior (MI), responsible for supervision, operated according to inadequate and backward criteria of assistance.[28]

Financing was also unsatisfactory. Of the 21 billion lire spent in 1952 by institutions of assistance, state and other public entities had contributed 15, while private charity had paid for the rest. This had proved inadequate in the face of the overwhelming need and unable to improve standards of care. Mediocrity, Montini commented, dominated 'every aspect of the organisation'. The outcome was a generalised state of decay, where poor education, low standards of hygiene, unsatisfactory recreational provisions, and lack of trained personnel constituted the norm. Montini advocated centralisation as the only means of guaranteeing uniform criteria of intervention, a clearer structure of responsibilities and the coordination necessary to promote the adoption of solutions more suitable to children's individual needs.[29]

Lack of political interest and complex political allegiances between the charitable sector, the Catholic Church and the ruling party hindered the cause of a comprehensive reform of the system of assistance, including the sector specifically concerned with child welfare. Montini's own influence within the Christian Democrat Party and as head of the AAI could do little to modify attitudes towards assistance throughout the 1950s, when the overcoming of the immediate post-war emergency contributed to the progressive disappearance of the question from the political debate.

State and voluntary associations in Britain: The 1948 Children Act

The war had had a dramatic impact on child assistance in Britain as well. In London and the country's other main urban areas most residential schools had been closed or used as 'transition centres' for children waiting to be transferred to safer areas. The larger premises outside the cities had been used to evacuate either very young children or children in care in the main urban areas, while the 'normal healthy children' who lived in them had been moved to private households.[30]

The re-opening of residential schools and children's homes in 1945 revealed shortage of staff, outdated premises, clumsy administrative machinery and over-lapping powers. At a Conference on Children Without Homes organised by the Women's Group on Public Welfare in February 1945, Rendell criticised the present system as leading to a 'chaotic state of affairs which often must of necessity allow abuses and injustices to go undetected'.[31] Her verdict was confirmed in the following year by the Curtis Committee, which criticised the lack of clear lines of responsibilities and coordination between government's departments, local authorities (LAs) and voluntary organisations.[32]

The findings of the report informed the Children Act of 1948, a landmark of British post-war social policy and a crucial point of reference and contestation for any reform in the sector of child assistance since. Among the main outcomes of the act were the organisation of a Children's department within the Home Office (HO) and the establishment of Children's Committees and Children Officers at local level.[33] The Act widened means of intervention, encouraging a greater use of boarding out and adoption and the restoration of children to their families whenever possible. It also recommended a more careful handling of children taken into residential institutions, starting with a careful assessment of their physical and psychological needs at the time of admission.[34]

Among the reasons why the 1948 Children Act has been seen as a turning point in the history of child welfare provisions in Britain is its support for casework and preventive care.[35] Among the measures intended to improve prevention was the possibility given to LAs to foster a child with one of his or her parents or relatives, a provision interpreted by Bob Holman as a challenge to the Victorian idea according to which 'once removed from their parent, children were best kept away from them'.[36]

Such a supposed upholding of the family, however, had at least two limitations. First, the act did not go as far as to envisage economic help for families in those cases where financial hardship constituted the principal source of problems within the household. (More often, economic difficulties were interpreted as symptoms of moral and temperamental defects in the parents.) Second, the Act effectively limited parental powers by allowing LAs to assume parental rights on the basis of a Children's Committee resolution, without need to apply to a court of law.[37] Finally, prevention might have been supported in principle but received little practical support, partly as a result of the limited resources available to the sector of child care as a whole. The dilemma was summed up effectively by a child welfare officer working in a voluntary organisation, who, in July 1949, commented:

> It is true to say that an ounce of prevention in this work is worth many pounds of cure. Unfortunately, there is no statutory provision whereby even the smallest expenditure can be made by the Children's Officer to avert the drastic step of removing the child from its home.

Once removed, the state is prepared to spend money on the child's upbringing.[38]

This, however, is not to deny that a shift in attitudes took place throughout the 1950s, culminating in a reassessment of the meaning of boarding out itself. Child Care Officers, originally appointed as Boarding Out Officers, were traditionally concerned with 'methods of care rather than the process of admission'.[39] Improved and longer assessments of the circumstances leading to children being taken into care represented the first stage of the attempt to keep a growing number of children either with their families of origin or with relatives or friends of the family. By the end of the 1950s, the common practice of placing children in residential establishments as the first step, with possible alternative solution sought only afterwards, was increasingly substituted by an attempt to seek solutions allowing children to remain with their parents or boarding them out with someone already known, leaving the transfer to an institution only to those cases where both alternatives had failed. This was partly the result of the medical establishment becoming increasingly doubtful of the consequence of separating young children from their families and concerned with the emotional as well as the physical well-being of young people, and partly the result of the difficulty of coping with existing pressure over inadequate facilities.

Public opinion, political awareness and the establishment of the Curtis Committee

The Report of the Care of Children Committee, the first British enquiry 'covering all groups of children' in care, has been described as the almost inevitable outcome of wartime concerns and solidarity.[40] The circumstances leading to the appointment of the Committee in 1945, however, question the idea of a state ready to mobilise in the name of solidarity. The public side of the campaign leading to the appointment is relatively well known.

In February 1944, Marjory Allen (later Lady Allen of Hurtwood) sent a letter to *The Times* describing the appalling conditions of children's homes throughout the country, and asking for a public enquiry. Allen had been the chairwoman of the Nursery Schools Association and a member of the Advisory Council on the Welfare of Mothers and Young Children, set up by the Ministry of Health (MH) during the war. Despite her political credentials as member of the Independent Labour Party, a pacifist activist and wife of the Labour MP Clifford Allen, her campaign was presented, at least publicly, as entirely motivated by her concerns as a private citizen.[41] The first groups to react to Allen's letter were ex-internees and workers. Most of their letters confirmed backward methods of care and inadequate premises and personnel. The letters received were collected and published by Allen in July 1944, in order 'to stir into action the Government, Members of Parliament, LAs, Governors of Charitable Organisations and the general public'.[42]

In a letter to Lord Woolton, then Minister of Reconstruction, Allen explained that she had 'hesitated for a long time' before bringing her findings to the 'public notice', in consideration of the engagement of the government 'with other urgent matters'. The government's lack of concern for children in care, however, had finally persuaded her to act.

> Since the Government is concerning itself with many fundamental reconstruction plans, I felt it is appropriate to draw attention to the fact that these particularly unfortunate children have, so far, found no place in the Education Bill, the White Paper on the Health Service, or in any other reconstruction plans.[43]

The popularity of the matter and its possible political implications captured the attention of the cabinet. Consultations between the HO and the Ministries of Health, Education and Reconstruction indicated that the 'public agitation about alleged conditions in children's homes' demanded the setting up without delay of a committee of enquiry, despite anticipated practical and political problems. In August 1944, in response to a suggestion to leave the matter until after the report on the Civil Service expected for 1946, the Permanent Undersecretary to the HO Sir Alexander Maxwell agreed on the desirability of postponing the enquiry. Nevertheless, he admitted that Herbert Morrison, the Home Secretary, felt that taking early action would most likely be inevitable 'in view of the correspondence in *The Times*, and of the pressure which will no doubt be exerted in Parliament when the House meet again'.[44] In November, the Home Secretary, the Secretary of State for Scotland, the Minister of Health and the Minister of Education issued a joint memorandum announcing the future establishment of the committee. The document explained that although 'variations of standards' were to be expected throughout the country, available evidence did not 'support any suggestion of general neglect and abuse'.[45] Despite the 'private citizen' image pursued by Allen, the success of her battle owned as much to her political skills and connections than to her perseverance. In a note to Frank Newsam at the end of October, Norman Brooke commented that Lady Allen was 'holding off temporarily' only because of Woolton's assurance that he was 'going into the matter with his colleagues in the Government'. However, it was 'already more than a month' since he had 'promised to let her know the result of his enquiries' and it was to be expected that 'before very long' she would have 'return[ed] to the charge'.[46] Marjory Allen herself recalled having been 'far from pleased when Herbert Morrison told me privately that he felt I overstated my case'.

The situation changed in January 1945 following the death of a young boy, Dennis O'Neil, for 'neglect' and 'ill-use' at the farmhouse in Pontesbury (Salop), where he had been boarded out an year before. The wave of public indignation that followed the case gave new grounds to Marjory Allen's denunciations. Among those who called for the appointment of a committee of enquiry into the death of Dennis O'Neil (and more generally over the state of child residential care) were the Women's Co-operative Guild, the Lambeth Trade Council and the Transport and General Workers Union, whose Bristol Branches declared that they were 'horrified at the revelation in the Pontesbury (Salop) case'. All agreed that the government could not 'escape responsibility for this tragic state of affairs'.[47] In February 1945, a deputation of members of parliament discussed the question of boarding out with the Home Secretary, the Ministry of Education and the Ministry of Health. A report on the circumstances that lead to the death of Dennis O'Neill was published in May 1945. The Chairman, Walter Monckton, criticised the lack of communication between the two LAs involved (Newport and Shropshire), neither of which had realised 'the direct and personal nature of the relationship between a supervising authority and boarded-out children'.[48]

However, public pressure was not sufficient to win over resistances to a widespread investigation. The departments concerned worried about the amount of work required by a 'lengthy and troublesome' enquiry at a time when 'Government Departments, LAs and voluntary organisations' were already 'understaffed and overworked'.[49] From a political point of view, concerns were expressed for the fact that a formal investigation could raise discontent among voluntary associations at a time when crucial issues concerning the respective roles of state and voluntary sector were been discussed. Such concerns were not unfounded, as showed by the adverse reaction of the Children's Society to the establishment of the Curtis Committee.

In 1944, a long article in the Society's Annual Report explained that in a situation where 'one cannot pick up a paper without seeing some new "revelation" or expression of opinion', the enquiry of the Committee on Children's Homes was welcomed by the Society. This was, however, on condition that 'the Inquiry will be an inquiry, not a trial'. The society emphasised that they had 'nothing to defend and nothing to hide', and that its homes were, 'as always, [...] open at any time to visitors who wish to see how our children live'.[50] Moreover, they maintained that they had 'a profoundly important part to play in the future of child care', in co-operation with government, statutory authorities and their welfare workers.

Already in the Annual Report for 1943, the Society had admitted that the voluntary movement was 'facing criticism and scrutiny as never before' and should 'stand or fall by its own real virtues'. In order to keep their role in the face of the expanding role of the state, voluntary organisations should stress their power to try things first, acting as 'a laboratory of social service'. It was part of the 'British tradition' that the voluntary sector should do 'the work of pioneering', and the government should learn 'by their success or failure'.[51]

The necessity of reaffirming the role of the voluntary sector became even more urgent after the introduction of the 1948 Act. Although welcoming the new legislation as a 'milestone' in child welfare, the Society criticised the press for having 'barely mentioned' the position of voluntary associations, giving the impression that there was 'now no need for the Society's existence and that everything will be attended to by the state'. This needed to be 'vigorously contradicted', not least because the 'many severe criticism of certain forms of child care' that had been 'very rightly brought to public notice' had 'cast a shadow' on the voluntary sector, which could result in a 'serious curtailment of financial support'.[52]

> We can say, humbly but confidently, that where the voluntary societies lead the State has followed. There is room – indeed a desperate need – for both, and one augments the other. Voluntary service is a worthy cause by men and women of Christian principles possessing an ideal, represents a tremendous driving force for good, and the State cannot possibly replace – and has no desire to suppress – such warm humanitarian impulses.[53]

In 1950, the Society made again the point that only the 'national but unnationalised work' of individual citizens could lay 'the foundation on which could be erected, strong and secure, the building of Christian life and character'.[54] The Annual Report for 1957 explained that people's 'simple desire [...] to help the children who suffer distress' and the incapacity of the welfare state 'to offer help as widely as it

[was] in demand' confirmed the importance of voluntary action in the sector of child assistance.[55] The role played by the Society was 'of great consequences' for the safeguarding of 'posterity', 'the nation' and 'the Commonwealth'.

> It is no mean record to have saved 76,000 children for the Nation. 'Saved' that is, from the environment and surroundings which would have made them a hindrance rather than a help to the community. 'Saved' in that there has been inculcated in their training a real meaning and understanding of that nation-wide code 'Fear God and Honour the Queen'.[56]

The many who had 'given their lives for their country' during the war and who had spent 'their earlier years under the Society's care' were the best proof of the good service the society provided.[57] Although from different perspectives, both the Church of England and Marjory Allen appealed to individual responsibility as the foundation of a cohesive society.

In her evidence to the Curtis Committee, Allen insisted that her involvement in the matter was that of 'a layman and a citizen'. Her motivations did not lie in any specialised knowledge, but in the duty to speak against 'tradition and vested interests' represented 'in the ministerial quarters, in religious organisations, in voluntary bodies and in the very Homes themselves'.[58] As she recalled in her memoirs, 'I had seen acts of grave injustice . . . and if I took no action I would become an accomplice'.[59] As members of a community, citizens were directly involved in the destiny of its more vulnerable members, ('for we pay for their (children's) upbringing either through taxes or by voluntary contributions') and had a duty to speak in their name. The state, on the other hand, had 'for too long, evaded its responsibility', creating 'an army of disillusioned and unhappy citizens', excluded by the new welfare entitlements, isolated 'from the main stream of life and education' and living 'under the chilly stigma of charity'.[60]

A world of its own? Child institutions and the reformation of the family

Who goes into care?

Both in Italy and in Britain, young people admitted to care could be divided into three main categories: those with 'particular needs', 'young offenders' and 'normal children in special circumstances'. As the Curtis Committee pointed out, these categories were far from being clear-cut and determined only marginally a child's destiny once in care.

A partly different case was that of young people taken into care only for short periods, following specific family emergencies. So-called 'short-term cases' attracted increasing attention in Britain in the mid-1950s, following an apparent rise in their incidence. In 1955, short-term cases constituted 'about half' of the total number of children taken into care in that year. New admissions, however, amounted only to 6 per cent of the total number of children in institutions, the great majority of whom remained long-term cases, likely to be retained until the age limit.[61] Rise in short-term cases was attributed variously to changes in social policy (particularly the fact that a growing number of women went now to hospitals to give birth under new National Health Service (NHS) provisions) and to the fact that fewer families lived sufficiently close to relatives able to help in the absence of the mother.

In both countries, inadequate procedures at the time of admission and the absence of agreed criteria of classification rendered it difficult to gain a clear picture of why children came into care. Nonetheless, occasional local studies showed relatively common paths. Poverty remained the main cause of admission in the Milanese province, where 33 per cent of children in institution were 'legitimate children coming from poor families'; the death of both parents constituted a reason for admission for a minority of children (8 per cent) while an even smaller proportion of admissions was caused by the child being an 'abandoned illegitimate'.[62] Similarly, a study conducted by Hilda Lewis on 500 children in care at the Mersham Reception Centre in 1954 found that most children came from families with low income, low occupational stability and overcrowded housing conditions. 'Children with no parents or no mother or deserted by the mother' constituted 13 per cent of the new reception and 23 per cent of the total. Children committed under a 'fit person order' represented 29.6 per cent of the total and 8.6 per cent of new admissions. Most of these court orders had followed charges of ill treatment and neglect, with only one-sixth of court orders having been caused by the child having committed an offence.[63] Mother's illness or death was seldom the direct cause of a child's admission. Usually 'the father or other relatives tried to care for him. It was only when these attempts failed that the children's officer entered the scene'.[64]

In search for definitions: State and voluntary organisations in the care of neglected children

According to Philp and Timms, the term 'problem family' was first consciously used in 1943 in an attempt to characterise a group of families 'living in squalor and unable or unwilling to make constructive use of the social services'.[65]

The identification of a particular group of families where social marginality and individual pathologies combined and were reproduced from generation to generation was intertwined with the attempt made in the post-war period to identify 'child neglect' as a specific, identifiable and treatable phenomenon.

An attempt to define what circumstances should be considered normal for the upbringing of a child was made in 1944 at a conference organised in London by the Women's Group on Public Welfare and the National Council for Maternity and Child Welfare. Normal circumstances could be summed up in being born into a married family, 'living in reasonable good housing conditions', having a mother who was 'well enough to look after her child' and was not 'compelled' 'to go out to work' for financial reasons.[66]

At the other end of the spectrum were family lives dominated by poor and 'dirty material conditions', and parental shortcomings that in the worst cases could culminate in 'child neglect'.[67] The 'neglected child' was the most dramatic example of a 'normal child' living in 'unsuitable circumstances'. After the war, the National Society for the Prevention of Cruelty to Children (NSPCC) estimated that the 100 000 children, with whom the society dealt annually constituted only the 'grossest cases' of an 'unexplored region of child suffering' existed in the country.[68] In the summer of 1949, following the passage of the new Children Act, the matter reached the attention of parliament.

In a letter to *The Times*, Eva Hubback explained that improved procedures were necessary to obtain earlier discovery of neglect, caused in the majority of cases by parents and especially mothers' 'inadequacy, ill health, limited mentality, ineducability, or apathy'.[69]

At the core of the problem was the absence of specific statutory duties for the treatment of child neglect. This left an overwhelming responsibility to voluntary organisations, themselves hampered by shortage of funds and personnel. The Ministries of Health and Education and the LAs appeared the most suitable bodies to take up the responsibility for neglected children, possibly through the creation of a specific family-care service employing trained social workers.[70] The Children's Department supported the idea, providing health visitors and housing managers with extra training necessary to deal with families at risk. Health visitors' training should be broadened to include work with mothers 'who through illness, discouragement, unemployment, or sheer callousness and indolence, fail[ed] to provide adequate care' to their children.[71] Housing managers, often women of 'wide social interests' trained 'on Octavia Hill lines', would benefit from more extensive domestic training. School attendance officers, school nurses and teachers could all contribute to the discovery and early treatment of symptoms of neglect. Voluntary agencies at the forefront of work with child neglect and abusive family life, such as the NSPCC and the Family Service Units (FSU), could provide useful models of intervention. Neither of them, however, proved entirely satisfactory.

The FSU, formed as a part of the Pacifist Service Units and operating in London, Liverpool and Manchester, had a unique style of work, based on the establishment of 'warm, personal and long-term' relationships between caseworkers and parents. The voluntary worker aimed to provide 'a stable, reliable' figure, able to understand parents' feelings 'without having to see things their way' and without 'be harmed by the phantasies [*sic*] which they find frightening'.[72] The FSU combined innovative methods of work with a traditional approach to family life made them a suitable model for state-sponsored intervention.[73] Their praxis based on 'daily, even hourly, example', however, proved difficult to incorporate into the work of a public department. In the case of the NSPCC, the main shortcomings of the approach found by officials in the Ministry of Health concerned the fact that none of the 'few women visitors' employed in preventive work by the Society were trained social workers and the fact that the NSPCC's overall attitude towards rehabilitation remained 'a not very whole hearted one'.[74]

Providing practical help and domestic training was crucial in a situation where most neglectful mothers seemed to be 'loving mothers and faithful wives, although thoroughly incompetent housekeepers'.[75]

Observations carried out in the Salvation Army's Training Home Mayflower, in Plymouth and Holloway prison in London suggested that most neglectful mothers shared a combination of below average intelligence, unusually difficult home circumstances and pregnancy before marriage.[76] According to a study conducted in Holloway prison during the mid-1950s, defective intelligence was so marked among these neglectful mothers that it was 'incredible' that they had 'remained in the ordinary community apparently undiagnosed, long enough to marry and have several children'. Nonetheless, the study admitted that many of them were 'temperamentally stable, and within their limited capacity...gentle, friendly, contented, and teachable'.[77]

Training (through practical education, but also through measures such as probation and fines) seemed a better option that imprisonment even for parents convicted for abuse.[78] This, however, remained a politically controversial and practically difficult strategy. The new welfare services could be precious in providing domestic training, and an expansion of domestic help could relieve many housewives from otherwise 'intolerable burdens'. This possibility was shattered by lack of financial resources shortage of 'trained women power'.[79] Probation officers in charge of convicted parents seemed hardly suitable to provide the kind of intensive training required.

Despite these difficulties, the government announced in 1951 that action against child neglect did not require any extension of statutory powers, but rather measures enabling the existing services to intervene at an early stage. Co-operation between different authorities at local level and the designation of an officer in charge of cases of neglect were recommended.[80] The implementation of both remained problematic and only partially implemented throughout the 1950s and 1960s.[81]

The state played an even more marginal role in Italy. Here as in Britain, social deprivation and maternal inadequacy recurred in representations of neglect, with poverty depicted as the most frequent cause 'of moral degradation, the breaking up of families, and the abandonment of children'.[82] The link between family size, poverty and neglect emerged clearly from available studies. In 1953, the *Commissione Parlamentare sulla Miseria* found that 15.5 per cent of families in the south and 11.6 per cent in Sicily and Sardinia lived in habitations with more than 4 people per room. Families constituted by more than 5 people represented 33.3 per cent of the total Italian population, 45.1 per cent of families with low standards of life (*disagiate*) and 50.4 per cent of those severely deprived (*misere*).[83] Practices such as child labour, the use of children for begging and the practice of having children raised by relatives or acquaintances were found to be widespread among these families.

In 1947, doctor Giuseppina Savalli asked ONMI to support the introduction of protective maternity legislation, and denounced the devastating effect of frequent pregnancies upon women and their families:

> Those who live in daily contact with mothers of 6, 8, 10 children, as
> do we doctors, know the Calvary of any new pregnancy for a woman

of the people, in a country where birth control is forbidden by law and practised only by better off families.[84]

The link between deprivation and family size was partly the consequence of a social policy inspired by Catholic values and hampered by economic shortage. Rather than stimulating intervention, however, the acknowledgement of the gravity of the situation resulted in an apparent greater tolerance for questionable practices, deemed necessary to the survival of the household. In 1952, a newspaper's campaign denounced the trafficking of children employed as 'professional beggars' in both the South to the North of the country. Despite the public outburst, a few commentators pointed out that the phenomenon was long established and socially accepted.[85] Already 2 years before, Veronese had explained in *Maternità e Infanzia* that begging was indeed a form of children's exploitation and misuse that should not be tolerated. And yet,

> If we take away those three exploited children to their unlucky mother, and we put them in an institution in the name of civility, any income of the family ends, and for those who remain at home then, is starvation. Unless we decide to take away all the children and older people in the family and we find a job for the unemployed man.[86]

Mothers' inadequacy, fathers' desertion, illness or imprisonment and mental or physical problems were identified as the main causes of child neglect both in Italy and in Britain. In both countries, despite ample evidence that poverty represented the first cause of family trouble, observers' attention concentrated on individual character and how to reform it. In both countries, the complex causes of neglect and the difficulty of defining the specific characters of the phenomenon justified the modesty of intervention by the state and the prominent role left to voluntary organisations. In Britain, expanded social services provided a possible means of intervention along lines traced by voluntary organisations. This remained largely impossible in Italy. The more limited influence exercised by medical expertise over social work and welfare approaches also meant that parental re-education received less attention in Italy and greater emphasis was put on poverty and marginality as the roots of child neglect. Indeed, such an acknowledgement became in certain cases a justification to avoid an intervention seen as a possible cause of greater ills.

Homeless children

Among the most striking examples of poverty leading to neglect and child exploitation was homelessness. Housing shortage in post-war Italy resulted in widespread overcrowding and homelessness, especially in the south of the country. The *Inchiesta sulla Miseria* estimated that in Naples alone around 18 000 people lived in caves and huts. Although unable to estimate the precise number of homeless families, the *Inchiesta* reported that 2354 families lived in schools and barracks destined to this use by the City Council, and 750 in ruined ex-warehouses in the city's industrial areas. A moderate estimate would suggest that at least 12 000 people lived in such premises. The description of the *Albergo dei Poveri* (hostel for the poor) in Naples was typical of similar institutions throughout the country, and justified the *Inchiesta*'s claim that the disheartening conditions in which homeless families lived prevented any possibility of improving either their way of life or their moral standards:

> The walls are filthy, the cobwebs as old as the Bourbons, the walls have not been painted for years. The partitions separating different families are made up of blankets, cardboard, sheets; everywhere there are children, Saints and lighted candles.[87]

Once again, however, moral outcry and denunciations were followed by little attempt to introduce measures to improve the situation. Housing program remained extremely modest in Italy throughout the post-war period, and responsibility to provide for homelessness, as well as any other form of poverty was left to council administration and to private charity.

The situation was significantly different in Britain, were both Labour and Conservatives identified the housing crisis as one of the most urgent emergencies and priorities of the post-war years and a crucial political issue. A particular dimension of the problem was represented by the consequences of homelessness over children.

In June 1950, British newspapers cried out against the apparent growing propensity of homeless parents to leave their children to the care of LAs.[88] In Croydon, the number of children in care had increased by ten within a week, because of 'family quarrels'. In Manchester, the City Council was 'seriously concerned' at the growing number of children taken into care under the Children Act deemed 'deserted by their parents'. For the tabloids, parents were 'not too poor to maintain their children, nor too ill to look after them'; they were 'young mothers and fathers trying to avoid the responsibilities of parenthood'.[89] Officials agreed that 'many of the desertions [were] of an artificial nature', where parents took advantage of the housing shortage to 'just dump' their children on the LA, and go off 'to live in furnished rooms'. Their selfishness and lack of moral sense was apparently showed by the fact that instead of using the temporary provisions available under the National Assistance Act, evicted parents left their children 'with neighbours' or in LAs' temporary accommodation, 'in circumstances which necessitate the children being taken into care'.[90] Resistance towards use of temporary accommodations provided under the National Assistance Act could be explained at least in part with the sense of stigma attached to premises still widely seen as the old workhouse under a different name. Charges of parental selfishness also concealed the different circumstances leading to homelessness and the structural causes behind it such as a largely unregulated renting market, and the financial difficulties encountered by many families with young children.[91] Nonetheless, a report issued by the Children's Department in 1953 concluded that eviction because of non-payment of rent was usually due to 'fecklessness and improvidence' rather than 'to misfortune beyond control'.

Although listing other specific causes of homelessness, linked to the structure of the labour market rather than to individual behaviour (particularly immigration in newly expanding industrial districts and the movements of seasonal workers), the report had little to say in terms of measures able to reduce the recurrence of the phenomenon.[92]

Although eviction rarely fit the conditions of 'urgent and unforeseeable need' required by the National Assistance Act of 1948, admission to temporary accommodation often represented the only solution available to LAs willing to keep children and their parents together.[93] Nonetheless, a wide agreement existed that Social Assistance Accommodations were unsuitable to children and that families' residence within them should be as short as possible. What limits should be laid down and how, however, was not easy to establish.

In 1951, the County Welfare Committee of Surrey imposed a limit of 6 months to families' permanence in temporary accommodation. The limit should apply regardless of whether the family had a place to move to at the end of its term. The aim was to discourage the perpetuation of 'a rather shiftless and aimless mode of life', and to make sure that children did not grow up in establishments unable to provide 'the environmental influences essential for their proper training and upbringing'. Moreover, the Surrey's Committee urged 'the Children's Department to take the children into care whenever parents made an application'.[94]

Following similar concerns, the Ministry of Health encouraged LA to provide accommodations aimed to meet 'reasonable standards', without making unattractive what families were 'likely to obtain for themselves'.[95] Fear that families would 'stay indefinitely if allowed' was widespread among LAs. Strategies designed to counteract this danger included admitting to temporary accommodations mothers and children only, providing 'bleak' lodgings, without 'comfort and privacy', and imposing charges 'deliberately pitched at so high [a] rate that families vacated them as soon as possible'.[96]

None of these methods proved entirely satisfactory, as many families, especially in the largest cities, remained unable to find an accommodation in the private market or, according to a HO's memorandum, 'unwilling to try, being content to live as long as they could at the expenses of the ratepayers, however low the standards were'.[97]

Officials admitted that the eviction of parents from National Assistance Accommodation and the reception of children into LAs' care did not constitute a wholly desirable alternative. According to the 1953 Children's Department's report, 'considerable evidence' showed that separation weakened family ties and might 'lead to a permanent disruption' of the household. Uncertain lengths of stay and frequent behavioural problems meant that only few homeless children were 'acceptable to foster parents [...] or to small voluntary homes'. The difficulty of visiting children placed in a distant home caused parents to progressively lose interest in them.[98]

Local Children's Committees complained that Welfare, Housing and Medical Departments put pressure on them 'to take evicted and homeless children into care', often with the support of the Police and the NSPCC. Lack of alternatives often succeeded in winning over their resistance. When Children's Departments remained unmoved, children were often brought before courts 'through neglect and deprivation' and therefore committed to the care of LAs by way of 'fit persons orders'. The result was to increase tensions between 'the Children's Officer, the Courts, and other social workers'.[99] In order to avoid such undesirable outcomes, the Children's Department stressed the need for improving prevention through co-operation between different LAs' sectors, a stronger involvement of the Housing Department, and the creation of support and training agencies for difficult families.[100] The call repeated many others in these same years, and as many others remained largely unattended in years to come, until the improvement of the housing situation contributed to the issue of homeless families gradually fading away from the political agenda.

Values in care

In July 1944, George Bernard Shaw explained in a letter to *The Times* that modern child care should combine scientific approach and maternal comfort, supplementing 'trained nurses with no time to spare for cuddling' with 'affectionate masseuses' to be found among 'motherly and grandmotherly' women.[101]

In the same year, the newly appointed Curtis Committee started to uncover the existence of institutions rarely in touch with updated conceptions of care and unable to give adequate attention to children's psychological and emotional needs.[102] While denying evidence of widespread 'neglect or harsh usage', the Committee pointed out that many institutions remained unaccountable to the public and outside the powers of control of the competent ministries. Most of the homes were found able to provide 'more material advantages' than 'the average poor family'; when their standards were 'below average' this was mostly the result of 'dirt and dreariness, drabness and over-regimentation'. In many cases, however, relative material comfort was accompanied by a 'shocking' 'lack of personal interest'. In most cases, the 'institutional child' was not 'an individual with his own rights and possessions, his own life to live and his own contribution to offer', but 'merely one of a large crowd' with no one 'vitally interested in his welfare or who cared for him as a person'.[103]

Both in Britain and in Italy, 'large gaunt looking buildings with dark stairways and corridors, high windows' and 'unadapted baths and lavatories' contributed to perpetuate the image of Victorian workhouses and the stigma associated with them.[104]

According to the Curtis Committee the use of large premises encouraged a military atmosphere, which accustomed children to 'the anonymity of collective life' and diminished their 'vivacity and natural ease'.[105] In Italy, Sigismondo Barbano agreed that institutions rationally organised could provide for the material needs of the children, but deprived them of the emotional and spiritual nurture necessary to their social life as adults.[106]

Despite a few 'admirable efforts', in both countries most homes continued to reflect the punitive approach associated with the admission to an institution. In the worst cases, the 'traditional chocolate and buff paint', the 'bare boards and draught' and 'the continuous smell of mass cooking, soft soap and disinfectant', as well as discipline and routines, constituted not only a side effect of institutional life, but also a symbolic demarcation between outside and inside worlds.[107]

In both countries, long-established institutional praxes rather than considerations of children's needs informed arrangements. Grouping children in different categories according to age, sex, physical and mental health had the aim of creating easy to run institutions. It also reflected moral, sanitary and educational criteria informed by fears of sexual promiscuity and normative notions of physical and moral health.

The division of children according to sex was increasingly criticised in Britain during the 1950s, particularly when this resulted in the separation of siblings, and for the negative effect that lack of contact with people of the other sex was bound to have on children at the time of discharge. A policy circular of the Children's Society explained in 1941 that mixing 'naturally with the opposite sex' was essential to teach girls 'to choose [their] friends with discretion, and be warned against the undesirable type of male acquaintance'.[108] Keeping together infants under two or three, toddlers and older children could also have positive effects, providing younger children with the kind of psychological and emotional stimulation that in a 'normal home' they would have received from their older siblings.

Much more resistant to challenge proved the idea that children should be divided according to criteria of physical and psychological 'normality'. In their evidence to the Curtis Committee, the Association of Municipal Corporations explained that different provisions should be made for 'normal children, that is, children normal in every way, normal intelligence, normal physique, normal habits and manners, and normal behaviour' and 'children who are not normal in all these respects'.[109] For the latter, the Association recommended the provision of 'special homes suited to their abnormality', where young people could be treated and transferred 'to foster parents or the ordinary children's homes if and when they become normal'.[110]

In the case of 'normal children', the Association recommended the adoption within the homes of a type of education that conformed to that available to the majority of the population; this included sending children 'to the ordinary schools of the district' whenever possible. They stressed that children's homes should 'be patterned as far as is practicable upon the normal life of ordinary citizens'. In particular, no attempt should be made to imitate boarding schools, which albeit considered 'the best possible form of education' by 'one section of the community', were nonetheless far away from the experience of the vast majority of the people.[111] Rather, institutions should try to recreate a home-like atmosphere, first of all discontinuing the use of 'large barrack type of homes' in favour of premises housing small numbers of children of mixed ages and sexes. This would make it possible to avoid the need to discipline large groups through the 'enforcement of rule and regulation'.[112]

The Church of England Children's Society had a long history of boarding in smaller homes and foster families.[113] The Society's Handbook for Workers, published in 1948, acknowledged that achieving a home-like environment required avoiding 'anything that savours of an Institution'. The handbook suggested privileging small buildings, using 'light cheerful colours for the walls, curtains and coverings', decorating the homes with 'suitable pictures' and adorning with flowers living rooms and dining tables.[114] Uniformity in food and clothing was to be avoided and daily routines should be as similar as possible to those followed in normal households. Children should not be made to get up before 7 a.m. and should not be sent to bed before 7 p.m.; family prayers should not be held more than once a day, preferably at breakfast; meals should be well presented and consumed in a pleasant atmosphere.[115] During the day, children should lead 'a happy and occupied life' and have access to different rooms for studying, hobbies and playing. Time should be found to teach 'proper manners', 'respect for the elderly', 'consideration for others', including 'good behaviour in queues', and how to show 'appreciation for anything given to or done for one'.[116] Housework should also be taught, but not used as a form of punishment. As the Curtis Report had pointed out, the practice of using housework as 'an instrument of repression, a means of keeping children out of mischief, a daily discipline and even punishment for misbehaviour' was widespread. Such a practice, however, was to be avoided, as it could 'only destroy any interest which boys and girls may have in looking after their homes'.[117]

During the 1950s, the introduction of mixed age groupings (or 'family groupings') under the care of individual nurses was presented as an important step towards a more family-like approach to care.[118] The Society's *Support Magazine* portrayed children playing happily and with 'no sign of irritability', singing while sweeping the floor or enjoying their favourite activities, and housemothers 'often more loving than wise' distributing extra sweets at any time of the day.[119]

Such a representation of life within the homes provided an idealised version of family life based on the idea that a combination of freedom, planned occupations and moderate discipline were the necessary elements of the transformation of deprived children into 'normal' citizens.

The possibility of translating these guidelines in everyday praxes, however, depended upon homes' resources in terms of premises, money and personnel. The London County Council Education Committee, for instance, reacted with scepticism to the remarks of the Curtis Committee against large institutions, refusing 'to bind themselves to a policy of closing a particular type of school'. They argued that children lived 'as happily' in barrack-type schools 'as in any other type' of residential provision. Large homes were easier to organise, helped superintendents and senior members of the staff 'to get to know the children individually', and allowed the employment of fewer personnel. Their institutional nature could be overcome by encouraging participation of children in the local community, particularly sending them to different schools.[120]

In the case of the Children's Society itself, economic stringency imposed a policy of austerity that rendered unavoidable a certain degree of regimentation. For many years after the end of the war, Headquarters invited homes to buy food in bulk, avoiding expensive items even if this meant planning ahead and little variety, and to exercise a 'constant and rigid economy' in the use of fuel and light, although trying to avoid 'spoiling the eyesight or making the house dim and gloomy'.[121]

Providing good quality and varied clothes proved equally difficult. In 1943, local branches were asked to let children choose their own clothes whenever possible; 2 years later, the Conference of Home Representatives stressed that 'children should be dressed like children in ordinary families' without 'distinctive features or dress' making them 'conspicuous'. The importance of overcoming the 'present tendency to regimentation' in clothing was stressed again in 1946 and repeated regularly during the following years. At the same time, Society's branches were asked to keep the buying of clothes to a minimum, recycling them whenever possible. Nonetheless, Headquarters criticised the custom of retaining children's best clothes when transferring them to a different home. A circular letter in February 1952 pointed out that giving children clothes of 'inadequate and . . . poor condition' was unfair and tended 'to make the child feel inferior on arrival at his new home'.[122] The recommended outfit for girls who were boarded out included throughout the 1950s two coats, of which one 'worn', two pairs of shoes, two dresses and one skirt, two jumpers and one cardigan. A similar number of outfits were recommended for boys.[123]

Italian institutions faced similar issues. Commenting on the conditions of children's institutions in Milan province, the lawyer Maria Lancellotti Mari affirmed that providing young people with 'clothes similar to those of anyone else' was 'dutiful rather that advisable'. Only this could end the 'parades of little grey orphans and old-fashioned girls, all looking the same in their mortifying uniforms', marching along the streets of Milan.[124]

The outside world

Both in Italy and in Britain, life in institutions remained too often repetitive and filled with housework; in the words of the Curtis Report, shortage of resources and 'lack of understanding of children's needs' brought 'with the best intentions to a dreary uninteresting life'.[125]

Promoting contacts between children in institutions and the outside world could help to avoid the creation of what Marjory Allen called 'complete closed' communities.[126] However, large homes providing their own schools and religious services made it unnecessary for children to go out. Moreover, as Lancellotti Mari pointed out, many homes avoided sending children to state schools because of their diffidence towards an environment extraneous to the life of the institution and the fear of exposing children to moral danger.[127] This was particularly the case in the religious institutions, which were predominant in Italy, but the problem was not unknown in Britain.

A report on the activities of Barnardo's Garden City at Woodford Bridge, Essex, in 1953, revealed that only some of the children attended outside sunday schools and only a few boys had been able to enter local scout troops. All the children attended religious services in the church located within the establishment.[128] The officer responsible for the supervision of 'the 20 local authority children' housed at Woodford Bridge found the houseparents 'definitely opposed to outside contacts', and hostile to her proposal of starting an 'uncles and aunts' scheme. According to the Children's Department, Barnardo's acted according to the belief that a child was 'better off' in its care than 'in a poor, dirty or immoral home'. There was therefore no interest in 'working with the parents for the child's ultimate good', no desire to integrate children in the activities of the neighbourhood.[129] Barnardo's failed 'to build their service round the needs of individual children', and tried instead 'to make children fit in to these services'.

In their passionate desire to form this mould into which they can put the children, they seem convinced that a child must be better off in clean hygienic surroundings than in its squalid or immoral homes. Once children are separated from 'bad parents' there seems little effort to return them, and we are even tempted to believe that there is resistance to the parents' wishes to have a child back.[130]

The making of reliable citizens

At the heart of many recommendations on how institutions should be run, there was the belief that any of the activities carried on should be informed by the aim of transforming children with unsuitable background into reliable citizens and parents. Children should be helped to acquire 'good social habits', developing their own interests, looking after themselves and their possessions and learning 'co-operation and general social adaptability'.[131] For this to be successful, institutional regimes needed to avoid praxes likely to produce rejection or apathy, while providing adequate education and professional training. Prejudice, lack of economic resources and shortage of trained personnel could easily hamper the success of such a strategy.[132] According to the Curtis Report only a few institutions allowed children to have personal possessions, and to keep pictures and photographs 'in their bedrooms and dormitories as children in ordinary households'. It was a common assumption that boys and girls in institutions 'were not of good enough calibre for skilled occupations, and that the best that could be done was to find them a job on a farm or in domestic service'. It was a 'long-standing tradition' that work placements could be arranged directly by the Matron, usually sending girls to domestic service without giving them sufficient opportunity to hear about or pursue other possibilities.

In both countries, the definition of reliable citizens included in many cases a religious dimension. Following the indication of the Curtis Committee, the 1948 Children's Act recommended that LAs made sure whenever possible that the person taking over the care of a child should either share the religious persuasion of the child's parents, or undertake to respect it in the education of the child. In most children's homes, the reference to the spiritual dimension of care meant communicating to children a sense of devotion to the church, through the achievement of 'a sure faith in God and a training in worship'.[133] Providing religious guidance was explicitly required by the HO, since 'a child who has to grow up away from his own parents needs even more then any other the comfort and help of a religious faith and the inspiration to right thinking and right doing which it gives'. Religious upbringing was to be rooted in examples, and if those who cared for the children were 'sincere in their convictions', even if they pertained to a different denomination, their guidance would have had 'an added significance'.[134] Such explicit calls were made redundant in Italy by the dominance exercised by catholic institutions in the sector of assistance.

In both countries, the effort of raising proper citizens was based on a normative definition of what constituted normality that implicitly limited children's choices. To be normal meant being polite and grateful, subscribing to a sexual morality acceptable to Christian ethics, and aspiring to a social position appropriate to one's conditions and to the creation of a family free from troubles.

Foucault has suggested that control of activities and the exhaustive use of the body are two essential components of the 'disciplinary method'. It could be argued that institutional children underwent a process of progressive loss of individuality, through a monotonous and rigid control of their time (in many case aimed at 'not wasting time'), limited access to unsupervised space, and restricted possibilities for developing individual interests.[135] This process was symbolically sanctioned by the little attention given to the causes that had brought children into care in the first place, and the 'irrelevance' of their previous lives to their experiences within the institution. As the Children Officer of Birmingham commented in January 1955,

> The original reason is sometimes rather obscure in the case of children admitted twelve or fifteen years ago. [...] Personally, I feel the original reason for admission become rather less significant than the course of subsequent events which lead to the assumption of parental rights.[136]

Conclusions

Two developments which took place during the post-war period had a lasting influence on the development of social policy towards children. The first was the unprecedented influence acquired by professional expertise in family matters, partly as a consequence of the expansion of specialised agencies, both at the state and voluntary level dealing with family problems. The second was the effort to present parenting as a prime civic responsibility by post-war welfare discourses. This implied that what actually happens at home becomes a public rather than merely private matter.

After the war medicine and psychoanalysis increasingly shaped understandings of family relationships and young people's needs, and oriented the policies of the 'social state'.[137] Medical and scientific knowledge had informed child's development studies already in the early 20th century.[138] In the post-war years, doctors' authority on family matters was strengthened further by the identification of the war as a major cause of psychological damage. In particular, the disruption of family life brought about by the conflict was used in post-war studies to define pathological aspects of the parent–child relationship and to set the parameters according to which domestic interactions could be assessed. The influence that the studies on evacuated children had over the development of emotional attachment theories in the 1950s is perhaps the best example of this phenomenon.

What made the flourishing of psychological and medical approaches to the family even more important, however, was the fact that this overlapped with a growing sense that what happened within the home was not just a matter of private responsibility. The post-war welfare state envisaged neatly distinct profiles for the desirable 'worker-citizen' (whose entitlements were based upon his work) and those dependent either on other members of their family (as in the case of women and children) or on the state (as in the case of the unemployed). Individuals' entitlements varied according to individuals' position in relation to family and work and were conditional to the ability to govern oneself and those dependent on him.[139] The disruption left behind by the war strengthened the link between individual and collective responsibilities and the family became the symbol of their entanglement. Parents' responsibility towards their children ceased to be a private concern and became relevant to society as a whole. Their duty was not only to bring children into adulthood, but also to form self-relying and democratically minded individuals able to make their contribution to the post-war order. When the family failed in this respect, alternative solutions had to be found.

Although major challenges have been brought to the post-war paradigm in the last three decades, the notion of conditionality has remained crucial to welfare policies and to the regulation of the family; entitlements have continued to depend on the individual's fulfilment of his or her duties as citizen. The rise of neo-liberal discourses and processes of welfare retrenchment in the 1980s reshaped narratives of individual and familial responsibility. Notions of choice and diversity were used to disengage the state from the provision of social services. At the same time, the family was once again presented as the main actor responsible for individual and social welfare.[140] New Labour's social agenda, based on an attempt to combine the construction of a fairer society with commitment to the market, relied heavily on the principle of conditionality, combined with strong expectations from the family as the main guardian of social values. Contemporary measures such as parenting orders and antisocial behaviour orders treat the family as having a near exclusive responsibility for the comportment of its younger members and penalise it for failing to regulate this behaviour in accordance with prevailing societal norms. In this sense, there is a strong element of continuity.

Although since the end of the Second World War the state's powers of intervention in social and family life dramatically increased, such powers were never deployed to substitute the family or to reduce its sphere of competence. On the contrary, new policies tended to promote even greater expectations in terms of families' performances and their responsibilities towards children's well-being. The contemporary Respect agenda of the Blair government works on the same assumptions.

The Italian case provides a useful counter narrative to the expansion of state's presence during the post-war period. In Italy the state provided quite modest social services, and a minimal engagement with family politics. At the same time, there was a continuously strong social contribution of the voluntary catholic sector. This, however, was not the result of a difference in investment in the family as a social institution, but rather the outcome of different social and political conditions, which affected the way in which state and voluntary agencies (particularly those connected to the Catholic Church) interacted in providing services for children in need.

5
Recreating the Family: Single Mothers, Maladjusted Children and the Search for a New Home

Chapter 4 looked at the family circumstances that could be considered as a reason for taking children into care, and at the relationship established between the state and the family in these cases. Chapter 5 concentrates on specific categories of children, considered as particularly at risk, and on adult behaviours deemed as an inevitable source of trouble. Maladjustment and illegitimacy are discussed in the chapter as 'pathological situations' requiring a special treatment and the involvement of specialised agencies. The chapter asks the question of how such 'extraordinary' types of intervention is related to established notions of normality in family life.

By focusing on the concepts of single motherhood and maladjustment, the chapter discusses the relationship between changes in family life and understandings of children's needs. Maternity outside marriage (particularly among younger women) was identified both as a sign of maladjustment and as one of its causes in post-war Britain and Italy. Despite the transformations that have taken place during the last 50 years, births outside marriage have continued to be seen as a sign of deterioration of family life, as a factor likely to increase young people's vulnerability, at the cost of society as a whole. This line of interpretation has proved successful in popular and academic debates and has influenced social policy making throughout the entire post-war period. Charles Murray's identification of lone mothers as the core of long-term welfare dependency epitomised the critique of state benefits that allowed single mothers to stay away from work.[1] Although born in the American context, Murray's analysis influenced welfare discourses outside the United States and had relevant echoes in the United Kingdom for the last 20 years. Even more interesting for my argument was Lawrence

Mead's theory according to which welfare dependency would have been not the result of a 'rational choice' (to continue receiving benefits rather than take up a badly paid job), as suggested by Murray, but rather the consequence of individuals' disordered lives. Mead identified sexuality, work and family as the areas manifesting individuals' inability to 'organise their personal lives'.[2] Neo-liberal focus on lone mothers and (unemployed) fathers of illegitimate children represented a means of emphasising individual accountability and reducing collective responsibility towards welfare. The popularity of these interpretations owed much to the fact that they built upon long-standing perceptions of what type of family life produced well-balanced and adjusted individuals able to behave like responsible citizens.

Here I seek to map how these perceptions were articulated and acted upon during the post-war period. My aim is to look not only at how normative notions of desirable family life influenced approaches to child welfare, but also at how children were treated as a means of influencing family life, particularly in relation to the performance of their mothers.

Although a large part of the chapter focuses on mothers as sight of social intervention, fathers are also important to my analysis. In many ways, the discussion presented here continues the examination started in chapter 3 regarding the meaning acquired by fatherhood in the post-war period. There I suggested that the emphasis on emotions that dominates post-war discourses unsettled traditional images of fathers as authority figures, without providing them with an alternative role, comparable to that of mothers. The examination of illegitimacy and its treatment presented in this chapter integrates that analysis and provides a powerful reminder of the importance maintained by the existence of a legal father in post-war discourses. Illegitimacy brings into focus the consequences that the absence of a father has not only for the child but also for the family as a whole: while the social role of fathers within the home became increasingly uncertain after the Second World War, the presence of a biological father remains paramount to the definition of the family as such.

The link between biological and legal paternity was crucial not only to the creation of categories such as illegitimacy, but also to institutions such as adoption, aimed to establish bonds between individuals substitutive of the 'biological relationships' that existed in a 'natural family'.[3] The second part of the chapter examines differences in approaches to adoption and fostering in Italy and Britain and discusses how these reflected differences in the conception of family relationships and the nature of the family.

Illegitimate children and their mothers

In the preface to her study on *The Unmarried Mother and Her Child*, published in 1960, Virginia Wimperis presented it as 'a first attempt' to gather information regarding 'who have illegitimate children, what happens to the children as they grow up' and 'the measures taken to help them in this and other countries'.[4] Non-communist Europe endorsed 'the courageous principle of faithful lifelong monogamous marriage' and adopted 'laws and morals and social sanctions' aimed to maintain it.[5] Nonetheless, in 1950 'every twentieth child' born in England and Wales was illegitimate, 'every eight was conceived outside marriage, every fourth mother conceived her first born before her wedding day'. Moreover, there were 'tens of thousands of "unofficial families" ' where children grew up 'with parents cohabiting without marriage', as well as 'tens of thousands' of unmarried women who resorted to abortion 'for fear that if they had their child they would be ostracized and treated with contempt'.[6]

Few other issues raised as many questions concerning the role of the family in relation to individual and social welfare as illegitimacy. From a legal point of view, 'illegitimate' children's unequal status was maintained on the basis of norms aimed to preserve the supremacy of marriage as the basis of the family.[7] In Britain, the 1872 Bastardy Laws Amendment Act continued to inform the status, custody and maintenance of the natural child, and the new forms of social protection established by the welfare state seemed to be of relatively little consequence as far as 'illegimate children' were concerned. The Affiliation Act approved in 1952 brought the weekly maintenance payment for illegitimate children to the same level of maintenance payment due to legitimate children following a divorce.[8] The outcome of the measure, however, was curbed by the limited extent to which affiliation orders were granted (in 1959, out of 38 161 births having been registered as illegitimate, only 4160 affiliation orders were awarded to mothers seeking them)[9] as well as by social policies that treated mothers as the unique responsible person for children born outside marriage. As Janet Fink has pointed out, the National Assistance Act of 1948 provides a telling example of the penalizing attitude of post-war welfare policies towards births out of wedlock. While according to the 1930 Poor Law Act (that the 1948 Act substituted) husbands were responsible for 'any child born to his wife prior to their marriage' – including illegitimate children – the National Assistance Act limited husbands' responsibility to his wife and his own children.[10] At the same time, being married to another man could prevent a woman from seeking an affiliation order for the father of her child, as she was no longer a single woman. The conclusion was that women should be considered as the sole bearers of responsibility towards children born outside marriage.

In Italy, the fact that the different status of legitimate and illegitimate children was affirmed in the new republican constitution represented both a means of conditioning successive social policy reforms and a symbolic reminder of the commitment of the state to the protection of the prerogatives of the family as a natural unit based upon marriage. Being 'illegitimate' was a status whose visibility was ensured and preserved in one's personal documents, as well as through the treatment reserved to 'illegitimate children' by social services. Moreover, the treatment of children born outside marriage symbolised the gender inequality that characterised the attribution of parental rights.

Until the reform of the family code in 1975, the mark of 'illegitimacy' remained independent from the acknowledgement of the mother, and men retained the right to acknowledge a 'natural' child independently of the will of the mother. As for married women, they could neither acknowledge a child born outside their marriage, nor reveal the name of the natural father, since paternity rights remained with the husband unless he renounced them. In Chiara Saraceno's words, 'the acknowledgement of the offspring was a right negotiated among men', without any power been left to the mother.[11]

Although abandoned illegitimate children constituted a minority of the children taken into care, birth outside marriage attracted much public attention and was often discussed as a benchmark against which to measure families' stability and society's moral fibre.[12] At the same time, little reliable information existed concerning the different situations to which the label of 'illegitimacy' applied, with the result that the phenomenon tended to be discussed in moralistic and generalising terms, with little attempt made to differentiate between individual circumstances.

In 1954, an enquiry conducted in Newcastle by the public health expert James Spence contradicted 'the common view that unmarried mothers live alone in a single room or flat, or that they are friendless in this situation'. Spence found that most illegitimate children belonged to a family circle, 'either through the parents, more often through the mother, or through the adopted parents'.[13] Nonetheless, Spence concluded that 'illegitimate infants' ran 'a far greater risk' than legitimate ones 'of living in a home where the maternal capacity, the family stability, and the physical environment and housing conditions' were unsatisfactory.[14] Even in the best scenarios, such as when parents lived together, the mother remarried, moved with her family of origin, or simply became self-sufficient, illegitimacy remained an abnormal situation likely to cause emotional, moral and physical hazard. The depiction of the illegitimate status as one of inevitable vulnerability was partly the consequence of the widespread assumption that an unmarried mother brought with her personal characteristics, either from a moral, social or psychological point of view, which were necessarily detrimental to the welfare of her child.

Rates of illegitimacy in Italy and Britain alike saw an increase during the war, followed by a slow down from the beginning of the 1950s. Throughout this period, illegitimacy rates remained about one point higher in Britain than in Italy (in 1954, the year of Spence's study, percentage of illegitimate births were 4.7 in Britain and 3.2 in Italy), and while the 1950s saw a constant diminution in the proportion of births outside marriage in Italy, these increased again in Britain after 1956. Although moral collapse and young women's behaviour dominated popular debates in both countries, reaching reliable conclusions on the social meaning of illegitimacy remained far from easy.

Rising numbers of illegitimate children during the war seemed relatively easy to explain. The Registrar General for England and Wales indicated in 'the enforced degree of physical separation of the sexes' imposed by the war the main cause behind the phenomenon.[15] A large proportion of those couples that would have normally married before the birth of a child conceived outside marriage had been prevented from doing so during the conflict by the recruitment of men. It was expected that many of these couples would marry after the war, securing to their children 'the normality of home life and upbringing of which they might otherwise have been deprived'. On the whole, 'the average increase of 6 per cent in the total number of irregularly conceived births' could 'hardly be regarded as inordinate', when taking into account 'the wholesale disturbance to customary habits and living conditions' and 'the temporary accession to the population of large numbers of young and virile men in the Armed Forces of our Dominions and Allies'.[16] Attitudes towards marriage rather than sexual immorality seemed to provide a crucial explanation of rising illegitimacy rates also in the second half of the 1950s. As Wimperis suggested, the new increase in births outside marriage observed in Britain after 1956 was not the result of moral decline, but rather of the fact that a growing proportion of children were now born to divorced women or to women living apart from their husbands.[17] In 1950, a study conducted in a Midland town by Valerie Hughes, of the London School of Economics, concluded that around 40 per cent of the illegitimate children born in that town in 1949 were born to couples who 'lived stably together' but were 'debarred from marrying by the still existing marriage of one or other partner'. The data were compatible with Spence's findings in Newcastle, and an even higher proportion (54 per cent) of mothers and children living with the putative father had been found by a study conducted by the Birmingham's Maternity and Child Welfare Department in 1955.[18]

Thoughtful analyses of the phenomenon, however, coexisted with impressionistic accounts of moral weakness, delinquency and psychological trouble as the factors inevitably associated with illegitimacy.[19] Readings mostly concerned with the moral dangers of illegitimacy, for instance, gave little space to evidence suggesting that in many cases the parents of an illegitimate child were involved in a long-term relationship at the moment of the conception.[20]

A memorandum submitted to Herbert Morrison in 1945 suggested that in matters of illegitimacy, 'sound common sense' was 'too often overlaid and smothered by inhumanity on the one hand and wholly sentimentality on the other'. With a few exceptions, 'little effort was made to distinguish between the trollops and foolish ex-virgins', causing an 'utter waste of time' and public resources 'on poor material'.[21]

As in the case of neglectful mothers discussed in Chapter 4, maternity outside marriage was also often associated with psychological trouble or 'low mentality'. The definition did not describe an identifiable syndrome, but rather a range of behaviours, among which stood out the inability to provide for their children's needs. The more cautious observers recognised that it was difficult to estimate to what extent such 'inability to cope with life' was the result of 'innate low intelligence' or the outcome of complex circumstances, including women's personal history and social environment.[22]

However, the circumstances surrounding the pregnancy were important in determining the type of treatment likely to be received by single mothers. Young mothers were those most likely to receive care in Mother and Baby Homes and by Moral Welfare Associations; only few Homes besides those run by the Salvation Army took in older women or women having their second illegitimate baby. In Wimperis' words, 'they [were] trying to rehabilitate the young and [did] not wish them to be confused or injured by contact with the more sophisticated or perhaps more hardened women'.[23] The situation could be even more difficult for the mothers of several illegitimate children.

Nonetheless, opinions remained divided as to how to care for 'expectant girls' and over the effects of pregnancy on young women. On the one hand was the idea that 'pregnancy, like VD' should not be seen as a problem in itself, but as a condition 'incidental to the girls' need for training, and a manifestation of moral and psychological weakness. On the other was a view of maternity as 'reforming influence', able to transform troubled girls into reliable and settled women. While the first interpretation supported the treatment of young mothers in correctional institutions, akin to reformatories, the second favoured the establishment of long-term voluntary maternal hostels. Among the criticism directed to the use of hostels to which women could return after work was the fact that allowing women to spend most of the day outside would have discouraged breast feeding and not promoted enough training in child care.

At a meeting of Chief Inspectors and Officers of Children Development held at the HO in 1947, most participants agreed that pregnancy itself should not be treated as something to be persecuted, and spoke instead in favour of extended training. Six months before birth and twelve months afterwards were considered appropriate, partly because, as explained by Dr Makepeace, of the HO, young women tended to become 'bored' with the child after the first six months and were unable to cope with the disturbance created by the prospect of caring alone for the child.[24]

Both in Britain and in Italy, the preoccupation for the welfare of the child overshadowed the concern for the needs and expectations of the mother, and the determination of affirming the deviant nature of maternity outside marriage prevailed over the possibility of a dispassionate analysis of single mothers' actual experiences.[25]

In 1956, the Church of England Moral Welfare Council (MWC) expressed their concern for the diffusion of illegitimacy among West Indian immigrants. In this case, the problem was not single motherhood as such, but rather the absence of marriage. 'Concubinage' was described as 'a socially accepted institution amongst a large section of the Caribbean working-class population', which regarded marriage 'as so expensive as to be almost a luxury'. Nonetheless, the Board lamented that in certain dioceses 'the provision of help for unmarried mothers and their children was being strained to breaking point by the influx of West Indian women'.[26] The report went on to affirm the desirability 'to bring about a change in their conception of marriage and parenthood' through 'social pressure and religious awareness'. In many ways, the problems described the result of social and economic marginality rather than family arrangements. It was 'the squalor of the housing conditions in which so many of them are living in this country' that undermined 'the possibility of decent family life and child care as we know it'. Nonetheless, the condemnation of 'concubinage' reinforced the nexus between illegitimacy, immorality and backwardness through the combination of racial and sexual stereotypes.[27]

In Italy, Catholic ideology permeated the language used to refer to illegitimacy, transforming it into a symbol itself of the family's moral collapse. Women who abandoned their babies were worse than the 'beasts of the desert' and could therefore deserve no sympathy.[28] Discriminating against the natural child could appear 'cruel', but it was 'just', and necessary to protect the institution of marriage against 'superficial and irresponsible attitudes'. The suffering caused by the stigma of illegitimacy could not be lessened by changes in the law if it was to remain a deterrent.[29] Rather, everyone should be aware that it was a duty to dissuade 'a brother, a friend, an acquaintance and even someone hardly known' from creating an illegitimate family. Only the unquestioned endorsement of 'family values' could reduce the number of 'unhappy, illegitimate children', and only the condemnation of procreation outside marriage could protect and perpetuate the legitimate family.[30]

In 1949, the Social Democrat MP Bianca Bianchi proposed a bill aimed to make it compulsory for mothers to acknowledge their child. On *Maternità e Infanzia*, Elvira Capace Elisi defined the proposal as 'generous and courageous', inspired by a conception 'of the responsibility attached to the most important act' in a woman's life; what was proposed was 'a deterrent not to do . . . and a redemption for having done'.[31]

Ultimately, the proposal was opposed and eventually rejected mostly on the ground that it would have encouraged abortions, putting at risk the future of an unwanted child. The argument that the implementation of the law would have 'put all the responsibility for children upon women' remained marginal in the debate. Much suspicion remained attached to the question of paternity search, seen mostly as a danger brought to legitimate families. In 1955, Lancellotti Mari explained that 'normal and healthy' children who had been acknowledged by neither of their natural parents were 'usually adopted by or affiliated to well off and morally strong families'. On the other side, life in an institution often constituted the only course open to most children acknowledged by the sole mother and admitted into care, because 'the very existence of a mother ready to assert her not always good reasons' had the effect of discouraging adoptions and affiliations. She concluded wondering whether.

It did not represent a better destiny for a child to be acknowledged by neither the father nor the mother, rather than having an indifferent and emotionally distant mother.[32]

The moral outcry that surrounded illegitimacy was paired in Italy with an almost complete lack of provision for single mothers. In 1954, a total of 11 maternity homes operated within the country, providing for 346 women; of these 3 were in Milan, 1 in nearby Como, 1 in Venice, 1 in Genoa, 3 in Rome and 1 in Cagliari (Sardinia). These were complemented by 19 Case per la Protezione della Giovane (Homes for the Protection of Young Women), providing for 850 women, concentrated in the north of the country, with only two premises operating in the south.[33]

It could be argued that lack of policies for single motherhood, reinforced the idea that marriage constituted the 'paradigmatic precondition for the generation of a distinction between legitimacy and illegitimacy' and that any arrangement other than lifelong official monogamy constituted imperfect and necessarily precarious situations.[34]

There is no perfect answer to illegitimacy because it goes against the divine plan. All we can do is to find the best answer to a situation which, from its very nature must give rise to suffering.[35]

The maladjusted child

In the welfare model of juvenile delinquency dominant during the post-war period, a fine line separated definitions and treatments of neglect, maladjustment and delinquency, the common aim of intervention being the protection of 'an existing social order by the containment and, at least theoretically, reform of potentially disruptive citizens'.[36]

In 1945, the British Ministry of Education defined a 'maladjusted child' as one showing 'evidence of emotional instability or psychological disturbance' and requiring 'special educational treatment in order to effect his personal, social or educational readjustment'.[37] A circular of the same year recognised that treatment was 'still in an experimental stage', and that approaches had to vary according to individual circumstances and needs.[38] Each case of maladjustment presented 'so many uncontrollable factors' that paradoxically 'cure [could] only be effectively determined when the child [grew] up into a mature citizen'.[39]

Despite disagreements on the intellectual abilities of 'difficult children', a certain consensus existed that poor educational facilities and the tendency to exclude 'troublesome' children from schools worsened the situation.[40] A memorandum submitted to the HO by the Advisory Council on the *Treatment of Offenders* in 1945 affirmed that a 'large number of children' could have been saved from appearing before the court 'had suitable advice, education or treatment been available for them or their parents'.

During the drafting of the 1948 Children Act, the question of maladjustment contributed to heating up the debate on whether approved schools and remand homes should be maintained under the Ministry of Education or passed to the HO. The fact that the new Education Act allowed education committees to make provisions for maladjusted children was presented as an important element stressing the educational definition of approved schools and their natural dependence on the Ministry of Education.[41] In 1950, a Committee was appointed under the Chairmanship of the Ministry of Education's Principal Medical Officer, Dr J. E. A. Underwood, to enquire into the treatment of maladjusted children within the educational system.[42] Their report, published in 1955, confirmed the ambiguity of the term and indicated as the main characteristic of maladjusted people a tendency 'to get on badly in their personal relationships, with father and mother, brothers and sisters, husband or wife, or their own children'.[43]

Despite the difficulty of reaching a satisfactory definition of maladjustment, home environment stood out as one of its most likely, and sometimes curable, causes. At risk family circumstances included loss 'of the normal emotional relationships of a good home' through death or breaking up, frustration and failure of the parents 'to give proper home training, example, or balanced nutrition'.[44] The Underwood Report emphasised that the early relationship between mother and child was 'of vital importance' and warned against the possible negative implications of mothers 'going out to work and being away from [young children] all day'.[45] 'The good mother' should be able to maintain 'a steady, secure intimacy with the child' while directing his or her interest 'away from herself' and encouraging a friendly relationship with other children. The role of the father became more important from the third year of the child, as he took 'his place as the embodiment of the authority in the family'.[46] The impact of loss of parents in maladjustment was worsened by the relative isolation of the contemporary nuclear family, which might prevent 'blood relations stepping into their place'. Because 'the family unit [was] now regarded primarily as father, mother and unmarried children', 'grandparents, aunts and uncles and other relatives' might 'be separated from the family emotionally as well as by distance'. The fact that families had tended 'to be smaller for the past two generations' had reduced the support available to individual households in case of need.[47]

The *Ascertainment of Maladjustment* report indicated parents among the agencies more likely to discover early signs of maladjustment within a child.[48] Difficulty in acquiring knowledge, physical and psychopathic 'inferiority', psychosis and disorders of the central nervous system were listed among the noticeable symptoms.[49]

In Italy, the definition closest to maladjustment was probably that of *bambini caratteriali*, children presenting different forms of behavioural problems, likely to develop in neuroses and delinquency.[50] The importance of the home environment was considered paramount in Italy as well as in Britain. Together with the usual considerations concerning the importance of stable affective relationships within the family, however, a different perspective was pointed out by the educationalist Origlia, based on the observation of 'disturbed adolescents' from middle- and lower-middle-class families. Origlia's interpretation was interesting because it moved the centre of attention from the role of the mother to that of the father and pointed out possible shortcomings of the male breadwinner model. He suggested that the 'peculiar situation of dependence of the whole family on the man' encouraged the 'unhappiness of the mother' and 'distracted' the father from domestic life, therefore depriving children of an influence essential to their psychological development.[51]

The collapse of morality and the young delinquent

Marriage and the war

Both in Britain and in Italy, one of the most common narratives associated with the war was that of a diminution of control and discipline. In the case of young people, this meant not only 'a sudden change from disciplined school life to responsibility', but also the possibility of making new and different experiences.[52] In the case of marital relationships, the war, the experience of evacuation and the 'calling up of women to industry and the uniformed services' was accused of relieving both husbands and wives of their traditional responsibilities.

> New independence and new interests other than home and family were discovered, and in some cases led to intolerance and to break up of the family.[53]

Since March 1942, Probation Officers had worked with the Army Welfare Service in dealing with 'domestic difficulties arising from the separation of members of the Forces from their wives and families'. As an extension to their work as conciliators in matrimonial cases, Probation Officers had been made responsible for reporting on the possibility of reconciliation in cases referred to them by Commanding Officers, Paymasters, Chaplains and so on. Probation Officers acknowledged that most of the cases they pursued concerned either 'allegations made to service men, often by ill-natured neighbours, that wives were unfaithful or were neglecting home and children', or wives' complaints about children, accommodations or financial difficulties.[54]

Nonetheless, their reports endorsed the view that throughout the war, men and women had had 'increased opportunity for meeting other people, and for forming illicit relationships'. A newly found independence had made it 'easier for women to maintain illegitimate children' and 'for men to keep other women, if they so wished'. 'Loss of companionship, of support, both financial and personal, and a sudden rise of unaccustomed responsibility' had encouraged 'some young women [to] fail their husbands'.[55] 'Hasty war marriages, on embarkation leave, sometimes between comparative strangers' had left 'both parties with little sense of responsibility or obligation towards one another'. The presence of American and Allied Servicemen had disclosed 'lack of control' and 'moral and intellectual' instability in family life, particularly among women:

> To girls brought up on the cinema, who copied the dress, hair style and manners of Hollywood stars, the sudden influx of Americans, speaking like the films, who actually lived in the magic country, and who had plenty of money, at once went to girls' head.[56]

American soldiers' propensity 'to build up, exaggerate, talk big and to act with generosity and flamboyance' had made them 'the most attractive boyfriends'. For soldiers coming from other countries, the appeal had been in 'the glamour of foreign accent, travel tales and of something different'.

Descriptions of the novelties and freedom brought by the war mixed misogynist stereotypes and normative definitions of family and sexual relationships. Moreover, it established a link between sexual behaviour, disrespect for authority and delinquency among young people that was to last throughout the post-war period.

The young delinquent

According to the paper *Children in Trouble*, published by the HO in 1968, juvenile delinquency had 'no single cause, manifestation or cure'. Its origins and symptoms were wide and in many circumstances the delinquent behaviour merged 'almost imperceptibly with behaviour which does not contravene the law'.[57]

In fact, the majority of children could be expected to behave 'contrary to the law' at some point, without this representing anything more than 'an accident in the pattern of a child's normal development'. The situation could became more serious as a result of 'genetic, emotional and intellectual factors' as well as a consequence of young people's family or social circumstances.[58] Delinquent behaviour could represent 'a result of boredom in and out of school, an indication of maladjustment or immaturity, or a symptom of a deviant, damaged or abnormal personality'.[59]

The Seventh Report on the Work of the Children's Department published in November 1955 indicated at 31 770 the total number of children found guilty of indictable offences in the previous year (1147 per 100 000 children). There had been a noticeable improvement since 1951, when the total number had been 47 473 (1678 per 100 000). The causes of this fall, however, remained unclear. The report mentioned as potentially positive factors 'the passing into a higher age group of those whose childhood was disturbed by war and evacuation', as well as improvements in housing and social services and the greater availability of employment in the country.[60] The performance of the family, however, continued to be considered the main variable affecting children's behaviour. Social services were of little use unless parents discharged 'effectively their unique responsibility for bringing up their children properly'.[61] Particularly damaging were the 'unwise handling' of the 'small emotional situations' that arose in family life, and 'parental indifference'. The first could create in a child 'an attitude of antagonism, first to the family and then to others in authority, the second might led a child 'into asserting himself' by 'apparently senseless delinquency, to test the interest and affection of his family'.[62] The report did not try to explain the fact that the overwhelming majority of young delinquents were male or why family life should affect boys more than girls.

In Italy as well post-war debates expressed anxiety for the attitudes of new generations, often portrayed as disengaged from the values of their families and caught in the conflicting messages generating by a fast-changing society.

More than in Britain, fear of unruly young generations acquired in Italy a particular political connotation as the Cold War increased the social consequences of the country's political polarisation. The analysis of the damages caused to children by the war became in the 1950s a means of stigmatising political confrontation and social mobilisation. The 'confrontation between opposite political tendencies unable to adopt disciplined forms of contest', 'magnified the echoes of the Cold War'. The result was to deprive young people of those 'ideal certainties, not yet poisoned by doubt or [...] scepticism', which they needed to grow into responsible adults: 'God, the country, the family, the neighbourhood'. This contributed to create anxious and excessively timid children who were prone to become delinquent.[63]

The signs of a maladjusted personality were found in stammering, tics, bed-wetting and a number of other 'physiological anomalies', which, according to the Director of the Milanese Centro di Rieducazione per Minorenni, still received a disproportionate attention in Italy.[64]

An enquiry into juvenile delinquency carried out by *Maternità e Infanzia* in 1953 described it as the result of individual and social factors, and as a phenomenon strongly associated to modernity. At individual level, risk factors included 'low intellectual abilities', 'abnormality of character' and 'physiological factors' such as tuberculosis, malnutrition and syphilis. From a social point of view, delinquency was portrayed as a predominantly urban phenomenon, often associated with deprived social groups and broken families.[65] The problem, however, was not extraneous to middle-class homes, where young people's antisocial behaviour seemed the expression of a moral crisis, which no material improvement could hope to solve.[66]

In Italy as in Britain, youth behaviour became the symbol itself of the contradictions associated to modernity. As in Britain, Italian social observers and practitioners found traditional means of intervention inadequate to tackle young offenders and called for approaches able to move beyond mere punishment and to bring together legal, educational and medical perspectives. Such calls, however, remained largely unattended. The main means of dealing with young offenders remained their admission to public and private institutions, which offered little in terms of education.[67] Limited resources left little space to the development of the 'early recognition and full assessment' of individual circumstances recommended by experts in both countries.[68]

Both in Italy and in Britain, the outcry surrounding young people's 'unruly' behaviour in the post-war period could be read as part of a much wider structure of feelings concerning the loss of traditional ways of life of which a particular view of family relationships constituted an essential character.[69] However, interpretations of youth unlawfulness changed to some extent between the 1950s and the 1960s, partly as a result of changes in economic and social circumstances. In Britain in particular, understandings of youth behaviour became increasingly influenced by the idea that the country's growing affluence would produce a negative transformation of family life, and result in a youth culture increasingly inspired by foreign (mostly American) models.

According to a paper published by the Conservative Research Department (CRD) in 1962, young criminals came from 'good homes' and 'new housing estates where wages [were] good and employment [was] satisfactorily'. 'Old theories' of 'poverty, mass unemployment, health and housing' no longer explained rises in criminality;[70] contemporary young people had more time and more money, but less 'sense of purpose and of personal responsibility'.[71] In a society where 'many of the old virtues such as piety, discipline and thrift' were 'giving away to a growing materialism', a 'moral crusade' was needed in order to bring people back 'to true spiritual values'.[72] Restoring parental role and authority was an essential element of such a crusade; this might require bringing back a moderate amount of corporal punishment. Speaking to a Conservative audience in 1961, R. A. Butler declared himself in favour of 'corporal punishment' administered 'in the heat of the moment', and with the right authority:

> I am not against the teacher using the cane and I think they should use it more. [...] I am in favour of the parents using the cane and I wish more of them had the moral courage to do it, or else a leather belt is often very effective for minor peccadilloes.[73]

'Unstable home life' and 'lack of discipline' had been indicated as the main causes of juvenile delinquency by the Committee on Parental Responsibility and Juvenile Delinquency, appointed by the Conservative Party's NWAC.[74] Working mothers carried the greatest share of responsibility, since 'overtired' and 'with frayed tempers', they had not 'enough time or energy left to give to the proper upbringing of their young'. The committee acknowledged that it was 'both impossible and undesirable to dictate to a woman whether she should take on work outside her home or not'. Rather, they proposed a range of solutions aimed to help to combine work and family life, including more shift work for married women employed in industry, allowing them to 'see their children off to school, and to be back again by the time they return'.[75] In praising the work of the Committee, the Minister of Education David Eccles added that he had done his best 'to get more married women teachers to return to the school when their own family responsibilities allow', in recognition of the importance of maternal influence in the experience of the child.[76] The issue of the link between mothers' work and juvenile delinquency was tackled again a decade later by the Association of Child Care Officers. In the occasion of their 1967s Annual Conference, the President of the Association J. W. D. Davies defined criticisms of working mothers as 'hypocrisy and nonsense'. Not only had married women's work become essential to the British economy, their presence was vital to the running of schools, hospitals and social services. Moreover, the real issue was not whether the mother worked. Rather social policy efforts should concentrate on making sure that 'the arrangements for the child when she is absent [were] satisfactory' and that mothers themselves 'should not be too tired to relate to the child'.[77] The creation of more day nurseries and nursery schools, 'not necessarily by the State but with State aid', was the most urgently needed type of intervention.[78] This was even more important in a situation where few families could count on the regular support of relatives. Again, this represented a long-lasting concern, which the Conservative NWAC had posed in very strong terms a few years earlier. Post-war transformations had caused many young families to live 'rootless, in a new community, with no experienced unofficial person to whom to turn when their children have outgrown the clinic.[79] They had improved their 'physical and material' situation, but this was no guarantee that they were able to support their children's 'emotional and mental development'.[80]

The strengthening of parental responsibilities emerged as a primary concern in relation to juvenile delinquency and young people's emotional adjustment from both liberal and conservative perspectives. Even reforms such as the reduction of the use of courts in relation to juvenile delinquency, increasingly favoured in Britain during the 1960s, had among their aims that of encouraging parents 'to fulfil the responsibilities which are properly theirs'.[81] This was part of a general movement in favour of prevention, on the basis of the identification of a close link between family life and young people's behaviour and of the assumption that 'children brought up in families which have failed themselves to "achieve a stable and satisfactory family life" would be those most likely to succumb to whatever adverse influence there may in the outside world'.[82]

The construction of new families: Fostering and adoption

In November 1943, HO inspectors explained that most children committed to the care of LAs by Juvenile Courts ended up in institutions due to foster parents' preference for 'poor law' cases. Moreover, they complained that the HO was being forced to grant permission to send these children to institutions ('more freely than we like') in the face of LAs' threat to refuse to take them into care.[83] A HO's attempt to change prospective foster parents' reluctance to accept 'court cases' by increasing their payments provoked widespread criticism and did little to change parental attitudes.[84]

In its evidence to the Curtis Committee, the Association of Municipal Corporation confirmed that boarding out with families rather than in institutions was hampered by shortage of suitable homes and the preferences expressed by foster parents 'as to the type of child they want'.[85] To these two factors, the Children's Society added that their policy of placing 'all normal children' with foster families, approved by the Executive Committee of the Society since January 1945, could not be carried out at present due to the inability or unwillingness of 'most Masters and Matrons'.[86]

According to the Curtis Report, 'a number of very suitable foster parents' had become unavailable after the war due to the 'strong desire' felt by many of those who had given hospitality to evacuated children during the conflict, 'to have their homes to themselves'. The housing situation, the fear of becoming too attached to a child who was then going to be removed, the uneasiness towards extensive controls and the increasing employment of women constituted further reasons for the reluctance of prospective foster parents to come forward. The question of whether better rewards should be used as a means of recruiting remained controversial.

Nonetheless, the Curtis Committee had encouraged a more extended use of fostering, although stressing that the shortage of suitable homes should not encourage accepting any candidate, and that not any child could be considered suitable for placement.[87] Moreover, their Report had warned that 'supervision and the possibility of removing the child from a bad or indifferent home' should not be regarded as a sufficient safeguard against the risk of bad placements. Removals were themselves 'bad for the child' and 'children undergoing several changes of foster parents [were] often worse off than if they had never been boarded out at all'.[88] It was necessary to acknowledge that 'a considerable proportion of children' were 'unsuited by habits, age, or by physical or mental condition to be placed in a private home'; that older children and boys were often difficult to place; and that 'coloured children' could 'hardly be placed at all'.[89]

The Children's Society considered it unsuitable for children with 'psychological or physical defects' requiring special care and those in regular contact with their parents – or whose parents objected to them being placed with a family – to board out. Moreover, the Society acknowledged that while 'pretty, docile girls with curly hair' were in great demand, 'foster-mothers of the real motherly sort' 'willing to tackle a brace of energetic young brothers [...] or a brother and sister' were difficult to find.[90] A census made at the beginning of 1949 revealed that of the total children available for fostering in the Society's branches, 35 were single girls under 5, 20 were girls over 5 and 18 were pairs or groups of sisters; the equivalent figures for boys were respectively 151, 110 and 40.[91] The attempt to render children more appealing by teaching good manners and education did little to correct the imbalance.[92]

A central consideration in the evaluation of possible placements concerned the relationship between foster families and natural parents.

In 1950, the Children's Society asked its branches to 'neither inform parents when their child was boarded out nor send to foster parents letters from parents'. The Society specified that this was not meant to 'cut off communications between a suitable parent and her child', but simply to protect foster families from inopportune interference. It was explained that natural parents' interference could easily result in the Society losing a foster home.[93] Moreover, a successful fostering (which is one resembling as much as possible normal family life) required a stable and exclusive relationship between foster parents and children, protected from the intrusion of the family of origin, often already diagnosed as unable to answer the child's needs.

The situation remained very different in Italy, where despite the relatively wide reference made by Italian professionals to the British act of 1948, fostering failed to be conceived as an alternative to institutional care throughout the 1950s.[94]

Two kinds of fostering were practised in Italy after the war. The first was placement without reward organised directly by children's homes, which retained full responsibility over the child. The second, defined as *collocamento familiare* or *collocamento mercenario* (paid fostering), was the closest equivalent to the kind of fostering practised in Britain. It consisted mostly in a form of nursling organised by maternity homes (*brefotrofi*) and paid for by Councils or Provinces. Although generally limited to very young children, this form of fostering was seen by some as a possible way towards more modern approaches to child care. Following Bowlby's theory, Lancellotti Mari explained that fostering allowed children to form the early emotional attachments upon which the future development of their whole nervous system depended. Moreover, a greater use of fostering could make it possible to overcome 'excessively standardised methods of care, harmful to children's physical and intellectual development'.[95] Lancellotti Mari stressed that greater efforts were necessary in Italy to extend the use of the system and to introduce reliable controls over foster parents. Similar observations were pointed out in the enquiry over assistance conducted by the AAI in 1954. This suggested that fostering was beneficial to children's physical and mental development and increased the possibilities of providing them with stable homes for the rest of their lives. The AAI's report also lamented that fostering was still neglected by most institutions, with the result that it was not unusual to find children of school age 'left' in young children and maternity homes.[96] The 1955 enquiry into the condition of child assistance in the Milan province confirmed that institutional care remained the inevitable destiny of most children deprived of family life, and that most children's homes resisted the idea of making a greater use of fostering.

The promotion of fostering and adoption was complicated by the existence of a complex and a restrictive legislation based on the Civil Code of 1942.[97] According to the Code, 'ordinary adoption' could take place exclusively between adopters without legitimate heirs and could not be used to acknowledge children born outside marriage. While the prospective adoptee could be of any age (although at least 18 years younger than the their adopter), childless adopters needed to have passed their reproductive age (with a minimum age for adopting usually fixed at 50). Either individuals or married couples had the right to adopt. Although adopting resulted in the attribution of the *patria potestas*, adoption remained revocable and the adopted person maintained his duties towards the family of origin. In all these respects, adoption created legal relationships that resembled but did not coincide with those existing within a 'natural family', in either quality or extension; adoption remained primarily a means of transferring name and patrimony to someone usually over the age of 18.

A more popular way of assuming the care of a child was through a form of *affiliazione* that did not include the transmission of rights of inheritance. According to Lancellotti Mari such a method was widely used not only by 'selfless people with modest economic possibilities', but also as a means of 'creating a legal relationship between the natural parent and the adulterine child'.[98] It is worth noticing that, as mentioned at the beginning of the chapter, the term affiliation had a different meaning in Britain, where it referred to a court order sought by the mother of an illegitimate child in order to obtain maintenance (of the child alone) from the father.[99]

Indeed, one of the most popular arguments used during the 1960s in support of the creation of a new system of adoption was the observation that *affiliazione* was increasingly used not to foster family-less children, but as a way of legitimising the position of 'children who are already part of the household of the *affiliante*'.[100] Nonetheless, *affiliazione* was defended as a solution able to offer the advantages of family life to a child 'in moral and material difficulties', creating symbolic as well as material links between the child and the family.

> The identity passed through the name contribute to the fraternal relationship established with the new comer; the word *affiliazione* itself shows that the child becomes part of the family, with great relief for the materially and morally abandoned child and the whole of society.[101]

However, the arrangement conferred hardly any right to the affiliated, whose position remained subordinated to the aim of safeguarding the superior legal status of the relationships taking place within the natural family.

Throughout the 1950s and 1960s, the modest use of adoption and affiliation seemed increasingly the unwelcome by-product of the determination to safeguard the prerogatives of the family as a 'natural institution', as well as the result of complex and expensive procedures. The reform of the legislation, finally adopted in 1967 (legge 5 giugno 1967, n. 431), aimed to make 'traditional adoption' easier by lowering the limits of the age of the adopters, allowing the adoption of more than one person and simplifying existing procedures. Such reforms, however, did not change the nature of the institution, which remained primarily intended to the transmission of name and patrimony to individual over the age of 18.

The main innovation introduced in 1967 was the creation of a new and parallel system, defined as 'special adoption' or '*adozione dei minori*'. The new institution regulated the adoption by married couples of children under the age of eight, whose state of abandonment had been established in court. Complex procedures were put into place, with the declared aim to protect the unique interest of the prospective adoptee, whose position within the household would then become analogous to that of a legitimate child. Unlike the *'adozione tradizionale'*, special adoptions aimed to 'protect not interests related to patrimony and descent, but exclusively the advantage of the adoptee', allowing him or her to grow up in 'a family to which he or she will be linked by bonds of affection'.[102]

Britain and Italy's different approaches to fostering and adoption were not only the consequences of the two countries' different legal systems. More importantly for my argument, they reflected different understandings of the nature of the family, its prerogatives and functions and a different conception of the possibility of correcting and recreating its foundations. Despite the many tensions that characterised the regulation of existing and reconstituted families in Britain, British social policy showed a degree of trust in the possibility of creating satisfactory forms of family life through the promotion of fostering and adoption and at the expenses of the 'natural family'. The possibility of encouraging the 'reconstitution' of different types of families was prevented in Italy by the overwhelming preoccupation to defend the prerogatives of the family as a natural institution based upon procreation within marriage. It was this concern that explained the reluctance to allow adoption where a legitimate succession already existed and to permit the adoption of one's own natural child.[103]

British intervention showed a greater confidence in the possibility of 'recreating' positive aspects of family life and a greater trust in the capacity of state and voluntary agencies to intervene in it. This implied the possibility of severing links of kinship if this was necessary to give the child a new and more suitable family, although not one based upon blood. In Italy, the legitimate family could share its privileges with someone 'less fortunate', but greater emphasis was put on the fact that the nature of its original relationships should remain different and superior.

Conclusions

Examining the duties of the state towards children, Lancellotti Mari explained that the interaction between state and family was both necessary and inevitable because it was 'through the family that the citizen becomes part of the state', and it was easy for the state 'to enter family life' through its economic, educational and health provisions. When the family was capable and trustworthy, then the state had simply the duty of complementing its functions, notably through the provision of education and health assistance. When the family was not suitable to answer the needs of the child, however, the state had the duty of taking over its responsibilities.[104]

Questions such as what responsibilities should be attributed to the state and the family respectively, where the power of intervention of the first ended, and how permeable private relationships should be to state and voluntary interventions are central to the examination of child care policy.[105] They assumed different contours in Britain and Italy.

In Britain, the post-war welfare state redefined (at least formally) the relationship between state and family, presenting welfare provisions as a new and constant companion to family life and a new means of individual support. Post-war rhetoric emphasised that the war had helped to make the presence of officials in individuals' private life increasingly acceptable. Probation officers, in particular, had become according to the HO a valuable support to family life in time of difficulty and had been 'often called on to give advice about education and even on postwar careers for the service men themselves'. Such 'friendly relations' were expected to continue after the war:

> It is felt that many young couples would now refer their matrimonial difficulties to the probation officers at an early stage, after having found them helpful during wartime difficulties.[106]

The experience of the post-war years showed that those expectations were over-optimistic. New welfare services sought to establish means of intervention in family life able to improve the performance of parents and of mothers in particular. Neglectful mothers and problem families were discussed increasingly in medico-social rather than in penal terms, yet the aim of controlling and limiting 'undesirable' behaviours remained at the centre of state and voluntary intervention. Incarceration and fines were increasingly substituted by rehabilitation, close supervision and skilled casework. Organisational problems, financial constraints and shortage of personnel held back the expansion of state's programs, leaving extensive responsibilities to the voluntary sector. Moreover, a flexible and dedicated voluntary intervention, free from bureaucratic hindrances and based on the work of strongly motivated individuals, was defended by many as a more appropriate means of dealing with troubled families. The best example in this sense remained the FSUs, often portrayed as a heroic organisation, able to compensate for its limited resources with the total commitment of its workers. The capacity of LA-based services to deliver equivalent social work was regarded with scepticism by the Children's Department itself, mostly as a result of lacking investments in the training of welfare workers.[107]

As I have already suggested in Chapter 4, a different situation was created in Italy by the more limited role assumed by the state in the provision of child assistance. In a situation in which voluntary, mostly Catholic, organisations maintained the almost complete responsibility over children's institutional care, and social work was in its infancy, the state took a less interventionist stance, leaving families to solve their own problems, often with the support of local voluntary organisations. Although episodic changes could be seen taking place in Italy as well, for instance, in relation to the re-education of young delinquents, welfare professionals played on the whole a smaller role in defining behavioural pathologies and criteria of interventions.

For all these differences, both in Britain and in Italy dominant discourses portrayed family values as the only possible basis of a morally strong society and stigmatised any behaviour likely to challenge such values. In both countries, supposed rises in juvenile delinquency were attributed first of all to lowering morality within the family, and 'illegitimacy' was condemned as a menace to the solidity of the institution of marriage. In both countries, women's individual capacities were deemed the most important factor within family life, often more important than economic and social conditions. Moreover, a significant convergence emerged during the 1950s between the Catholic ideology dominant in Italy and the values promoted in Britain by the Conservative Party on matters such as parental authority, marriage and the identification of the ideal family with a middle-class, conservative household broadly informed by religious principles. In both countries normative definitions of moral values and acceptable behaviour were used to construct a strong idea of normality in family life. This was based upon an idealised view of legitimate, stable and monogamous families as the only environment suitable to the development of a child. Most 'child welfare services' aimed to preserve and occasionally recreate such environment through a range of interventions intended to educate, punish or substitute unsuitable parents.

Conclusions

Because of its relevance to a number of different political and social processes, the regulation of family life offers a privileged perspective through which to look at the transformations taking place within the political and social sphere.

More than any other institution the family has been at the centre of the main issues confronted by the state in the post-war period. The regulation of family life has had extensive implications in relation to the creation of citizenship entitlements and gender policy. It is mostly through interventions addressed to the family that social policy has shaped personal lives. Moreover, no other institution has proved as effective as the family as an instrument of political propaganda and as an amplifier of social concerns. However, while an extensive body of work has dealt with the family in terms of demography, sexuality and intimacy, few historians have used the family as the main analytical category through which to analyse the development of political processes. This is what this book has sought to do.

As this book goes to print, the family is once again at the centre of legislative changes and political controversies both in Britain and in Italy. In the latter, issues such as women's reproductive rights, the legal treatment of same sex couples and the possible relaxation of existing laws on divorce played an important role in the 2006 electoral campaign and remains a contentious terrain of legislation for the centre-left coalition led by Romano Prodi presently in power. In a polarised and fragmented political landscape, these themes prove to be a hazardous terrain of confrontation not only between opposing factions, but also between allied parties. In particular, secular and catholic parties have assumed in Italy sharply different positions, with the Catholic Church playing an important role in shaping the debate. In Britain, New

Labour's eagerness to deal with social issues such as anti-social behaviour has encouraged a wide debate on the prerogatives of the family in contemporary society. Much of the rhetoric embraced by the government in this area has stressed the centrality of the family as the guardian of social cohesion and reinforced normative definitions of the kind of family life most suitable to support society's collective welfare. At the same time, legislative measures such as the Civil Partnership Bill have to some extent modified dominant understandings of what constitutes a family, by introducing new sets of rights and obligations for individuals involved in stable same sex relationships.

In any of these debates the relationship between the family and the state has represented a critical area of confrontation.

Throughout the post-war period, the definition of the respective prerogatives of state and family represented a primary consideration in social policy reforms, particularly when dealing with families' dependent members such as children. As Gillian Pascal has pointed out, interventions aimed to 'support' the family in its responsibility represented also a means of defining such responsibilities and of distinguishing them from those of the state.[1] The way in which families' rights and duties were defined and upheld in social policy reforms was shaped throughout the post-war period by political interests as well as by long-term cultural and social factors. The treatment of the family represented a defining characteristic of post-war politics, not only because it set the agenda for social policy, but also because it informed the language through which 'social problems' were defined and confronted. Both in Italy and in Britain, the family was used as a political tool; the way in which social policy was used to shape family life differed in the two countries, partly as a result of the differences that characterised their political and social landscapes. Differences in the extent and shape of welfare policies, in the rules followed by political competition and in the role played by the major religious institutions have been explored in this book as the main causes of Britain and Italy's diverging approaches to the regulation of family life.

It has been a common assumption that the development of the welfare state has irrevocably changed the relationship between citizens and state, making an extended social presence of the latter a necessary and inevitable characteristic of modern Western societies. More than any other area of social intervention, measures dealing with child welfare pointed out the tensions and contradictions that characterised the approach to the family at political level. In 1942, William Beveridge summed up with remarkable clarity the two principles that should shape the development of welfare policies in relation to children: 'first, that nothing should be done to remove from parents the responsibility of maintaining their children, and second that it is in the national interest for the state to help parents to discharge that responsibility properly'.[2] Both principles have informed (more or less openly) the development of social intervention both in Britain and in Italy during the post-war period.

Despite policymakers' clear unwillingness to replace functions and responsibilities traditionally attributed to the family with social services, the transformation and expansion of the functions of the state within society has been seen often as a threat to the family and its social role. The growth of welfare services, in particular, has been seen by 'pro-families' positions as a more or less overt attack to the autonomy of the family, particularly within 'New Right' discourses in Britain and in the United States. The idea that social security programmes were bound to impinge upon families' commitment to self-reliance and to undermine individuals' sense of responsibility permeated the action of groups such as the Conservative Family Campaign in 1980s Britain. Although coinciding with the dominant position acquired by the New Right in the Conservative Party and despite being influenced by contemporary developments taking place in America (particularly by the work of authors such as Charles Murray), 'pro-traditional-family values' campaigns articulated tensions and dilemmas that had accompanied the development of social policy in Britain throughout the post-war period.[3]

In Italy, the modesty of social intervention was accompanied by a rhetoric emphasising the irreplaceable role of the family in the construction of networks of solidarity and support. The absence of a clearly oriented family policy was supported by an enduring representation of the Italian family as a strong institution based on extended kinship networks. The supposedly 'familistic' nature of the Italian society was used to justify a lack of social provisions that left upon (loosely defined) families the burden of personal care and support.[4]

Nonetheless, both in Britain and Italy the family was used by the state as a means of shaping social and economic relations. Both states showed determination to regulate what 'the family is' (i.e. a social institution based upon marriage and having the nurturing of children as its first aim) through legislative interventions that defined which sexual and intimate relationships should be considered as acceptable. Although to different degrees, both states sought to use social policy as a means of shaping family life according to values and standards formulated outside the family itself.

In both countries, professional, political and religious discourses interacted in creating dominant understandings of the family and its responsibilities. However, the specific characteristics that such discourses assumed in Britain and Italy led to different outcomes in relation to the regulation of the family. Different political and social factors either encouraged or hindered a transformation of the notion of the family in the two countries.

Despite the many similarities that characterised the way in which the family was regulated at the legislative level, significant differences existed in the hegemonic discourses according to which the family was conceptualised in the two countries. This was the result of the fact that different authorities asserted their dominant expertise over the family in post-war Britain and Italy. In Britain, psychological and medical expertise emerged as the dominant paradigm according to which the family was understood and treated. In Italy, approaches to the family continued to be shaped by the enduring influence exercised by the Catholic Church. This discrepancy had far-reaching implications. It affected the way in which the relationships taking place within the home were conceptualised in the two countries' main public discourses. It also influenced the regulation of the family in legislative processes, especially those related to social policy.

It was the greater extent of social intervention in Britain that gave new and far-reaching opportunities to social and medical experts to intervene in family life. In turn, medical and psychological knowledge and professional expertise became the greatest authority in questions of family welfare. In Italy, the modesty of social intervention and the greater social presence of the Church delayed such a transformation, leaving family matters to be discussed primarily in terms of morality.

Similar issues captured the attention of professionals and politicians both in Italy and in Britain, namely late marriage, falling birth rates and the increased participation of women in the labour market. In Britain, such concerns were accompanied by a sense that problems within the family could be understood and solved through scientific knowledge and expertise. In Italy, anxieties and moral concerns filled public debates, but failed to promote extensive family-oriented policies. It could be suggested that Britain and Italy expressed two different ideas of social and political progress, reflecting, in one case, post-war optimism and confidence in the possibility of 'putting things right' through social intervention, and, in the other, the strong role maintained by the Church's dystopic view of modernity. Both attitudes included a strong notion of what families should be about and tried to promote a society where such (ideal) households could thrive.

Both in Britain and in Italy, the churches claimed that they had a natural responsibility over matters concerning family life. Their role, however, differed widely. While the role of the Catholic Church has dominated studies of the family in Italy, the influence of the Anglican Church has hardly figured as a relevant factor in existing analyses of the British family after 1945. The comparison with the Italian Catholic Church demonstrates the usefulness of bringing it back into the picture. It suggests that far from playing no role in the shaping of post-war British social transformations, the Anglican Church tried to deal with wider processes of change rethinking its role and its responsibilities in the context of the welfare society. While the Roman Catholic Church used its political influence to oppose the transformations taking place in the context of sexual and domestic relationships, the Anglican hierarchy showed a greater willingness to accept social changes underway. This may have been the consequence of the Anglican Church's weakness, but it contributed to support (at least indirectly) changes in attitudes towards sexuality and what has been described as a shift 'from the idea of marriage as an institution to marriage as a relationship'.[5] If the post-war period was characterised in Britain by the consolidation of the 'symmetrical family' (at least as an ideal), this was also the result of the stand taken by the Anglican Church.[6] The acceptance of family planning in marriage, for instance, was based on a more positive evaluation of the importance of sex and emphasised the spouses' shared responsibilities and co-operation. The Catholic Church's enduring suspicion towards sexuality as inherently sinful and its disregard for sexuality in marriage remained inextricably linked to a view of marriage as a hierarchical institution that left little space for a positive evaluation of the transformation of conjugal roles.

Equally significant were differences in attitudes expressed by the two churches towards state intervention in social policy. As I have suggested in Chapter 3, while the Church of England was forced to come to terms with a situation that saw professional social workers taking up much of the work that the church itself had traditionally carried out, in Italy, the Catholic Church maintained a near-monopoly over social assistance and with it a direct and unquestioned involvement in family life. Moreover, while the Italian church remained on the whole opposed to an expansion of state power in the sector of assistance, important elements within the Anglican Church supported and embraced the reform agenda which was at the basis of the new welfare state. This affected how the two churches considered issues such as families' responsibility for the care of their members and the relative duties of men and women within the household.

Differences in attitudes towards the family reflected not only different dogmatic positions embraced by the two churches. Equally influential were differences in institutional nature and the different relationship established by the Catholic and the Anglican Church within the political sphere.

Both in Italy and in Britain, the family proved to be highly relevant to political interests and emerged as a potential terrain of conflict between political and religious powers. In both countries, this potential conflict was resolved with the establishment of more or less stable (although not necessarily equal) partnerships between the main Churches and the political power, aimed to the pursuing of common interests. In Britain, this took the shape of the Anglican Church's supporting and trying to contribute to the shaping of the post-war welfare state. In Italy, it resulted in the Catholic Church taking an active political role in party politics, lending its support to the DC and becoming a leading advocate of the necessity to resist the possible ascendance to power of the Communist Party. The different political strategies pursued by the Catholic and the Anglican Church (as well as their different social influence) affected the way in which different political parties addressed issues related to the family across the political spectrum.

Unsurprisingly, Italian and British politicians and experts expressed similar concerns about the erosion of the traditional family and the subsequent decline in moral standards throughout the post-war period. On the left of the political spectrum, the Labour Party and the PCI declared themselves to be as concerned as their political opponents about the fate of the family in contemporary society. In Italy, the explicit appeal to family values represented an essential means of counterbalancing the anticommunist propaganda put out by the DC and the Catholic Church. By speaking of the moral and material ruin which affected post-war Italian families the leader of the PCI Palmiro Togliatti pointed to the common roots that united catholic and communist masses and reassured its audience that his party had no intention to pursue policies aimed to a far-reaching reform of the family as an institution. Cultural values and political opportunism perpetuated the endorsement of the family as the bulwark of Italian society, and postponed the consideration of controversial issues like divorce.

In Britain, the Labour Party had no similar need to reassure and appease, its model of family life been well in tune with mainstream ideas of what family life should be. Indeed, strengthening the family had been central to the commitment to welfare legislation that defined Labour's political project at the end of the war. Following Beveridge's approach to social intervention, the party subscribed to a view of the family as a team based on different roles normatively defined and promoted it through its politics. Nonetheless, throughout the 1950s and 1960s, Labour intellectuals expressed concern for the transformation of the 'traditional' working-class family and community, the social fragmentation they threatened and the undesirable political effects they were likely to have upon the party. Such a concern was part of the larger question of how to avoid that an increasingly rich society became also ever more individualistic and therefore socially costly. It was a dilemma that confronted political parties throughout the post-war period across the political spectrum.

In both Italy and Britain, it was the moderate parties that put most emphasis on the family in their public discourse. Both Conservatives and Christian Democrats described the family as the primary sphere of individual engagement and as the main guarantor of society's morality and cohesion. The preservation of a society based on sound moral values depended upon the capacity of individuals to act as free agents: the family was essential to preserve individual freedom and therefore freedom within society. Moreover, for centre right parties in both countries, the family had an invaluable political role to play: the family constituted a bastion against the dangers supposedly coming from extremist left wing parties and revolutionary ideologies. Traditional family life and private property represented an indissoluble unit and together provided the best protection against the temptations of socialism and communism.

Both Conservatives and Christian Democrats advocated a state that promoted freedom of enterprise and individual success while being able to provide care for those in need. Both parties used the family to justify their attitudes towards social intervention: namely, their support for a minimal amount of social services (useful to promote family welfare) and their opposition to their extended use, seen as having the potential for undermining individual responsibilities.

In both cases, however, these doctrinal positions were only partially reflected in political practice and the attempt to govern the transformation undergone by the family as an institution proved often an unachievable goal. Although the reference to the family fitted well with a rhetoric that promised to combine a degree of social intervention with a discernibly conservative view of society and economic liberalism, individual behaviours challenged legal definitions and normative expectations in terms of sexuality, family life and life expectations. Centre right parties used the reference to the family to defend policies promoting widespread property and individual spending against socialist collectivism, austerity and planning. They soon worried, however, that increasingly prosperous families seemed to find less time not only for public engagement, but also for properly fulfilling their primary function as agencies of socialisation and providers of care. Individualism and materialism, two terms increasingly popular in the political discourse since the second half of the 1950s, seemed to be harboured within those same families that should constitute the backbone of an efficient and stable society.

Throughout the post-war period, the behaviour of women and young people posed a radical challenge to the expectations attached to the nuclear family. The 'disaffection' of young people was (and still is) read mostly as the consequence of the deterioration of family life. The continuous growth in the number of married women seeking employment was at odds with public discourses emphasising the importance of the presence of the mother for the development of the child. The stated dissatisfaction of many housewives called into question the image of the couple as a team carrying out different but equally satisfying roles. Falling birth rates in Italy proved the growing inability of the Catholic Church to influence individuals' behaviour, particularly among women. Moreover, declining fertility suggested that larger families were becoming incompatible with the models of consumption increasingly proposed by the media and sustained by the DC. Liberalisation of morality and social behaviour stigmatised by the Catholic Church seemed an unstoppable by-product of the modernisation of the country promoted by the DC. While the supposed disintegration of the family provided (and continues to provide) a unique source of political propaganda, the identification of an ideal model of family life suitable to the requirements of effective liberal democracies and the creation of social policy able to promote such models of family life remained an elusive quest throughout the post-war period.

Notes

Introduction

1. M. Daly and K. Rake, *Gender and the Welfare State, Care, Work and Welfare in Europe and the USA*, Cambridge, Polity, 2003, p. 175.
2. Among those suggesting an irreversible transformation of family life and sexual relationships A. Giddens, *The Transformation of Intimacy: Sexuality, Love, and Eroticism in Modern Societies*, Oxford, Policy Press, 1995 and J. Lewis, *The End of Marriage? Individualism and Intimate Relationships*, Aldershot, Elgar, 2001.
3. G. Therborn, *Between Sex and Power. Family in the World, 1900–2000*, London, Routledge, 2004, p. 2.
4. Ibid., p. 3.
5. L. H. Hall, *Sex, Gender and Social Change in Britain since 1880*, Basingstoke, Macmillan, 2000, pp. 150–152.
6. J. Finch, *Family Obligations and Social Change*, Cambridge, Polity, 1989, p. 4.
7. A noticeable exception remains; for example, S. Pederson, *Family, Dependency and the Rise of the Welfare State*, Cambridge, Cambridge University Press, 1993.
8. Of particular interest to this book are studies of the relationship between welfare and gender that adopt a comparative perspective, in particular J. Bock and P. Thane (eds), *Maternity and Gender Policy. Women and the Rise of the European Welfare States 1880s–1950*, London, Routledge, 1991, J. Lewis (ed.), *Women and Social Policy in Europe. Work, Family and the State*, Aldershot, Elgar, 1993, and M. Daly and K. Rake, *Gender and the Welfare State, Care, Work and Welfare in Europe and the USA*, Cambridge, Polity, 2003.
9. See, for instance, C. Mancina, *La famiglia*, Roma, Editori Riuniti, 1981, M. Mitterauer and R. Sieber, *The European Family. Patriarchy to Partnership from the Middle Ages to the Present*, Oxford, Blackwell, 1982, J. Elshtain, *The Family in Political Thought*, Amherst, University of Massachusetts, 1982, B. Thorne and M. Yalom, *Rethinking the Family, Some Feminist Questions*, New York, Longman, 1982, D. H. J. Morgan, *The Family, Politics, and Social Theory*, London, Routledge, 1985, Id., *Family Connections. An Introduction to Family Studies*, Cambridge, Polity, 1996, and D. Cheal, *Family and the State of Theory*, London, Harvester Wheatsheaf, 1991.
10. In particular, L. Caldwell, *Italian Family Matters, Women, Politics and Legal Reforms*, Basingstoke, Macmillan, 1991, also M. Barbagli, *Sotto lo stesso tetto: mutamenti della famiglia in Italia dal xv al xx secolo*, Bologna, Il Mulino, 1984; for the fascist period, V. De Grazia, *How Fascism Ruled Women. Italy 1922–1945*, Berkeley, University of California Press, 1992 and M. Quine, *Italy's Social Revolution. Charity, and Welfare from Liberalism to Fascism*, Basingstoke, Palgrave, 2002. Sociologists have proved more prolific than historians, although only few have adopted a comparative perspective or focused specifically on the family; among the exceptions are P. Donati, *Famiglia e politiche sociali*, Milano, Franco Angeli, 1981 and C. Saraceno, *Mutamenti della famiglia e politiche sociali in Italia*, Bologna, Il Mulino, 1998.

11. Among the others, G. Allan and G. Crow, *Home and Family. Creating the Domestic Sphere*, Basingstoke, Macmillan, 1989, H. Corr and L. Jameson (eds), *Politics of Everyday Life. Continuity and Change in Work and the Family*, Basingstoke, Macmillan, 1990, W. Webster, *Imagining Home. Gender, 'Race', and National Identity, 1945–1964*, London, UCL, 1998, Davidoff, L., Doolittle, M., Fink, J. and Holden, K., *The Family Story. Blood, Contract and Intimacy, 1830 – 1960*, London, Longman, 1999, and M. Peplar, *Family Matters. A History of Ideas about the Family since 1945*, London, Longman, 2002.

12. An idea powerfully represented in P. Higgins, *Heterosexual Dictatorship: Male Homosexuality in Post-war Britain*, London, Fourth Estate, 1996.

13. Among the works that have concentrated specifically on the interactions between family and state in relation to the development of social policy, see J. Finch and D. Grove, *A Labour of Love. Family, Work and Caring*, London, Routledge, 1983, and F. Williams, *Rethinking Families*, London, Calouste Gulbekian Foundation, 2004.

14. It remains relevant here the classification of welfare regimes put forward by G. Esping Andersen, *The Three Worlds of Welfare Capitalism*, Princeton, Princeton University Press, 1990.

15. See, for instance, J. Finch, 'Kinship and friendship', in Jowell, Witherspoon and Brook (eds), *British Social Attitudes. Special International Report*, quoted in P. Ginsborg, *L'Italia del tempo presente*, Torino, Einaudi, 1998, pp. 132–133.

16. For a contextualised discussion of the transformations underwent by the Italian family in the last 20 years see Ginsborg, *L'Italia del tempo presente*, pp. 132–179.

17. H. Glennerster, *British Social Policy since 1945*, Oxford, Blackwell, 1995, pp. 3–4.

18. M. Pugh, *State and Society. A Social and Political History of Britain 1870–1997*, London, Arnold, 1999 (1st edn 1994), p. 281.

19. P. Thane, *Foundations of the Welfare State*, London, Longman, 1996, pp. 246–247.

20. For a discussion of the transformation of the Italian demographic structure, see M. Livi Bacci and M. Breschi, 'La Fecondità', in M. Barbagli and D. I. Kertzer (eds), *Storia della Famiglia Italiana 1750–1950*, Bologna, Il Mulino, 1992, p. 30. The effect of the industrialisation upon family structures was put forward by M. Anderson, 'Famiglia e Rivoluzione Industriale', in M. Barbagli (a cura di), *Famiglia e Mutamento Sociale*, Bologna, Il Mulino, 1977, pp. 13–29.

21. For an analysis of the Italian economic development during the 1950s and 1960s see M. Paci, *La struttura sociale italiana*, Bologna, Il Mulino, 1982.

22. C. Saraceno, 'The Ambivalent Familism of the Italian Welfare State', *Social Politics*, 1 (1994), 1, pp. 60–82.

1   Family, state and democratic development in Britain and Italy

1. J. La Palombara, *Democracy, Italian Style*, New Haven, Yale University Press, 1987, p. 3.

2. R. Putnam, *The Beliefs of Politicians. Ideology, Conflict and Democracy in Britain and Italy*, New Haven, Yale University Press, 1973, p. 9.

3. Ibid., pp. 84, 138.

4. G. A. Almond and S. Verba, *The Civic Culture. Political Attitudes and Democracy in Five Nations*, Princeton, Princeton University Press, 1963, p. 8.
5. For an extensive discussion of Italy's 'dual' political culture see Joseph La Palombara, *Interest Groups in Italian Politics*, Princeton, Princeton University Press, 1964, in particular Ch. 3
6. Ibid., pp. 9, 39.
7. E. C. Banfield, *The Moral Basis of a Backward Society*, Glencoe, The Free Press, 1958, p. 7. The study was published in Italy for the first time in 1961 (E. C. Banfield *Una comunità del Mezzogiorno*, Bologna, Il Mulino, 1961), and again in 1976, as *Le basi morali di una società arretrata*.
8. Banfield defined his notion of ethos as 'the sum of the characteristic usage, ideas, standards, and codes by which a group is differentiated and individualised in character from other groups', W. G. Sumner, *Folkways*, Boston, Ginn & Co./the Athenaeum Press, 1907, p. 36. In the case of Montegrano, 'amoral familism' was the result of 'a high death rate, certain land tenure conditions, and the absence of the institution of the extended family', Banfield, *The Moral Basis*, p. 10.
9. Ibid., p. 15.
10. Ibid., pp. 85–90.
11. W. Bell, 'Familism and Suburbanisation: One Test of the Social Choice Hypothesis', *Rural Sociology*, 21, 1956, pp. 276–283.
12. Ibid.
13. R. F. Winch, 'Some Observations on Extended Familism in the United States', in R. F. Winch and L. W. Goodman (eds), *Selected Studies in Marriage and the Family*, New York, Holt, Rinehart and Winston, 1968, pp. 127–138.
14. Extensive critiques of Banfield's study can be found in the 1976 Italian edition of the work; among them Domenico De Masi's essay, according to which Banfield's study had become 'a concrete example of how research should not be conducted, but also a model with which everyone with an interest in Southern Italy was forced to engage', D. De Masi, 'Arretratezza del Mezzogiorno e Analisi Sociologica', Banfield, *Le Basi Morali di una Società Arretrata*, Bologna, Il Mulino, 1976, p. 9. Also, on Banfield's use of the notion of ethos see A. Pizzorno, 'Familismo amorale e marginalità storica ovvero perché non c'è niente da fare a Montegrano', ibid., pp. 237–252.
15. La Palombara, *Interest Groups*, p. 65.
16. Ibid., pp. 64–65.
17. Ibid., p. 66.
18. Ibid., p. 67.
19. J. La Palombara, 'Italy: Fragmentation, Isolation, Alienation', in L. N. Pye and S. Verba (eds), *Political Culture and Political Development*, Princeton, Princeton University Press, 1965, pp. 318–319.
20. R. Rose, 'England: A Traditionally Modern Political Culture', ibid., p. 106. In his *Studies of British Politics*, Rose explained, 'beginning in early childhood, a young Englishman learns through formal and informal instruction the basic outlook of his society. This process of socialisation helps to differentiate the individual Englishman from a German, Russian or American [...]. The family constituted the main agency through which such a culture was passed through the generations', R. Rose (ed.), *Studies in British Politics*, London, Macmillan, 1966, p. 1.

21. Ibid.
22. L. Pinna, *La famiglia esclusiva. Parentela e clientelismo in Sardegna*, Bari, Laterza, 1971, pp. 7, 19–22.
23. C. Tullio-Altan, *La Nostra Italia. Arretratezza socioculturale, clientelismo, tras-formismo e ribellismo dall'Unità a oggi*, Milano, Feltrinelli, 1986, p. 83; G. Campanini, *Potere politico e immagine paterna*, Milano, Vita e Pensiero, 1985, pp. 119–120; the idea of a prevailing Italian particularistic ethos has been recently re-stated by Tullio-Altan in *Gli Italiani in Europa. Profilo storico comparato delle identità nazionali europee*, Bologna, Il Mulino, 1999, pp. 156–159.
24. P. Ginsborg, 'Family, Culture and Politics in Contemporary Italy', in Z. G. Barański and R. Lumley (eds), *Culture and Conflict in Post-War Italy. Essays on Mass and Popular Culture*, Basingstoke, Macmillan, 1990, p. 21, see also P. Ginsborg, 'Famiglia, società civile e stato nella storia contemporanea: alcune considerazioni metodologiche', in *Meridiana*, 17, Maggio, 1993, pp. 179–208 and id., 'Familismo' in P. Ginsborg (ed.), *Stato dell'Italia*, Milano, Il Saggiatore, 1994, pp. 78–82.
25. G. Gribaudi, 'Images of the South', in D. Forgacs and R. Lumley (eds), *Italian Cultural Studies*, Oxford, Oxford University Press, 1996 , pp. 83–85.
26. Similar consideration apply to the closely related idea of 'particularism', M. Eve, 'Comparing Italy: The Case of Corruption', ibid., p. 46.
27. A possible declination of familism as a relationship between family, civil society and state rather than as specific ethos has been suggested by Paul Ginsborg in his recent *Il tempo di cambiare, Politica e potere della vita quotidiana*, Torino, Einaudi, 2004, p. 124. Here too, however, the inherently comparative dimension of the concept remains underplayed.
28. Saraceno, 'The Ambivalent Familism of the Italian Welfare State'.
29. For a discussion of the state as an organisation, G. Poggi, *The State. Its Nature, Development and Prospects*, Cambridge, Polity Press, 1990, p. 18.
30. J. Donzelot, *The Policing of the Family*, Baltimore and London, The John Hopkins University Press, 1997, p. 7, originally published as *La Police des familles*, Paris, Les Éditions de Minuit, 1977. Also, C. Lasch, *Haven in a Heartless World; The Family Besieged*, New York, Basic Books, p. 197.
31. F. Mount, *The Subversive Family. An Alternative History of Love and Marriage*, London, Jonathan Cape, 1982, p. 173. From the opposite side, the development of social services has been seen as an encouragement to individuals to go back to the family to protect themselves from too pervasive society and state, A. Ardigò, 'La crescita dell'uomo nella società industriale', in AA. VV., *Il problema della società industriale*, Milano, Vita e Pensiero, 1979, p. 424, Campanini, *Potere politico*, pp. 110–113. On the presumed fragility of the family in post-war Italy, partly as a result of the power acquired by controlling agencies, Campanini, *Cattolici e società fra dopoguerra e post-concilio*, Roma, AVE, 1990, pp. 2, 8–9, and Id., *Le stagioni della famiglia*, Milano, Ed. San Paolo, 1994, p. 28.
32. Finch, *Family Obligations*, p. 4.
33. L. Fox Harding, *Family, State and Social Policy*, Basingstoke, Macmillan, 1996, p. xi; because of these difficulties, Harding resolved to avoid 'on the whole' the term 'the family' in her work.
34. D. Gittins, *The Family in Question*, London, Macmillan, 1985, p. 2.

35. L. Balbo, 'Crazy Quilts: Rethinking the Welfare State Debate from a Woman's Point of View', in A. S. Sassoon (ed.), *Women and the State*, London, Hutchinson, 1987, p. 48.

36. Morgan, *The Family, Politics, and Social Theory*, London, Routledge and Kegan Paul, 1985, pp. 283–285.

37. Campanini, *Potere Politico*, pp. 96–97.

38. J. Gillis, *A World of Their Own Making. Myth, ritual, and the quest for family values*, Cambridge Mass., Harvard University Press, 1997 (first published, 1996), p. xv.

39. Finch, *Family Obligations*, p. 7.

40. E. W. Burgess and H. J. Locke, *The Family*, New York, American Book Company, 1945, p. 27.

41. Gillis, *A World of Their Own Making*, p. 149.

42. T. H. Hareven, 'The History of the Family and the Complexity of Social Change', *American Historical Review*, 96, 1 (1991), p. 120. The paradigm of the conjugal nuclear family as the type of household inevitably associated to modernity was set most powerfully by William J. Goode, *World Revolution and Family Patterns*, New York, Free Press of Glencoe, 1963; for a critique of Goode's interpretation, see Therborn, *Between Sex and Power*, pp. 3–4.

43. R. Fletcher, *Britain in the Sixties: Family and Marriage. An Analysis and Moral Assessment*, Harmondsworth, Penguin, 1962, p. 19.

44. Classic formulations of this perspective are T. Parsons and R. F. Bales, *Family, Socialisation and Interaction Process*, London, Routledge and Kegan Paul, 1956, and W. Thomas and F. Znaniecki, *The Polish Peasant in Europe and America. Monograph of an Immigrant Group*, 5 vv., Boston, Richard G. Badger, 1918–1920.

45. In particular, see P. Laslett, *The World We Have Lost*, London, Methuen, 1965 and J. Hajnal, 'European Marriage Patterns in Perspective', in D. V. Glass and D. E. C. Eversley (eds), *Population in History*, Chicago, Chicago University Press, 1965, and J. Hajnal, P. Laslett, R. Wall, et al., *Family Forms in Historic Europe*, Cambridge, Cambridge University Press, 1983. Peter Laslett contrasted the 'western family' model to the southern European and Mediterranean family type, characterised by complex household structures and early marriage; David Kertzer later refined Laslett's hypothesis, criticising the link between type of household organisation and age at marriage and emphasising instead the connection between family organisation and type of land tenure, D. I. Kertzer and D. Hogan, *Family, Political Economy and Demographic Change: The Transformation of Life in Casalecchio, Italy, 1861–1921*, Madison, Wisconsin, University of Wisconsin Press, 1989.

46. See, in particular, M. Anderson, *Family Structure in Nineteenth-Century Lancashire*, Cambridge, Cambridge University Press, 1971, T. K. Hareven, *Family Time and Industrial Time. The Relationship between the Family and Work in a New England Community*, Cambridge, Cambridge University Press, 1982.

47. T. Parsons, 'The Social Structure of the Family', in R. N. Anshen (ed.), *The Family: Its Function and Destiny*, New York, Harper and Brothers, 1959 (first ed. 1949), pp. 241–274.

48. Particularly interesting here is Goldthorpe's interpretation of how the growing investment in family life had encouraged the acquisition of middle-class values among industrial workers, eroding traditional proletarian solidarity in J. H. Goldthorpe, *The Affluent Worker. Industrial Attitudes and Behaviour*, Cambridge, Cambridge University Press, 1968, in particular, pp. 149, 175–176. For a critique of Goldthorpe's interpretation see F. Devine, 'Privatised Families and Their Homes', in G. Allan and G. Crow, (eds) *Home and Family*, Basingstoke, Macmillan, 1989, pp. 84–85 and id., *Affluent Workers Revisited*, Edinburgh, Edinburgh University Press, 1992.

49. Following this line of interpretation, the early emergence of system of social protection in western and northern Europe has been seen as a possible consequence of the processes of nuclearisation of the family and a characteristic European phenomenon, see H. Kaelble, *Verso una società europea. Storia social dell'europa, 1880–1980*, Bari, Laterza, 1990, pp. 14–15. (first ed. *Auf dem Weg zu einer europäischen Gesellschaft. Eine Sozialgeschichte Westeuropas. 1880–1980*, C. H. Beck'sche Verlagsbuchhandlung, Munich, 1987).

2   The family in the political debate

1. For a compendium of existing legislation up to 2003 see K. Boele-Woelki and A. Fichs (eds), *Legal Recognition of Same Sex Couples in Europe*, Antwerp, Oxford, New York, Intersentia, 2003.
2. N. Gray and D. Brazil, *Blackstone Guide to The Civil Partnership Act 2004*, Oxford and New York, Oxford University Press, 2005, p. v.
3. Ibid., pp. 7–8.
4. Unione, *Per il Bene dell'Italia, Programma di Governo 2006–2011*, p. 72.
5. The centre-left coalition includes far left parties (such as Rifondazione Comunista) and moderate catholic ones (such as Margherita).
6. C. Lasch, *Haven in a Heartless World*, p. 15.
7. The decision to focus on parties with a large social presence penalises the space given in my account to the so-called 'secular' parties in Italy. Nonetheless, secular parties played on occasions an important role in fostering political reforms, as in the case of radicals' campaigns for family reforms in the 1970 and their role had been more extensively analysed in other works, such as L. Caldwell, *Italian Family Matters, Women, Politics and Legal Reform*, London, Macmillan, 1991.
8. D. Sassoon, *One Hundred Years of Socialism. The West European Left in the Twentieth Century*, London, Tauris, 1996, p. 124.
9. The definition, taken from Art. 29 of the Constitution, was used by the Christian Democrat MP Franca Falcucci as a title for her intervention at a Symposium organised by the *Movimento Femminile della Dc* in February 1963.
10. G. Tupini, 'Verso il Congresso. La Nostra Unità', in *Il Popolo*, 14 April 1946, quoted by M. S. Piretti, 'La stampa democristiana; tra prospettiva personalista e preoccupazione garantista', in R. Ruffilli (a cura di), *Costituente e lotta politica. La stampa e le scelte costituzionali*, Firenze, Vallecchi, 1978, p. 52.
11. On De Gasperi's political project in relation to the Catholic Church see G. Martina, *La Chiesa in Italia negli ultimi 30 anni*, Roma, Studium, 1977,

pp. 21–22. See also P. Scoppola, *La proposta politica di De Gasperi*, Bologna, Il Mulino, 1977.

12. The Assembly was formed by 556 elected members; 75 of them consti-tuted the Commission responsible for the preparation of the text to be later approved by the full Assembly. The *Commissione dei 75* was organised in three subcommittees responsible respectively for 'rights and duties of the citizens', constitutional matters, and social rights and duties. The question of the family was discussed within the first sub-committee.

13. In P. Pombeni, *La Costituente*, Bologna, Il Mulino, 1995, p. 130.

14. This included the difficult agreement found concerning the inclusion within the new Constitution of the Concordat signed between the Vatican and the Fascist state in 1927 (now Art. 7), G. Ambrosini *Costituzione Italiana*, Torino, Einaudi, 1975, pp. xli–xliii.

15. R. M., 'Temerari soliloqui', in *Avvenire d'Italia*, 23 Aprile 1947, quoted in Piretti, 'La Stampa Democristiana', p. 68.

16. D. Barbero, *Matrimonio Fondamento della Famiglia*, VII Convegno Nazionale di Studio dell'Unione Giuristi Cattolici Italiani, Roma, 3–5 November 1955, p. 66. Barbero was a Professor at the Università Cattolica di Milano and member of the Unione Giuristi Cattolici Italiani.

17. F. Falcucci, 'La famiglia, società naturale fondata sul matrimonio', in *La famiglia e le trasformazioni della società Italiana*, Movimento Femminile della DC, Rome, 10–11 February 1963, pp. 9–11.

18. Ibid., pp. 13–14.

19. Ibid., pp. 33–35.

20. A. Ardigò, 'Le trasformazioni della società Italiana: Riflessi nella Vita della Famiglia', in *La Famiglia e le Trasformazioni della Società Italiana*, pp. 39–42.

21. Ibid., pp. 52–54.

22. Dianella Gagliani has suggested that an 'anti-paternalistic' transformation took place after the war among sharecropping families, linked to changes in the role and attitude of women, D. Gagliani, 'Welfare State come Umanesimo e Antipatronage. Un'Esperienza delle Donne nel Secondo Dopoguerra', in D. Gagliani and M. Salvati (eds), *La Sfera Pubblica Femminile. Percorsi di Storia delle Donne in Età Contemporanea*, Bologna, CLUEB, 1990, pp. 163–177, in particular pp. 166–167.

23. On this point, Sassoon's observation is only partially convincing: 'Christian Democrats, precisely because they enjoyed the support of many women, were more sensitive to women's issues than was generally acknowledged', D. Sassoon, *Contemporary Italy. Politics, Economy and Society since 1945*, Harlow, Longman, 1997 (first published, 1986), p. 120.

24. This session owes much to the work of Lorenzo Cinatti and to many discus-sions held while both were students in Florence, for a detailed examination of the ideology of the PCI in relation to the family, L. Cinatti, *Il Partito Comunista Italian e la Famiglia: Ideologia, Modelli e propaganda fra il 1921 e il 1948*, Unpublished tesi di Laurea, Firenze, Facoltà di Lettere e Filosofia, 1998.

25. On the 'doctrinal approach' of the party to the question of the position of women within the home during the 1920s, G. Chianese, *Storia Sociale della Donna in Italia*, Napoli, Guida, 1980, p. 61.

26. D. Sassoon, *The Strategy of the Italian Communist Party. From the Resistance to the Historic Compromise*, London, Frances Pinter, 1981, p. 29.

27. Party membership grew from 401 960 in 1944 to 1 770 896 in 1945, imposing the creation of a complex structure and new ways of communication, R. Martinelli *Storia del Partito Comunista Italiano. VI. Il 'Partito Nuovo' dalla Liberazione al 18 Aprile*, Torino, Einaudi, 1995, pp. 17–19.

28. P. Togliatti, 'Per la Difesa della Famiglia Italiana', *L'Alba*, 18 March 1944, in Togliatti, *Opere*, Vol. IV, 2, Roma, Editori Riuniti, 1979, pp. 534–537.

29. Ibid., p. 156.

30. P. Togliatti, speech at the Conference of Communist Women, Rome, 2–4 June 1945, in Togliatti, *Opere*, Vol. V, Roma, Editori Riuniti, 1984, p. 154.

31. G. Gozzini and R. Martinelli, *Storia del Partito Comunista Italiano. VII. Dall'Attentato a Togliatti all'VIII Congresso*, Torino, Einaudi, 1998, pp. 297–300. Also M. Weber, 'Italy', in J. Lovenduski and J. Hills (eds), *The Politics of the Second Electorate*, London, Routledge & Kegan Paul, 1981, pp. 193–196.

32. Ibid., pp. 156–157.

33. Ibid., pp. 161–162.

34. L. Castellina, 'Quali Compromessi', in A. Sartogo (ed.), *La Donna al Muro. L'Immagine Femminile nel Manifesto Politico Italiano, 1947–1977*, Roma, Savelli, 1978, pp. 13–14

35. Archivio PCI, Istituto Gramsci (from now on APC), Comitati Centrali, Mf.039, 1946; 27 April 1946. At a Central Committee held in September 1946, Terracini warned that the DC was likely to oppose measures intended to introduce greater equality within the family, and expressed the hope that the Christian Democrats would have decided to leave aside the question of the indissolubility of marriage.

36. G. Dossetti, N. Iotti, and M. Ruini, *Interventi alla Costituente*, Bologna, Analisi-Trend, 1986, p. 51.

37. R. Martinelli, *Storia del Partito Comunista Italiano*, pp. 258–259, 265, 276–277.

38. APC, Comitati Centrali, 27–28 February 1947.

39. A later reconstruction wrongly described Umberto Grilli not as a Socialist but as a little known Communist rebelling against Togliatti's line; an authoritative example of this version is in U. Terracini, *Come Nacque la Costituzione*, Roma, Editori Riuniti, 1978, pp. 55–59. An extended discussion of the question can be found in Cinatti, *Il Partito Comunista Italiano e la Famiglia*, pp. 135-138.

40. Camera dei Deputati, *La Costituzione della Repubblica nei Lavori Preparatori dell'Assemblea Costituente*, Vol. II, Roma, 1976, p. 971.

41. According to the authors the transformation of the PCI into a 'party for families' reflected the 'stability of values proper to the Italian families' and their 'lasting role in the process of political socialisation', Gozzini and Martinelli, *Storia del Partito Comunista*, p. 299.

42. Quoted in C. Pavone, *Una guerra civile. Saggio storico sulla moralità della Resistenza*, Torino, Bollati Boringhieri, 1991, p. 526.

43. Makarenko, 'Upbringing in the Family (Lectures on the upbringing of Children)', in A. Makarenko (ed.), *Selected Pedagogical Works*, Moscow, Progress Publishers, 1990, p. 251. The lectures, commissioned from Makarenko by the *Pedagogical Propaganda for Parents*, went on the air on September 1937, following the publication of *A Book for Parents*. Makarenko's *Poema pedagogico* (*Pedagogicheskaia poema*) was published in Italy by the Communist publisher Rinascita in 1955.

44. Ibid., p. 253.

45. Ibid., p. 309.

46. A. Minella, N. Spano, and F. Terranova, *Cari bambini vi aspettiamo con gioia*, Milano, Teti Editore, 1980, p. 167.
47. A. Cervi and R. Nicolai, *I miei sette figli*, Roma, Editori Riuniti, 1956. The book sold 500 000 copies by 1957 and was successively published in 14 languages.
48. From the commemorative speech given by Piero Calamandrei in January 1954, P. Calamandrei, *Uomini e città della Resistenza*, Milano, Linea D'Ombra, 1994, p. 108.
49. Cervi and Nicolai, *I miei sette figli,* p. 97.
50. See, Gozzini and Martinelli, *Storia del Partito Comunista*, p. 297.
51. See, for instance, Ginsborg, *A History of Contemporary Italy*, p. 197.
52. G. A. Almond, *The Appeals of Communism*, Princeton, Princeton University Press, 1954, p. 308.
53. Chianese, *Storia sociale della donna*, p. 91.
54. R. Barker, *Political Ideas in Modern Britain*, London, Routledge, 1997, p. 233.
55. The issue has received greater attention in relation to earlier periods, for instance, in P. Williamson, *Stanley Baldwin. Conservative Leadership and National Values*, Cambridge, Cambridge University Press, 1999, pp. 283–293. On the predominance of the 'secular stream' in twentieth-century Conservatism, J. Barnes, 'Ideology and Factions', in A. Seldon and S. Ball (eds), *Conservative Century: The Conservative Party since 1900*, Oxford, Oxford University Press, 1994, pp. 320–321.
56. F. O' Gorman, *Conservative Thought from Burke to Thatcher*, London, Longman, 1986, p. xii, also, P. W. Buck (ed.), *How Conservative Think*, Harmondsworth, Penguin, 1975, pp. 26–28. Among contemporary studies see P. Goldman, *Some Principles of Conservatism*, London, Conservative Political Centre, 1961 (first published 1956), pp. 5–14 and H. Cecil, *Conservatism,* London, William & Norgate, 1912, pp. 116–117.
57. R. J. White, *The Conservative Tradition*, London, Nicholas Kaye, 1950, p. 3.
58. White, *The Conservative Tradition*, p. 8.
59. R. K. L. Coleraine, *For Conservatives Only*, London, Tom Stacey, 1970, p. 32.
60. Cecil, *Conservatism,* pp. 116–117.
61. T. U. Utley, *Essays in Conservatism*, quoted in R. Barker (ed.), *Political Ideas in Modern Britain*, London, Routledge, 1997 (first published, 1978), p. 203.
62. Q. Hogg, *The Case for Conservatism*, Harmondsworth, Penguin, 1947, p. 97.
63. I. Gilmour, *Inside Right: A Study of Conservatism*, London, Quartet Books, 1978 (first published, 1977), p. 149.
64. Hogg, *The Case*, p. 64.
65. Quoted in M. Francis, ' "Set the People Free?" Conservatives and the State, 1920–1960', in M. Francis and I. Zweiniger-Bargielowska (eds), *The Conservative and British Society, 1880–1990*, Cardiff, University of Wales, 1996, p. 62.
66. CUCO, *A True Balance: In the Home, in Employment, as Citizens* (1949), ibid.
67. CPA, CCO 4/8/379, WNAC, Report on a Working Party on Parental Responsibility and Juvenile Delinquency.
68. The number of indictable offences recorded in 1955 was 438 085, this had grown to 743 713 in 1960; one third of such crimes had been committed by people under 17 and half by people under 21, T. Morris, *Crime and Criminal Justice*, Oxford, Blackwell, 1989, pp. 90–91.

69. CPA, CCO 4/8/379, National Union of Conservative and Unionist Organisation, WNAC, Report on a Working Party on Parental Responsibility and Juvenile Delinquency, 1959.
70. Hogg, *The Case*, p. 19.
71. CPA, CCO 4/409, 'The Tasks that Lie Ahead', notes of a discussion held at a meeting of the Women's National Advisory Committee on the 2 September 1954.
72. Ibid.
73. The question was considered in similar terms in a pamphlet published by the Conservative Political Centre in 1956 and dedicated to the needs and expectation of young couples, *The Young Marrieds*, London, Conservative Political Centre, 1956, pp. 11–14.
74. M. Pugh, *Women and the Women's Movement in Britain, 1914–1999*, Basingstoke, Macmillan, 2000, p. 298, A. Myrdal and V. Klein, *Women's Two Roles, home and work*, London, Routledge and Kegan Paul, 1956.
75. The concern expressed by Conservative women for the supposed weakening of women's domestic/maternal role in modern society had been underplayed in interpretations stressing Conservatives' 'feminist agenda', as in I. Zweiniger-Bargielowska, 'Explaining the Gender Gap: The Conservative Party and the Women's Vote', in Francis and Zweiniger-Bargielowska, *The Conservative and British Society*, pp. 210–211. For the 'mixed attitudes' of the Conservative Party towards women as voters and party members see J. Lovenduski, P. Norris, and C. Burness, 'The Party and Women', in Seldon and Ball (eds), *Conservative Century*, pp. 611–635.
76. *The Right Road for Britain. The Conservative Party's Statement of Policy*, London, Conservative and Unionist Central Office, 1949, p. 9.
77. Ibid., p. 43.
78. CPA, CCO 4/8/377, Women's Annual Conference, 1961, extended summary of the Prime Minister speech Albert Hall, on 20 April 1961.
79. Parliamentary Papers, *Report by Sir William Beveridge on Social Insurance and Allied Services*, Cmd.6404, 1942–1943, VI, p. 53.
80. S. Kingsley Kent, *Making peace. The Reconstruction of Gender in Interwar Britain*, Princeton, Princeton University Press, 1993, p. 107.
81. On the need for the party to recover 'a sense of direction', R. Crossman, 'Towards a Philosophy of Socialism', in id. (ed.), *New Fabian Essays*, London, Turnstile Press, London, 1952, pp. 1–4. Martin Francis has pointed out that neither family allowances nor equal pay were confronted by the Labour Party in terms of gender difference alone, but in relation to questions of excessive state intervention within the labour market, M. Francis, *Labour and Gender*, in D. Tanner, P. Thane, and N. Tiratsoo (eds), *Labour's First Century*, Cambridge, Cambridge University Press, 2000, pp. 204–205.
82. On the division arising within the Labour Party on the definition of socialism and the means of realising it, S. Fielding, *The Labour Party, Socialism and Society Since 1951*, Manchester, Manchester University Press, 1997, p. 8.
83. R. Hoggart, *The Uses of Literacy*, Harmondsworth, Penguin, 1960, p. 20 (first published, 1957).
84. E. Durbin, *The Politics of Democratic Socialism*, London, Routledge, 1940, p. 30. A critique of Durbin's political vision is in G. Foote, *The Labour Party's*

Political Thought. A History, Basingstoke, Macmillan, 1997 (first published, 1985), pp. 193–194.

85. Ibid., pp. 37–39. In 1938, Bowlby and Durbin had written together 'Personal Aggressiveness and War', in E. Durbin and Catlin, G., *War and Democracy. Essays on the Causes and Prevention of War*, London, Kegan Paul, 1938, pp. 3–150, some central ideas of which were represented by Durbin in 1940. On the space found within the Party by an approach to socialism looking at 'social relations' and non-material needs rather than economics, in the late 1940s, M. Francis, *Ideas and Policies Under Labour, 1945–1951*, Manchester, Manchester University Press, 1997, pp. 50–57.

86. Durbin, *The Politics*, p. 55.

87. Ibid.

88. Ibid., p. 68.

89. P. Townsend, 'A Society for People', in N. Mackenzie (ed.), *Conviction*, London, MacGibbon, 1959, p. 120.

90. Ibid. The reference was to the Soviet experience of the 1920s, also indicated by Richard Crossman as a time of lowering morality, later restored by Stalin's intervention, R. H. S. Crossman, *Plato Today*, London, George Allen & Unwin, 1937, pp. 202–203.

91. R. Titmuss, *Essays on Welfare State*, London, George Allen and Unwin, 1958, pp. 101–102.

92. Crossman, *Plato*, p. 183. (My italics).

93. Ibid., pp. 196–197.

94. Ibid., pp. 202–203.

95. Ibid., pp. 199–200.

96. Francis, *Labour and Gender*, p. 209.

97. A. Crosland, *The Future of Socialism*, London, Jonathan Cape, 1956, pp. 148–153.

98. Ibid., pp. 151–152.

99. Townsend, 'A Society for People', p. 112.

100. J. Bourke, *Working-Class Cultures in Britain 1890–1960. Gender, class, and ethnicity*, London, Routledge, 1994, p. 137.

101. Townsend, 'A Society for People', p. 112.

102. Young and Willmott, *Family and Kinship*, London, Routledge and Kegan Paul, 1957, p. 25.

103. Bourke, *Working Class Cultures*, pp. 142–155, 169.

104. P. Thompson, 'Labour's "Gannex Conscience"? Politics and Popular Attitudes in the "Permissive Society"', in R. Coopey, S. Fielding, and N. Tiratsoo (eds), *The Wilson Governments, 1964–1970*, London, Pinter, 1993, pp. 136–150.

3   Moral and scientific discussions

1. Marco Politi, 'I Diritti vengono da Dio, non dallo Stato', *La Repubblica*, 16 October 2005, p. 7.

2. M. D. Jordan, *Blessing Same-Sex Unions. The Perils of Queer Romance and the Confusions of Christian Marriage*, Chicago and London, The University of Chicago Press, 2005, p. 4.

3. My analysis concentrates on the Catholic Church in Italy and the Anglican Church in Britain, as the two organisations with established links with the political power of the state.
4. Questions of co-operation between 'moral welfare workers and other voluntary and statutory social workers' had been discussed by the Church of England Advisory Board for Moral Welfare Work since 1940, as a consequence of wartime welfare development, Church of England Archive (CEA), MWC/REP, Annual Report, 1940, p. 5. Also, *The Church and The Family, Recent Developments in the Moral Welfare Work of the Church of England*, The Church of England Moral Welfare Council, London, 1947, Church of England Archive, Pamphlet.
5. CEA, MWC/M/2, Church of England Moral Welfare Council, Minutes Book, July 1949–November 1955, 1 July 1949.
6. Eugenio Pacelli was born in 1876 to a family of Roman jurists closely connected with the Vatican. He was Secretary of State since 1930 and was elected Pope in 1939 after a Conclave lasted only one day. His coronation, on 12th March, took place at the St. Peter's loggia to allow greater visibility and was transmitted via radio, H. Jedin, 'Popes Benedict XV, Pius XI, and Pius XII, Biography and Activity within the Church', in H. Jedin, K. Repgen and J. Dolan (eds), *History of the Church*, Vol. X, London, Burns & Oates, 1981, pp. 29–31.
7. Jedin, Popes, pp. 32–33. Traditionally newly married couples would go to Rome to receive a special blessing by the Pope. Since the beginning of its pontificate, Pacelli received large numbers of newly weds in the so-called *Wednesdays of the Spouses*; audiences reached their peak between April 1939 and May 1943.
8. P. Barberi and D. Tettamanzi, *Matrimonio e famiglia nel magistero della Chiesa. I documenti dal Concilio di Firenze a Giovanni Paolo II*, Milano, Massimo, 1986.
9. A. Riccardi, 'Governo e profezia nel Pontificato di Pio XII, in A. Riccardi (a cura di), *Pio XII*, Bari, Laterza, 1984, pp. 53–57.
10. By the mid-1950s, Catholic propaganda included a large number of pamphlets and handbooks written by priests and Catholic personalities, and the magazine *Famiglia Cristiana*, published since 1931, which sold one million copies in 1961, M. Marazziti, 'Cultura di massa e valori cattolici: il modello di Famiglia Cristiana', in A. Riccardi (ed.), *Pio XII*, pp. 307–333, in particular p. 316 and M. Schmolke, 'Information and the Mass Media', in Jedin, Repgen and Dolan (eds), *History of the Church*, Vol.X, pp. 422–423. On Pius XII's centralisation and control over local churches, P. Scoppola, 'Chiesa e società negli anni della modernizzazione', in A. Riccardi (a cura di), *Le chiese di Pio XII*, Roma-Bari, Laterza, 1986, pp. 3–19.
11. Pius XII, 'Al mondo cinematografico', 28 October 1955, in *Discorsi e radiomessaggi di S.S. Pio XII* (from now on *DR*), Città del Vaticano, Tipografia Poliglotta Vaticana, 1941–1958, Vol. XVII, p. 352. (My translation).
12. Pius XII, 'Address to Married Couples', 22 April 1942, in *The Dignity and Happiness of Marriage. Selected addresses of Pope Pius XII to Married Couples*, London-Dublin, Campion Press, 1959, p. 79.
13. The question of the hierarchy of ends within marriage had been stirred up by the publication of M. H. Doms, *Vom Sinn und Zweck Der Ehe*, in 1935 (*The Meaning of Marriage*, London, Sheed and Ward, 1939), E. Ruffini, 'Il

matrimonio alla luce della teologia cattolica', in V. Melchiorre (a cura di), *Amore e matrimonio nel pensiero filosofico e teologico moderno*, Milano, Vita e Pensiero, 1976, pp. 101–103, 108–111. Only the Vatican II affirmed the existence of parallel ends within marriage, in the encyclical letter *Gaudium et Spes*, published in 1965.

14. Pius XII, 'Address to Newly-Weds', 29 October 1951, in M. Chinigo (ed.), *The Teachings of Pope Pius XII*, London, Methuen & Co., 1958, p. 29.

15. Among the many texts explaining the method and analysing its moral content, L. Oldani, 'Il Metodo Ogino dal punto di vista morale', *Questioni Matrimoniali. I Tre Giorni di Teologia Morale*, Facoltà di Teologia dei PP. Gesuiti, Torino, L.I.C.E., 1949, pp. 47–69.

16. 'Because Conceiving, Giving Birth, and Educating is the Gift of the Mother', A. Bianchi, *Matrimonio Cristiano. Istruzioni*, Bergamo, Sant' Alessandro, 1948 (third edn), p. 51.

17. Pius XII, 'Address to Newly-Weds', 29 October 1951, in Chinigo (ed.), *The Teachings*, p. 29.

18. Martina, *La Chiesa negli ultimi 30 Anni*, pp. 21–22 and C. Dau Novelli, 'La famiglia come soggetto della ricostruzione sociale', in G. De Rosa (a cura di) *Cattolici, Chiesa, Resistenza*, Bologna, Il Mulino, 1997, pp. 485–486.

19. P. Luzzatto Fegiz, *Il volto sconosciuto dell'Italia, 10 anni di sondaggi Doxa*, Milano, Giuffré, 1956, pp. 377–836, Id., *Il volto sconosciuto dell'Italia. Seconda serie, 1956–1965*, Milano, Giuffré, 1966, p. 344.

20. Luzzatto Fegiz, *Il volto sconosciuto*, pp. 304, 356 and id., *Il volto sconosciuto. Seconda serie*, pp. 337–338.

21. In 1947, 35 per cent of men declared to be favourable to divorce against 19 per cent of women; the proportions had grown respectively to 40 per cent and 28 per cent in 1949, Luzzatto Fegiz, *Il volto sconosciuto*, pp. 397–398.

22. *The Family Today. The report of Committee 5 of the Lambeth Conference 1958 together with the text of the relevant Resolutions passed by the Conference*, London, SPCK, 1958, p. 11.

23. Ibid., p. 4.

24. Ibid., p. 6.

25. Ibid., p. 7.

26. Church of England Archive (from now on CEA), MWC/EX/1, *The Church of England and Family Planning*, Revised draft, 2 September 1949, p. 7.

27. *The Family Today*, p. 12.

28. Against accusation that the Report of the Royal Commission on Marriage was *godless*, the Rev. G. R. Dunstan remarked in April 1956, that 'an attempt to frame just laws, to deal justly between conflicting parties, even in a matrimonial dispute or after matrimonial breakdown, was an entirely godly activity'. A similar co-operative attitude would have been inconceivable in the case of the Italian Catholic Church, CEA, MWC/D/5, *A First Impression on the Report of the Royal Commission on Marriage and Divorce*, by the Rev. G. R. Dunstan, Council meeting, 12 April 1956, p. 1.

29. J. W. C. Wand, *The Church Today*, Harmondsworth, Penguin, 1960, pp. 123–124.

30. Pius XII, 'Address to Married Couples', 10 September 1941, in *The Dignity and Happiness of Marriage*, pp. 48–52.

31. Pius XII, 'Address to Married Couples', 25 February 1942, ibid., p. 62.

32. *Woman's Place in the World. Address by His Holiness Pope Pius XII*, Catholic Truth Society of Ireland, 1946, p. 6; address delivered by Pius XII to the women of Rome on 21 October 1945.
33. Ibid.
34. The suggestion was part of a decalogue published by *Famiglia Cristiana* in 1948, ibid., pp. 318–319.
35. Pius XII, 'Alle Lettrici della Rivista Alba', 17 May 1942, in *AD*, Vol. IV, p. 147.
36. *Woman's Place in the World*, 21 October 1945, pp. 5–6.
37. Bianchi, *Matrimonio Cristiano*, p. 151.
38. Pius XII, 'Agli uomini di AC', 20 September 1942, in *AD*, Vol. IV, p. 224.
39. The advice was given in 1959 to a reader of *Famiglia Cristiana* who had hit his wife for having used 'obscene language' in front of the children, in Marazziti, 'Cultura di massa e valori cattolici', p. 318.
40. *The Family Today*, pp. 23–24.
41. *The Family Today*, p. 12.
42. Ibid.
43. *The Family Today*, p. 14.
44. *Moral Welfare in Christian Social Service*, Annual Report of the Church of England Moral Welfare Council, London, The Church Assembly, 1948, pp. 11–12. Also, CEA, MWC/REP, *The Church, the Family and the Welfare State. What the Moral Welfare Council is Doing*, report prepared for presentation to the Church Assembly, in June 1955,
45. Ibid., p. 2. The question of how 'the Church should be and is yet of service in the welfare state' was discussed at the Swanwick Conference in June 1956.
46. *The Family To-day*, p. 27.
47. According to J. W. C. Wand, no 'Christian party' was necessary in England because of the existence of an established church and the presence of 'noteworthy Christian representatives in all the main political parties'. The presence of Bishops in the House of Lords guaranteed the opportunity for 'official Christianity to make its voice heard in the legislature', Wand, *The Church Today*, p. 35.
48. C. Garbett, *In an Age of Revolution*, London, Hodder & Stoughton, 1952, p. 153. William Temple, *Christianity and Social Order*, Harmondsworth, Penguin, 1942, constituted the best example of the social concern expressed by the Anglican Church.
49. Wand, *The Church Today*, p. 19.
50. CEA, MWC/REP, Church of England Advisory Board for Moral Welfare Work, Annual Reports, 1956, p. 3.
51. J. W. C. Wand, *What the Church of England Stands For*, London, Mowbarry & Co., 1951, pp. 13–14.
52. The contradictory results that a large diffusion of parental education could have were pointed out by M. Creak, 'The Age of the Expert', in J. Bowlby, *Rediscovery of the Family and Other Lectures*, Sister Maria Hilda Memorial Lectures, 1954–1973, Aberdeen, Aberdeen University Press, 1981, pp. 22–40 (Creak's essay had been originally written in 1960). The title of the collection was taken by Bowlby's opening lecture 'The Rediscovery of the Family' (1954), ibid., pp. 1–7.
53. C. Trabucchi, *Parole chiare di un medico agli sposi*, Milano, Istituto La Casa, 1955, p. 13.

54. Bowlby, 'The Rediscovery of the Family', p. 2; the lecture was originally written in 1954.

55. D. Burlingham and A. Freud, *Young Children in War Time in a Residential War Nursery*, London, George Allen and Unwin, 1942, p. 41. Also, J. Macnicol, 'The Effect of the Evacuation of Schoolchildren on Official Attitudes to State Intervention', in H. L. Smith (ed.), *War and Social Change. British Society in the Second World War*, Manchester, Manchester University Press, 1986, pp. 7–8. On the experiences of evacuated children, R. Inglis, *The Children's War: Evacuation, 1939–1945*, London, Fontana, 1990 (first published, 1989), pp. 49–68 and A. Calder, *The People's War. Britain 1939–1945*, London, Pimlico, 1992 (first published, 1969), pp. 35–50.

56. N. Rose, *Governing the Soul: The Shaping of the Private Self*, London, Routledge, 1990, pp. 159–163.

57. John Bowlby's work on evacuated children was part of a study commissioned by the World Health Organisation, the results of which were published in 1951 under the title *Maternal Care and Mental Health*. The report constituted the basis of *Child Care and the Growth of Love*, Harmondsworth, Penguin, 1953.

58. D. Burlingham and A. Freud, *Infants Without Families, the Case For and Against Residential Nurseries*, London, George Allen & Unwin, 1943, p. 7. The Hampstead Nurseries (two houses in London and one in Chelmsford, Essex) operated under the American Foster Parents' Plan for War Children; they developed from a Children's Rest Centre, opened in Hampstead by a number of refugees from Austria, Germany Czechoslovakia, Italy and Holland; Burlingham and Freud, *Young Children in War Time*, pp. 3–6. Also, A. Freud, 'Why Children Go Wrong', in W. D. Wall and A. Freud (eds), *The Enrichment of Childhood*, London, The Nursery School Association of Great Britain, 1962, p. 23.

59. See, for instance, the observations on the institutional treatment of 'difficult children' in Ministry of Health, *Hostels for 'Difficult' Children. A Survey of Experience under the Evacuation Scheme*, London, HMSO, 1944.

60. Hostels for 'difficult' children were opened by the Government in co-operation with the Child Guidance Clinics since 1941, as alternative to billeting, and were later extended to 'difficult children' resident within the area. Among the best-known examples were the hostels opened by D. W. Winnicott in Oxfordshire, M. Bridgeland, *Pioneer Work with Maladjusted Children*, London, Staples Press, 1971, p. 205.

61. T. L. Crosby, *The Impact of Civilian Evacuation in the Second World War*, London, Croom Helm, 1986, p. 9. Crosby suggested that the major consequences of evacuation was that of showing to the working class 'the advantages of the few', contributing to shift political attitudes leftwards since 1940, ibid., p. 10.

62. Macnicol, 'The Effect of the Evacuation of Schoolchildren', p. 24.

63. The question of how to create 'modern social services' was discussed in 1957, at the First National Conference of the ONARMO (*Opera Nazionale per l'Assistenza Religiosa e Morale degli Operai*), by the responsible for the Social Services of the Opera, V. Delmati, 'Natura e scopi del servizio sociale', in ONARMO, *Atti del Primo Congresso Nazionale*, Rome 16–17 April 1956, pp. 67–78.

64. ONMI's activities have received significant attention for the fascist period, as one of the instruments by which the Fascist regime promoted specific conceptions of social relations in which women's role in the family was 'defined as first and foremost a social role', Saraceno, 'Women, Family, and the Law, 1750–1942', *Journal of Family History*, XV, 4 (1990), p. 438. Also, Quine, *Italy's Social Revolution*, pp. 132–133. Little attention has been given to the Onmi in the post-war period.

65. I. Gueli and G. Pezzali, 'Ripresa', *MI*, xix, 1, September–October (1947), p. 3. Ignazio Gueli and Stefano Pezzali were respectively the Commissioner (*Commissario Straordinario*) and the Director of the Opera. To the journal, published by the ONMI, contributed some the best known paediatricians and gynaecologists of the country, as well as moralists and academics concerned with questions of maternity, child health and family welfare and morality.

66. F. Godano, 'Per una migliore protezione dell'infanzia', ibid., xx, 2, March–April (1949), pp. 83–84.

67. L. D. Veronese, 'Per una maggiore tutela del lattante', *MI*, xvii, 4–5, July–October (1942), p. 107.

68. Ibid.

69. Among the few articles dedicated to the necessity of promoting better paediatric preparation among doctors was G. Bentivoglio, 'Ancora troppi pregiudizi, troppi errori a danno dei bambini', *MI*, xx, 2, March–April (1949), p. 75.

70. R. Calogero, 'L'inchiesta sociologica', in ONARMO, Atti del Primo Congresso Nazionale, p. 82.

71. Bowlby, *Child Care*, (first edn), p. 95.

72. Ibid., (first edn), pp. 94, 131.

73. Ibid., (first edn), p. 95.

74. J. C. Spence, *The Purpose of the Family. A Guide to the Care of Children*, London, The Epworth Press, 1947 (first published, 1946), pp. 49–51. James Spence was Professor of Child Health at Durham University and author of much-quoted studies on child health in relation to family life. Spence's definition of family was subscribed by John Bowlby, who borrowed the title of Spence's lecture for the seventh chapter of his *Child Care*.

75. Bowlby, *Child care*, p. 13. In the second edition of the book, published in 1965, 'the infant thrive' was changed to the more explicit 'her infant thrive', J. Bowlby, *Child Care and the Growth of Love*, second edition, Harmondsworth, Penguin, 1965, p. 15.

76. R. Jemma, 'Morbilità nell'infanzia nel Dopoguerra', *MI*, xix, 1, September–October (1947), p. 10.

77. M. V. Pugliaro, 'Essere madre', ibid., xxiii, 1–3, January–March (1959), p. 15.

78. Trabucchi, *Parole franche*, p. 16.

79. *The Neglected Child and His Family. A study made in 1946–47*, with an introduction by J. B. Priestley, London, Oxford University Press, 1948, p. xi. The report was the result of the work of a Committee set up in 1945 by the Women's Group on Public Welfare in association with the National Council of Social service under the Chairmanship of Eva Hubback. It was planned to appear soon after the Curtis report, of which it was said to be 'a kind of sequel-cum-preface', breaking off 'at the point where the Curtis Committees begins'. In 1943, the Women's Group on Public Welfare had produced the influential *Our Towns* dedicated to the condition of children evacuees.

80. Ibid., p. 34.
81. O. Moscucci, *The Science of Woman. Gynaecology and Gender in England, 1800–1929*, Cambridge, Cambridge University Press, 1990, p. 40.
82. A. Boschi, *Nuove questioni matrimoniali*, Torino, Marietti, 1952 (first published, 1949), pp. 32–41. In a handbook originally written to advise priests on question of sexual morality and becoming soon very popular among doctors, Boschi argued that large families presented moral, educational, psychological and demographic advantages.
83. *The Neglected Child*, p. 22. The report suggested that some of the worst cases of neglect could be found among 'high income' families, with an average of L.6–7 per week.
84. F. Zweig, *The British Worker. A Social and Psychological Study, Presenting the Problems, Difficulties and Struggles of the Ordinary Men at Home, Work, and in His Leisure Hours*, Harmondsworth, Penguin, 1952, p. 22.
85. J. Spence, *A Thousand Families in Newcastle-Upon-Tyne. An Approach to the Study of Health and Illness in Children*, London, Oxford University Press, 1954, p. 121.
86. *The Neglected Child*, pp. 59–67.
87. *The Neglected Child*, p. 70.
88. A recent and authoritative version of this interpretation is offered by Hera Cook, *The Long Sexual Revolution*, pp. 318–337.
89. Bianchi, *Matrimonio Cristiano*, p. 157.
90. Bianchi stressed the importance of following the advice and judgement of the parents, 'enlightened by their experience of life and not blinded by passion', Bianchi, *Matrimonio Cristiano*, p. 84.
91. Bianchi, *Matrimonio Cristiano*, p. 89.
92. Ibid., p. 93.
93. *The Neglected Child*, p. xi.
94. Bowlby, *Child care*, (first edn), pp. 87–88.
95. *The Neglected Child*, p. 60. A similar point could be found in J. Bowlby, *Child care*, (first edn), p. 89.
96. Bowlby, *Child Care*, (first edn), pp. 77, 79–80.
97. Trabucchi, *Parole Chiare*, pp. 29–31.
98. Ibid., pp. 21–24.
99. P. M. Lewis, 'Mummy, Matron and the Maids. Feminine presence and absence in male institutions', in M. Roper and J. Tosh (eds), *Manful Assertions, Masculinities in Britain Since 1800*, London, Routledge, 1991, pp. 168–189.
100. Post-war fathers have been largely ignored also in studies of gender and masculinity. Only Victorian fathers are discussed in Roper and Tosh's *Manful Assertions*, while Lewis's examination of post-war 'institutions in which masculinity is developed' focuses on the role of the 'feminine presence and absence in male institutions', ibid. Although Lewis acknowledges that 'it is in the institution of the *family* [sic] that [masculinity] is first formed', the above-mentioned sketch of his own father is the only reference made to such 'male influence', ibid, p. 173.
101. D. W. Winnicott, *Getting to Know Your Baby*, London, Heinemann / The New Era, 1945.
102. Bowlby, *Child Care*, (first edn), pp. 75–76.

103. Ibid., p. 13.
104. The alternative view that mothers' employment did not put children under five in a position of disadvantage was sustained in a study conducted between 1946 and 1958, J. W. B. Douglas and J. M. Bloomfield, *Children under five. The results of a national survey made by a Joint Committee of the Institute of Child Health (University of London), the Society of Medical Officers of Health and the Population Investigation Committee*, London, Allen & Unwin, 1958, pp. 117–126.
105. M. D. Salter Ainsworth 'Conclusions from Recent Research, in J. Bowlby (ed.), *Child Care and the Growth of Love*, (second edn., 1961), pp. 210–211.
106. Spence, *The Purpose of the Family*, p. 50.
107. Ibid., p. 51.
108. Pius XII, 'Alle donne rappresentanti delle Associazioni Cristiane Italiane' (Address to the Female Representatives of Italian Christian Associations), 21 October 1945, in *DR*, Vol. viii, p. 225 [my translation].
109. I. Petrone, 'Madri che lavorano nella società moderna', *MI*, xxii, 9, November (1951), p. 3. The fact that women were in large part excluded from the labour market, and that their access to education remained significantly inferior to those of men was ignored in Petrone's argument, S. Ulivieri, 'Alfabetizzazione, processi di scolarizzazione femminile e percorsi professionali, tra tradizione e mutamento', in S. Ulivieri (a cura di), *Educazione e ruolo femminile. La condizione delle donne in Italia dal Dopoguerra ad oggi*, Scandicci, La Nuova Italia, 1992, pp. 205–206.
110. The diminishing role of men within the home fits G. L. Mosse's suggestion that a 'change through erosion not confrontation' took place in the masculine identity after the Second World War, G. L. Mosse, *The Image of Man. The Creation of Modern Masculinity*, New York–Oxford, Oxford University Press, 1996, p. 183.
111. Parsons, 'The American Family: Its Relations to Personality and to the Social Structure', in T. Parsons and R. F. Bales (eds), *Family Socialization and Interaction Process*, London, Routledge and Kegan Paul, 1956, p. 26.
112. A. Oakley, 'A Case of Maternity: Paradigms of Women as Maternity Cases', in *Signs, Journal of Women in Culture and Society*, 4, 4 (1979), p. 621.
113. For a discussion of the emergence of the 'new father' 'as someone who assumes a more active role in parenting' in response to the growing participation of women to the workforce, W. Marsiglio, *Procreative Man*, New York and London, New York University Press, 1998, pp. 42–43. Also R. La Rossa, *The Modernization of Fatherhood: A Social and Political History*, Chicago, University of Chicago Press, 1997. Both Marsiglio and La Rossa concentrate their research on contemporary American society.
114. T. Parsons, 'The American Family' pp. 3–33, 16.
115. D. Riley, *War in the Nursery. Theories of the Child and Mother*, London, Virago, 1983, p. 77.
116. R. D. Laing and A. Esterson, *Sanity, Madness and the Family*, London, The Tavistock Institute of Human Relations, 1964 and R. D. Laing, *The Divided Self*, London, The Tavistock Institute of Human Relations, 1960.

4   The edges of the family: State, citizens and the 'Children deprived of a normal home life'

1. F. Furedi, *Therapy Culture. Cultivating Vulnerability in an Uncertain Age*, London and New York, Routledge, 2004, p. 63.
2. Ibid., pp. 64–65.
3. Ibid., pp. 75, 84.
4. 'Blair Spells Out his Masterplan for a Safer, Fairer Society', *The Guardian*, 11 January 2006, p. 6.
5. B. Dobson, 'Children, Crime and the State', in Golson, B., Lavalette, M. and McKechnie, J. (eds), *Children, Welfare and the State*, London, Sage, 2004 (first published, 2002), pp. 120–121.
6. The main reference remains here P. Aries, *Centuries of Childhood*, Harmondsworth, Penguin, 1962; for an overview of current interpretations, see also H. Cunningham, *Children and Childhood in Western Societies since 1500*, London, Longman, 1995.
7. In particular H. Hendrick, *Child Welfare: England 1872–1989*, London, Routledge, 1994.
8. Ambrosini, *La Costituzione Italiana*, Art. 29, p. 9.
9. L. Rendel, 'The Administrative Framework', *Children Without Homes*, Proceedings of a Conference called in London by the Women's Group on Public Welfare, 8–9 February 1945, London, The National Council of Social Service, 1945, p. 2.
10. M. King, 'Welfare and Justice', in M. King (ed.), *Childhood, Welfare and Justice. A critical examination of children in the legal and childcare systems*, London, Batsford Academic and Educational, 1981, pp. 109–110.
11. J. Heywood, *Children in Care. The Development of the Service for the Deprived Child*, London, Routledge and Kegan Paul, 1978 (first published, 1959), pp. 148–149. Also, N. Middleton, *When Family Failed. The Treatment of Children in the Care of the Community During the First Half of the Twentieth Century*, London, Victor Gollancz, 1971, p. 18.
12. King, 'Welfare and Justice', p. 110.
13. M. Lancellotti Mari, 'Breve studio su alcuni concetti di ordine etico e giuridico', in *Relazione della Commissione Speciale per un'Indagine sulle Condizioni dell'Infanzia nella Provincia di Milano*, Milano, Giuffré, 1955, p. 142.
14. Ibid., p. 145.
15. Article 403 of the Civil Code dealt specifically with provisions for young people in need, on the basis of Article 21 T.U. of R.D. 24.12.1934, concerned with maternity and child protection.
16. According to an inquiry conducted in 1954, only 5 per cent of the institutions operating in Italy (for children and adults as well) were run by the state or local government, AAI, *Guida Nazionale degli Istituti di Assistenza con Ricovero*, Roma, Stabilimento Tipografico Fausto Failli, 1954, p. vii.
17. A. Napoli, *MI*, 1, January–February (1948), pp. 25–26 and Ibid., 4, July–August (1948), pp. 201–202. Napoli was the chairman of the Association of the ONMI's Federation of Catanzaro in Southern Italy.
18. A. Vigorelli, 'Orfanotrofi', *MI*, 3, May–June (1948), p. 135.

19. I. Pini, 'Duecentomila bambini negli Istituti Italiani per l'Infanzia', *MI*, 2, March–April (1951), p. 8.
20. *L'Amministrazione per gli Aiuti Internazionali*, Roma, 1952, p. 33.
21. From a letter quoted in I. Pini, 'Duecentomila bambini', p. 8.
22. Ibid., p. 6.
23. Camera dei Deputati, *Atti della Commissione Parlamentare d'Inchiesta sulla Miseria in Italia e sui Mezzi per Combatterla*, Roma, 1953, Vol. III, pp. 28–29.
24. Ibid., pp. 65–75.
25. *Guida Nazionale degli Istituti di Assistenza con Ricovero*, Roma, 1954.
26. Ibid., pp. 9–11, 26–31, Table 2.
27. Ibid., p. 17.
28. Ibid., pp. viii–ix.
29. Ibid., pp. x–xiii.
30. PRO, MH 102/1447, LCC, *Care of Children Committee – Evidence*, 19 February 1946.
31. Rendel, 'The Administrative Framework', p. 2.
32. LAs – under the supervision of the Ministry of Health – were responsible for 'Poor law cases' and for the supervision of children under nine fostered for rewards or placed for adoption 'by private persons'. Welfare authorities' child protection visitors inspected institutions receiving children under nine years of age 'for rewards', while the HO held responsibility over children sent to 'approved schools' for remedial training or placed in 'remand homes' awaiting a Court's decision. No public authority was responsible for children over nine and for those placed without rewards, and no powers of inspection existed in the case of homes not receiving public contributions and not dealing with Poor Law cases, *Report of the Care of Children Committee*, London, HMSO, 1946, Cmd.6922, para. 95–99, pp. 24–27; also, Heywood, *Children in Care*, pp. 143–144. Similar points were made for Scotland by the Clyde Committee, *Report of the Committee on Homeless Children*, Edinburgh, HMSO, 1946, Cmd.6911, para. 13, pp. 31–33.
33. Children's Officers were responsible for the care and supervision of children maintained for reward, third part adoption cases, registration of adoption societies, appearance of children before Juvenile Courts and the care of children committed by Courts, and provision and management of remand homes and approved schools.
34. In 1954, Hilda Lewis defended the role of reception centres in the childcare system against suggestions that their use could be harmful to children and encouraged hasty removal from the family (the second objection had been advanced by John Bowlby in 1951 in J. Bowlby, *Maternal Care and Mental Health*, Geneva, WHO, 1951), H. Lewis, *Deprived Children. The Mersham Experiment. A social and clinical study*, Oxford, The Nuffield Foundation/Oxford University Press, 1954, pp. 128–134. Also, O. Stevenson 'Reception into Care – its Meaning for all Concerned', (1963), in R. J. N. Tod (ed.), *Children in Care. Papers on Residential Work*, London, Longman, 1976 (first published, 1968), pp. 8–17.
35. Among the others, R. Lowe, *The Welfare State in Britain Since 1945*, Basingstoke, Macmillan, 1999 (first published, 1993), p. 263 and Hendrick, *Child Welfare in England*, p. 219.

36. B. Holman, *Putting Families First. Prevention and Child Care*, London, Macmillan, 1988, pp. 35–36.
37. *Hansard, House of Commons, Standing Committees*, session 1947–1948, Vol. III, coll. 10–18, also R. Parker, 'The Gestation of Reform: the Children Act 1948', in P. Bean and S. MacPherson (eds), *Approaches to Welfare*, London, Routledge & Kegan Paul, 1983, p. 202.
38. P. Atkin, Magnolia House, Suffolk, *The Times*, 15/7/49, in PRO, MH 102/1961.
39. J. Stroud, *An Introduction to the Child Care Service*, London, Longmans, 1965, p. 11.
40. N. Frost and M. Stein, *The Politics of Child Welfare. Inequality, Power and Change*, London, Harvester Wheatsheaf, 1989, p. 33.
41. M. Allen and M. Nicholson, *Memoirs of an Uneducated Lady. Lady Allen of Hurtwood*, London, Thames and Hudson, 1975, Chapters 7–12 in particular.
42. *Whose Children?*, London, The Favil Press, 1944, p. 1. In order to substantiate the content of the letters, Allen asked every sender to make themselves available to give evidence in case of a public enquiry and left out the letters of those who refused, PRO, MH 102/1449, *Care of Children Committee. Evidence submitted by Lady Allen of Hurtwood*, 11 June 1945.
43. PRO, MH 57/297, letter dated 28 July 1944.
44. PRO, MH 102/1161.
45. Ibid., War Cabinet Record Committee, Joint Memorandum by the Home Secretary, the Secretary of State for Scotland, the Minister of Health and the Minister of Education, Whitehall, 30 November 1944.
46. Allen and Nicholson, *Memoirs of an Uneducated Lady*, p. 184. The disappointment with Morrison grew when Allen discovered she had not been included in the Committee set up under the Chairmanship of Myra Curtis, ibid., p. 189.
47. PRO, MH 57/297.
48. *Report by Sir Walter Monckton on the circumstances which led to the boarding out of Terence and Dennis O'Neill at Bank Farm, Minsterley and the steps taken to supervise their welfare*, London, MHSO, May, 1945, Cmd. 6636, para. 50, pp. 16–17.
49. PRO, MH 102/1161, note from A. Maxwell to N. Brook, 22 August 1944.
50. Children Society's Archive (from now on CSA), *Annual Report for 1944*, Report of the Executive Committee for the year ended 31 December 1944, p. 2.
51. Ibid., *Annual Report for 1943*, p. 2.
52. Ibid., *Annual Report for 1948*, p. 2. The Society's Report for the following year lamented that '18 months after the passing of the Children Act', the general public had still not fully realised that the voluntary child-care organisations had not been 'absorbed into the State' and were therefore still dependent on 'voluntary support', ibid., *Annual Report for 1949*, p. 2.
53. Ibid., *Annual Report for 1950*, p. 6.
54. Ibid., *'Laying Foundations', Annual Report for 1955*, p. 321.
55. Ibid., *Annual Report for 1957*, p. 513.
56. Ibid., *Annual Report for 1958*, p. 605.
57. Ibid.
58. PRO, MH 102/1449, *Care of Children Committee, evidence submitted by Lady Allen of Hurtwood*, 11 June 1945. Also, *Whose Children*, p. 1.
59. Allen and Nicholson, *Memoirs of an Uneducated Lady*, p. 176.

60. Ibid.

61. PRO, BN 29/4 *Reasons why children come into care*.

62. Lancellotti Mari, 'Breve rielaborazione dei dati statistici e note aggiunte alla precedente relazione', *Relazione della Commissione Speciale*, p. 156.

63. Lewis, *Deprived Children*, pp. 20–31.

64. Ibid., p. 27.

65. A. F. Philp and N. Timms, *The Problem of the 'Problem Family'. A critical review of the literature concerning the 'problem family' and its treatment*, London, Family Service Units, 1957, p. vii.

66. PRO, MH 102/1158 *Post War Provisions for the Care and Education of Children up to 7 Years of Age*, Conference of the Women's Group on Public Welfare and National Council for Maternity and Child Welfare, 22–23 February 1944.

67. Philp and Timms, *The Problem of the 'Problem Family'*, pp. 8, 12, 14.

68. *The Neglected Child and His Family*, pp. 17–19.

69. PRO, 102/1961, *Mrs. Ayrton Gould and others. Neglected Children*, cutting from *The Times*, 6.7.49.

70. *Hansard*, House of Commons, Vol. 467, 22 July 1949, pp. 1740–1745. Following Ayrton Gould's motion, a working party of officials met for the first time on 4th November 1949.

71. PRO, MH 102/1961, Adjournment Debate on 6th July 1949, Note for parliamentary Under-Secretary of State.

72. A. F. Philp, *Family Failure. A study of 129 Families with Multiple Problems*, London, Faber and Faber, 1963, pp. 288–289. Philp indicated failure to earn and manage money, bad housing, poor health of the parents, poor affective relationships with their larger families, problems in marital relationships, petty crime and poor care as the more characteristic traits of the family upon which the FSU was called to intervene, ibid., *passim*. For an example of the FSU's approach, T. Stephens (ed.), *Problem Families: An Experiment in Social Rehabilitation*, Pacifist Service Units, Liverpool, 1947.

73. P. Starkey, *Families and Social Workers. The work of the Family service Units, 1940–1985*, Liverpool, Liverpool University Press, 2000, pp. 32, 45.

74. PRO, MH 102/1961, Adjournment Debate, 6 July 1949.

75. PRO, MH 102/1964, *Cruelty and Neglect of Children. Note for the Secretary of State on the Motion to be taken on 12th December, 1949*. The Salvation Army's training home *Mayflower* had been opened in January 1948 and housed 24 mothers.

76. Ibid.

77. M. D. Sheridan, 'The Intelligence of 100 Neglectful Mothers', *BMJ*, 14 January 1956, p. 91. Follow up studies showed that improvement had occurred in the majority of cases, but also that this had revealed more difficult in the case of women of higher intelligence and greater emotional instability.

78. In 1948, probation had been used in 16 per cent of the cases, imprisonment in 42 per cent and fines in 26 per cent. During the same period, 610 people had been committed under Sect. 1 of the Children and Young Persons Act, 1933 for 'wilfully assaulting, ill treating, neglecting, abandoning or exposing or procuring a child to be exposed in a manner likely to cause him unnecessary suffering or injury to health', PRO MH 102/1964, *Motion on Cruelty and Neglect of Children*. During the preparation of the 1948 Children act, consideration had been given to the possibility of imposing a penalty on parents whose

children were received in care and on those who failed to take over child care when asked to do so by the LAs. The proposal was ultimately rejected on the grounds that inducing a parent to keep a child 'through fear of prosecution' could lead to unsatisfactory conditions of life for the child. However, Sect. 10 of the Act established that the parents of a child in care should keep the appropriate LAs informed of their circumstances and whereabouts, PRO, MH 102/1967, 21 June 1950, letter to Geoffrey Williamson, Odhams Periodical.
79. Ibid., 19 July 1949, Note by the Ministry of Health.
80. Circular Home Office 157/50, Ministry of Health 78/50, Ministry of Education 225/50, quoted in Sixth Report of the Children's Department, Home Office, May 1951.
81. D. Donnison, *The Neglected Child and the Social Services. A study of the work done in Manchester and Salford by social services of all kinds for 118 families whose children came into public care*, Manchester, Manchester University Press, pp. 121–123.
82. U. M. Colombo, 'Osservazioni sui dati statistici relativi agli ECA', in *Relazione Della Commissione Speciale per in'Indagine sulle Condizioni dell'Infanzia nella Provincia di Milano*, p. 21.
83. Camera dei Deputati, *Atti della Commissione parlamentare d'Inchiesta sulla Miseria*, Vol. I, pp. 77, 78.
84. G. Savalli, 'Maternità e lavoro', *MI*, xix, 1, September–October (1947), pp. 35–37.
85. Ibid., pp. 111–112.
86. L. D. Veronese, 'Bambini mendicanti', *MI*, xxii, 1, January–February (1950), p. 14.
87. *Inchiesta sulla miseria in Italia (1951–1952)*, Materiali della Commissione Parlamentare, a cura di Paolo Braghin, Torino, Einaudi, 1978, p. 83.
88. Clause 13 of the 1948 Children Act gave power to LAs to provide temporary accommodation for children in Public Assistance Accommodation – together with their parents – (for a maximum of 14 days for children over 3), before sending them to a Child institution.
89. PRO, MH 102/1967, cut from the *Daily Mail*, 5/6/1950, 'Thousands of parents "dump" their children'.
90. D. G. Stewart campaigned for legislation against desertion, and against the fact that the 1948 Children Act prevented LAs from take proceedings against parents leaving their children, as foreseen in Sect. 4 of the Vagrancy Act, 1824.
91. PRO, MH 102/1967, Letter sent by Mrs Williams, 6 June 1950.
92. PRO, MH 57/561, 'The Children of Homeless Families', memorandum prepared by the Children's Department Inspectorate, circulated in May 1953, para. 4.
93. PRO, MH 57/561, National Assistance Act 1948, Temporary Accommodation, Correspondence between J. Ross (HO) and W. H. Boucher (MH), November 1949.
94. PRO, MH 57/557, National Assistance Act 1948, Temporary Accommodation under section 21 (1) (B) Homeless Families, 1948–1957.
95. PRO MH 57/558, National Assistance Act 1948, February 1958–June 1958, Notes sent to Mr Dodds, Tuesday, 11 February 1958.
96. PRO, MH 57/561, 'The Children of Homeless Families', para. 9.

97. Ibid., para. 2.
98. Ibid., para. 14.
99. Ibid., para. 18.
100. Ibid., para. 22.
101. 'A contrast in method: Connemara and Berlin', letter by George Bernard Shaw, *The Times*, 21 July 1944, cutting, in MH 102/1160.
102. The Committee visited once without pre-warning, a sample of homes estimated to give care 'to some 30 000 children'. Commenting on the 'surprise factor', the report noted that 'it [was] perhaps a measure of the care taken in the care of children that a large number had not heard of the appointment of the committee to enquiry into these questions', *Report of the Care of Children Committee*, para. 101, p. 28.
103. Ibid., para. 418, p. 134.
104. Ibid., para. 141, p. 39.
105. Ibid., para. 241, p. 78 and PRO, MH 102/1448, *Care of Children Committee*, evidence of the Association of Municipal Corporations, 11 April 1946.
106. S. Barbano. 'Occorre rivedere il metodo', *MI*, 9 (1953), p. 17.
107. *The Report on the Care of Children*, para. 141, p. 39. On the lasting inheritance left by 19th century approach to the organisation of children's institutions, S. Millham, R. Bullock and K. Hosie, *Locking up Children. Secure provision within the child-care system*, Westmead, Saxon House, 1978, p. 17.
108. CSA, *Policy Circulars*, 1939–54, letter circulated to Homes in 1941.
109. PRO, MH 102/1448, *Care of Children Committee*, Evidence of the Association of Municipal Corporations, para. 45.
110. Ibid.
111. Ibid., para. 39–40.
112. Ibid., para. 33.
113. The name of the Society was changed in 1945, following the consideration that the original title, 'The Church of England Incorporated Society for Providing Homes for Waifs and Strays', was 'no longer symbolic' of the Society's work, CSA, Policy Circular, Conference of Homes Representatives, St. Anselm's Hall, 20 September 1945.
114. CSA, 85.110/11, *Handbook for Workers*, 1948, p. 2.
115. Ibid., pp. 14–15. The recommendation was advanced again, unchanged, 10 years later, ibid., 85.110/14, *Handbook for Workers*, 1959, p. 38.
116. Ibid., *Handbook for Workers*, 1948, p. 18.
117. *Report on the Care of children*, para. 247, p. 80.
118. For instance, K. Wood, *The Story of St. Mary's Cold Ash*, Child Care Study Paper n. 7, London, Church of England Children's Society, 1981, pp. 10–11.
119. On the situation of playing facilities in children's homes, E. Ingram, 'Play and Leisure Time in the Children's Home', *Case Conference*, Vol. 7, January 1961, in Tod (ed.), *Children in Care*, pp. 40–54.
120. PRO, MH 102/1447, *Curtis Committee*, Statement of Evidence Submitted by the London County Council, p. 4.
121. CSA, Policy Circular, 25 November 1943, ibid., Conference of Homes Representatives, St. Anselm's Hall, 20 September 1945, ibid., *Important Memorandum (H/JCH/17)* 1 May 1949, and H/RI/JCH/1, 14 February 1952.
122. Ibid., circular letter, 14 February 1952.

123. Ibid., Boarding out outfits, 1 October 1950.
124. Lancellotti Mari, 'Breve rielaborazione', p. 158.
125. *The Report of the Care of Children Committee*, p. 63.
126. PRO, MH 102/1449, *Care of Children Committee. Evidence submitted by Lady Allen of Hurtwood*, p. 3.
127. Lancellotti Mari, 'Breve rielaborazione', p. 157.
128. PRO, HO 361/1, Woodford Bridge Garden City was a large establishment housing 116 boys and 20 girls in 7 permanent houses, with 60 children in 3 nursery houses, and 80 girls in the 'Princess Margaret School'.
129. Ibid., *Summary of Points for Barnardo's Discussion* on 8th December, 1953.
130. Ibid., *The Chief Inspector, Dr. Barnardo's Homes*, December 1953.
131. Ibid., para. 207, p. 62. In 1949, the Children's Society stressed the importance of teaching 'good manners' as a means of improving the chances of boarding out children, since foster parents expected 'a child to be trained up to its age', CSA, Children's Society, *Bulletin*, n. 13, August (1949), p. 1.
132. Ibid., para. 222, p. 70.
133. CSA, 85.110/14, *Handbook for workers*, 1959, p. 86.
134. CEA, Board of Education/CC/WP/4/1, Central Training Council in Child Care, paper for meeting on Friday, 15 May 1953, 'Notes on the training of housemothers and housefathers of children's homes', p. 5.
135. M. Foucault, *Discipline and Punish. The Birth of the Prison*, London, Allen Lane, 1977 (originally published, 1975), pp. 149–156.
136. Ibid., letter sent by E. J. Holmes, Children's Officer of the City of Birmingham, to Miss Rosling, Children's Department, Home Office on 19th January 1955.
137. J. Donzelot, *The Policing of Families*, quoted.
138. See, for instance, M. N. Bloch, 'Becoming scientific and professional: historical perspectives on the aims and effects of early education and child care' in Popkewitz, T. S. (ed.), *The Formation of School Subjects: The Struggle for Creating an American Institution*, New York, Philadelphia and London, Falmer Press, 2000, pp. 25–62.
139. For a discussion of conditionality in relation to citizenship and welfare, P. Dwyer, *Welfare, Rights and Responsibilities: contesting social citizenship*, Bristol, the policy press, 2000, pp. 4–5, 129–169.
140. G. Lewis, 'Coming Apart at the Seams: The Crises of the Welfare State', in G. Hughes and G. Lewis (eds), *Unsettling Welfare: the Reconstruction of Social Policy*, London, Routledge, 1998, pp. 39–80.

5 Recreating the family: Single mothers, maladjusted children and the search for a new home

1. C. Murray, *Losing Ground: American Social Policy, 1950–1980*, New York, Basic Books, 1984.
2. L. Mead, 'From Welfare to Work: lessons from America', in A. Deacon (ed.), *From Welfare to Work: Lessons from America*, London, Institute of Economic Affairs, 1997, p. 12.

3. For a discussion of the link between the establishment of paternal rights and political interests see X. Martin, 'The Paternal Role and the Napoleonic Code', in L. Spaas (ed.), *Paternity and Fatherhood, Myths and Realities*, Basingstoke and London, Macmillan, 1998, pp. 27–35.
4. V. Wimperis, *The Unmarried Mother and Her Child*, London, George Allen & Unwin, 1960, p. 13.
5. Ibid., p. 11.
6. Ibid.
7. For England see J. Fink, 'Natural Mothers, Putative Fathers, and Innocent Children: The Definition and Regulation of Parental Relationships Outside Marriage, in England, 1945 – 1959, *Journal of Family History*, 25, 2 (2000), p. 181.
8. The latter were regulated by the 1949 Married Women (Maintenance) Act and by the 1951 Guardianship and Maintenance of Children Act.
9. Fink, 'Natural Mothers, Putative Fathers and Innocent Children', p. 183.
10. Ibid., p. 185.
11. Saraceno, *Mutamenti della Famiglia*, p. 41 (my translation). Also, Ambrosini, *La Costituzione Italiana*, pp. xlvi–xlviii. Family legislation derived largely from the Codice Rocco, adopted by the fascist regime in 1942 and largely based, as far as the treatment of the family was concerned, on the 1861 Pisanelli Code, itself inspired by the Napoleonic Civil Code, introduced in the Italian states in 1804, C. Saraceno, 'Women, Family and the Law, 1750–1942', *Journal of Family History*, xv, 4 (1990), pp. 431–432.
12. On 'the principle of legitimacy' as 'universal sociological law', B. Malinowski, 'Parenthood – the Basis of the Social Structure', in V. F. Calverton and S. D. Schmalhausen (eds), *The New Generation. The Intimate Problems of Modern Parents and Children*, London, George Allen and Unwin, 1930, pp. 113–168, in particular pp. 137–139.
13. J. Spence, *A Thousand Families in Newcastle-Upon-Tyne*, p. 144.
14. Ibid., p. 145.
15. Statistical Review for England and Wales, 1940–1945, quoted in Wimperis, *The Unmarried Mother*, p. 31.
16. Ibid., pp. 31–34.
17. Wimperis, *The Unmarried Mother*, p. 29.
18. The findings are quoted in Wimperis, *The Unmarried Mother*, pp. 68–69.
19. CEA, MWC/EX/4. The question of the behaviour of American soldiers in Britain continued to be discussed by the CEMWC throughout the 1950s, ibid.
20. Wimperis, *The Unmarried Mother*, pp. 55–56. Wimperis based her account on a study conducted in 1950 by Valerie Hughes, a researcher of the LSE, 'in one midland city – here known as Midboro'. According to the study, fewer than 20 per cent of mothers of illegitimate children 'had known the man less than a year', while almost half of them said that they had known the father of the child for at least 2 years. *Midboro* had over 250 000 inhabitants and had an illegitimacy rate of 5.6 per cent in 1949, when the 278 mothers studied in the survey had given birth to their children.
21. PRO, MH 102/1164, Co-ordinating Provision for the Care of Children, memorandum sent to Herbert Morrison on 12th March 1945.

22. Wimperis, *The Unmarried Mother*, p. 64.

23. Ibid., pp. 184–185.

24. PRO MH 102/1576, Meetings with Chief Inspectors and Officers of Children Development, Chief Inspectors' monthly meetings, note of a meeting held on 9th September 1947, at the HO, to consider the question of special approved school for maternity cases. Similar conclusions were contained in memoranda prepared by HO officers and voluntary associations and circulated between 1945 and 1947.

25. On the necessity of both parents for the successful socialisation of the child, S. Foster Hartley, *Illegitimacy*, Berkeley, University of California, 1975, p. 15.

26. CEA, MWC, Advisory Board for Moral Welfare Work, Annual Report for 1956, p. 5., CEA, MWC/M/3 Church on England. Moral Welfare Council, Minutes Book, 1956–1957, meeting held on 12th April 1956. Plans for taking children into care were recommended, although no wishes in this sense were reported to exist among children's mothers.

27. G. Reekie, *Measuring Immorality. Social Inquiry and the Problem of Illegitimacy*, Cambridge, Cambridge Univerity Press, 1998, pp. 90–91, pp. 67–72.

28. R. di San Secondo, 'Bimbi senza nome', *MI*, y.xix, n. 1, September–October (1947), pp. 12–13.

29. According to the Italian Civil Code, a *filiazione legittima* existed in the presence of four concomitant factors: the marriage between the parents, the birth of a live child, the conception of the new born within the same marriage and the biological paternity of the husband, A. Violante, *I rapporti di filiazione e le azioni di stato*, Napoli, Jovene, 1983, p. 2. The definition survived the reform of Italian family law in 1975.

30. V. Gatti, 'Dura lex, sed lex', ibid., pp. 23–30.

31. E. Capace Elisi, 'Sulla obbligatorietà del riconoscimento materno', *MI*, xxi, 4 (1949), pp. 223–225.

32. Lancellotti Mari, 'Breve rielaborazione', p. 160.

33. *Guida Nazionale degli Istituti di Assistenza*, Tab. 1, pp. 22–25, 17–18.

34. J. Teichman, *Illegitimacy. A Philosophical Examination*, Oxford, Basil Blackwell, 1982, p. 80.

35. CEA, Notes on the Address on Adoption by the Hon. Mrs Edwards, Chairman of the Standing Conference of Societies Registered for Adoption, 6 November 1951.

36. J. Eekelaar, R. Dingwall, and T. Murray, 'Victims or Threats? Children in Care Proceedings', *Journal of Social Welfare Law*, March 1982, p. 73 and R. Harris and D. Webb, *Welfare, Power and Juvenile Justice. The Social Control of Delinquent Youth*, London, Tavistock, 1987, pp. 55–57.

37. Handicapped Pupils and Schools Service Regulations, 1945, Sect. 8(2) and 34 of the Education act, 1944, quoted in London County Council, Report of the Special Education Sub-Committee to the Education Committee on 5 December 1945, PRO, MH 102/2270.

38. Ibid.

39. PRO, MH 102/2281, *Treatment of Maladjusted Children*, LCC, Maladjusted Children-Treatment, Joint Report by the Education Officer and the School Medical Officer, 20 December 1948, p. 2. In 1964, the Working Party set up by the Scottish Education Department acknowledged that the term *maladjustment* lacked precision, but considered that it remained the more

useful definition available, *Ascertainment of Maladjusted Children*, Edinburgh, HMSO, 1964, p. 8.

40. PRO, HO 45/25144, *Juvenile Delinquency – Problems of Diagnosis and Treatment Met by Juvenile Courts*, Report submitted to the Home Secretary by the Advisory Council on the Treatment of Offenders, 13 October 1945, para. 2. Also, PRO, MH 102/2270, *London – Special Education Treatment for Maladjusted Pupils. Report of the Special Education Sub-Committee*, 5 December 1945.

41. *Hansard*, Commons, Standing Committee, 8 June 1948, coll. 165–190.

42. John Bowlby criticised the mandate of the Committee as inadequate to promote a thorough consideration of the medical problems involved in maladjustment and likely to encourage fragmentation in interventions and the perpetuation of a 'piecemeal legislation', J. Bowlby, letter to *The Times*, 18 October 1950, PRO MH 102/2283.

43. Ministry of Education, *Report of the Committee on Maladjusted Children*, London, MHSO, 1955, Para. 14, p. 3. The Committee had been appointed 'to enquire into and report upon the medical, educational and social problems related to maladjusted children, with reference to their treatment within the educational system', ibid., para. 1, p. 1.

44. PRO, MH 102/2281, LCC, Maladjusted Children-Treatment, p. 1.

45. *Report of the Committee on Maladjusted Children*, para. 119, 121, p. 30.

46. Ibid., para. 65, 67, pp. 16–17.

47. Ibid., para. 120, p. 30.

48. *Ascertainment of Maladjustment*, pp. 11–12.

49. MH 102/2281, LCC, Maladjusted Children-Treatment, pp. 1–2.

50. V. Porta, 'Relazione Conclusiva della Sotto-Commissione per la Profilassi e Cura delle Affezioni Psichiche dell'Infanzia', *Relazione della Commissione Speciale per un'Indagine sulle Condizioni dell'Infanzia nella Provincia di*, Milano, pp. 37–39.

51. D. Origlia, 'Relazione sugli adolescenti irregolari', *Relazione della Commissione Speciale*, p. 63.

52. PRO HO 45/25198, *Report on the Work of the Children Branch and Probation*, pp. 3–4. The number of boys under 17 under probation was 14 780 in 1938 and 19 609 in 1946 the number of girls was 1134 in 1938 and 1820 in 1945. Despite the disproportion existing between the figures for males and females, the report commented that the war had affected mostly the moral customs of young women, while boys had caused 'on the whole…fewer problems'.

53. Ibid., p. 6.

54. Ibid.

55. Ibid., pp. 6–8.

56. Ibid., *Summary of Probation Officers' Reports on Social Work During the War*, 1945, p. 2, para. 5.

57. *Children in Trouble, presented to Parliament by the Secretary of State for the Home Department by Command of Her Majesty, April, 1968*, London, HMSO, Cmnd. 3601, para.5, p.2.

58. Ibid.

59. Ibid., para. 6, p. 4.

60. *Seventh Report on the Work of the Children's Department*, London, HMSO, 1955, para. 152 and 153, p. 33 .

61. Ibid., p. 33.
62. Ibid.
63. F. Della Valle, 'Nubi sul mondo sereno dei piccoli', *MI*, xxiii, 7, September (1951), p. 11.
64. A. Giordano, 'Prevenzione e Trattamento per i minorenni di sesso maschile Dissociali, discoli, delinquenti nella provincia di Milano', *Relazione della Commissione Speciale*, p. 79.
65. E. Gastaldi, 'Il giovane delinquente', *MI*, xxv, 3, March (1953), pp. 19–22. On the effect of urban living on young people's life, F. Fasolo, 'Il fanciullo e la città', *MI*, xxv, 11, November (1953), pp. 30–33.
66. The paradigmatic case were the Milanese Teddy Boys described by Enrica Capussotti, 'Scenarios of Modernity. Youth Culture in 1950s Milan', in R. Lumley and J. Foot (eds), *Italian cityscapes. Culture and urban change in contemporary Italy*, Exeter, University of Exeter Press, 2004, pp. 169–184.
67. AAI, *Guida Nazionale degli Istituti di Assistenza*, pp. 12–13. Also, M. Costa, 'L'Italia Non Può Lasciare che un Solo Fanciullo Si Perda', *MI*, xxv, 1, January (1953), pp. 17–18.
68. *Children in Trouble*, para. 6, p. 4.
69. For Britain, G. Pearson, *Hooligan. A History of Respectable Fears*, Basingstoke, Macmillan, 1983, p. 19 and R. Hoggart, *The Uses of Literacy*, Harmondsworth, Penguin, 1960 (first published, 1957), pp. 211–224.
70. CPA, CRD 2/44/12, *Crime and Penal Reform*, p. 3.
71. Ibid., *The Question of Crime* (1962), p. 4.
72. Ibid., *Juvenile Delinquency*, 1959–1961, Some Minutes for Mr Butler: Oxford University Conservative Association, 14 October 1960.
73. CPA, CCO 4/8/375, NUCUA, Women's Annual Conference, Central Hall, Westminster, 19 April 1961, speech by R. A. Butler.
74. CPA, CCO 4/8/375, NUCUO, WNAC, *Report on a Working Party on Parental Responsibility and Juvenile Delinquency*, pp. 3–4. The report stressed the importance of establishing a good relationship between families and schools, and suggested that introducing sex education should be considered for the 'definite link' existing between 'the fact that sexual maturity [was] coming earlier, when still at school, and juvenile delinquency'.
75. Ibid., p. 2, and CPA, CRD 2/44/12, *The Question of Crime*, p. 5.
76. CPA, CCO 4/8/155.
77. Association of Child Care Officers, *Child Care in the Seventies, A Report of the Annual Conference*, The Oxford House, London, June 1967, para. 3, p. 3.
78. Ibid.
79. Ibid., p. 6.
80. CPA, CCO 4/8/375, NUCUO, WNAC, *Report on a Working Party on Parental Responsibility and Juvenile Delinquency*, pp. 1–2.
81. *Children in Trouble*, para. 12, p. 5.
82. B. J. Kahan, *Prevention and Rehabilitation*, An address at the Association of Children's Officers Annual Conference, Reprinted from the December 1961 issue of the Approved School Gazette, p. 8.
83. PRO, MH 57/300, Letter sent from Odgers (Children's Branch) to Miss MacKinnon, 10 November 1943.
84. Ibid., letter sent from Howell Jones to Mr Beckett, 10 March 1944.

85. PRO, MH 102/1448, *Care of Children Committee, Evidence of Association of Municipal Corporation*, January 1946, para. 25.
86. CSA, *Policy Circulars*, Conference of Home Representatives, St. Anselm Hall, 20 September 1945.
87. Jane Packman has suggested that evacuation, Bowlby's theories and economic considerations contributed to fostering been seen as 'the ideal method' of childcare during the 1950s, J. Packman, *The Child Generation, Child Care Policy in Britain*, Oxford, Blackwell and Robertson, 1981 (first published, 1975), pp. 21–23. According to the 1955 *Boarding Out of Children Regulations* foster parents' living conditions and age, and number and sex of the members of the household should be compatible with the aim of creating foster families resembling as closely as possible normal households. The Regulations lifted up statutory regulations on the maximum number of children in a foster home, and introduced greater flexibility in the procedures to be adopted in local situations, therefore increasing the powers of LAs.
88. *Report of the Care of Children Committee*, para. 461, p. 153.
89. Ibid., para. 460, p. 152.
90. CSA, 'No Place Like Home', *Our Waifs and Strays*, Children's Society Support Magazine, XL, 680, Christmas (1946), p. 52.
91. Ibid., *Bulletin*, 11, April (1949), p. 1.
92. Ibid., *Annual Report for* 1945, p. 8 and *Annual Report for* 1955, p. 327.
93. Ibid., *Bulletin*, 17, May (1950), p. 1 (My italics).
94. L. Rocchi's intervention in *Matrimonio fondamento della famiglia*, Atti del VII Convegno Nazionale di Studio dell'Unione Giuristi Cattolici Italiani, Roma, 3–5 Novembr 1955, pp. 86–87.
95. Lancellotti Mari, 'Breve Studio', pp. 148–149.
96. AAI, *Guida Nazionale degli Istituti di Assistenza*, p. 17.
97. G. Tamburrino, *La filiazione,* Torino, UTET, 1984, p. 207.
98. Lancellotti Mari, 'Breve Studio', p. 150.
99. For a wider discussion of affiliation orders in Britain see Fink, 'Natural Mothers, Putative Fathers and Innocent Children', pp. 182–186.
100. Tamburrino, *La filiazione*, p. 249.
101. *Lancellotti Mari*, 'Breve studio', p. 150.
102. Cass. 5-1-1971, n. 11, in *Foro pad.*, 1973, I, 364, quoted in Tamburrino, *La filiazione*, p. 252. A further reorganisation of fostering and adoption took place in 1983, with the Legge 184 (Legge 4 maggio 1983, n. 184 – in Suppl. ordinario alla Gazz. Uff. n. 133, del 17 maggio, Disciplina dell'adozione e dell'affidamento dei minori). According to the new law, fostering with a family or individual people should represent the privileged instrument of intervention, leaving the use of institutions only to cases where the *affidamento familieare* could not be pursued (Art. 2). As far as adoption was concerned, the reform transformed the 'adozione tradizionale' (traditional adoption) in 'adozione di persone maggiori di età' (adoption of people of full age). 'Adoption' as such indicated now the adoption of people under 18 in accordance with the procedures established in 1967 (with the noticeable change of the abolition of the limit of 8 years for the adoptee).
103. In 1967, the European Convention on adoption sanctioned the right to adopt an illegitimate child when this is in the interest of the child (Art 12, para. 3). Although the Convention was ratified in Italy in 1974 (legge

22.5.1974, n. 357), such a disposition was rejected, and the adoption of one's natural child prohibited. The exception was confirmed by the reform of 1983, on the basis of a 'principio di veridicità' ('principle of truth'), aimed to affirm the incompatibility between adoption and the existence of ties of blood: 'nel senso che nell'adozione non puo' esistere un vincolo di sangue, onde quando esso effettivamente esiste non può parlarsi di adozione', Tamburrino, pp. 218–219, 306.

104. Lancellotti Mari, 'Breve Studio', pp. 142–143.
105. L. Fox Harding, *Perspectives in Child Care Policy*, London, Longman, 1997 (first published, 1991), p. 4–5.
106. Ibid., para. 6, p. 2.
107. PRO, MH 102/1961, Children's Department, 5/7/49, Adjournment debate, 6 July 1949, Note for the Parliamentary Under-Secretary of State, p. 3.

Conclusions

1. G. Pascall, *Social Policy. A Feminist Analysis*, London, Tavistock, 1986, p. 38.
2. W. Beveridge, *Social Security and Allied Services*, London, HMSO, Cmnd. 6550, 1942, p. 14.
3. C. Murray, *Losing Ground. American Social Policy 1950–1980*, New York, Basic Books, 1984.
4. See C. Saraceno, *Mutamenti della famiglia e politiche sociali in Italia*, Bologna, Il Mulino, 1998, pp. 8–9.
5. J. Finch and P. Summerfield, 'Social Reconstruction and the emergence of Companionate Marriage, 1945–59', in D. Clark (ed.), *Marriage, Domestic Life and Social Change. Writings for Jaqueline Burgoyne*, London, Routledge, 1991, pp. 7–8.
6. The definition was introduced in G. Gorer, *Sex and Marriage in England Today*, London, Nelson, 1971 and adopted, with different emphases by M. Young and P. Willmott, *The Symmetrical Family. A Study of Work and Leisure in the London Region*, London, Routledge & Kegan Paul, 1973.

Bibliography

Archival collections

Archivio centrale dello stato, Rome

    Presidenza del Consiglio dei Ministri (PCM), 1944–1961.

National archives, London

    Cabinet: Miscellaneous Committees; Minutes and Papers (CAB 130).

    Ministry of National Insurance and Predecessors: Committee on Social Insurance and Allied Services (Beveridge Committee), Correspondence, Papers and Registered Files (PIN 8)

    Ministry of National Insurance, Chief Insurance Officer's Branch and Successors: Policy Files (PIN 61).

    Home Office: Registered Papers (HO 45).

    Home Office and Department of Health and Social Security: Children: General Files (HO 361).

    Ministry of Health – Health Division: Public Health and Poor Law Services, Local Government Administration and Finance, General Registered Files (MH 53).

    Home Office: Children's Department, Registered Files (MH 102).

    Ministry of Health: Social Welfare Services, Registered Files (MH 130).

    Ministry of Health: Local Authorities Services: Registered Files (MH 134).

Archivio del Partito Comunista Italiano, Istituto Gramsci, Rome.

Archivio Giulio Pastore, Rome.

Archivio Fondazione Sturzo, Rome.

Archivio Opera Nazionale Maternità e Infanzia, Rome.

Church of England Archive, London.

Church of England Children's Society Archive, London.

Conservative Party Archive, Bodlean Library, Oxford.

Government documents and publications

AAI, *L'Amministrazione per gli Aiuti Internazionali. Origini, Ordinamento, Funzioni, Attività*, Roma, 1952.

——, *Organi ed Enti di Assistenza Pubblica e Privata in Italia*, Roma, Tipografia Abete, 1953.

——, *Guida Nazionale degli Istituti di Assistenza con Ricovero*, Roma, Stabilimento Tipografico Fausto Failli, 1954.

Camera dei Deputati, *Atti Parlamentari, Discussioni*, 1947–1960.

——, *Atti della Commissione Parlamentar e di Inchiesta sulla Miseria in Italia e sui Mezzi per Combatterla*, Roma, 1953.

——, *La Costituzione della Repubblica nei lavori preparatori dell'Assemblea Costituente*, Roma, 1976, 8 vol.

Hansard, Parliamentary Debates, 5th series, 1945–1960.

Hansard, Standing Committees, 1947–1948.

Ministero del Lavoro, Piano Incremento Occupazione Operaia, Case per Lavoratori, *Suggerimenti, Esempi e Norme, per la Progettazione Urbanistica. Progetti Tipo* Roma, Ministero del Lavoro, 1950.

Ministry of Health, *Hostels for 'Difficult' Children. A Survey of Experience under the Evacuation Scheme*, London, HMSO, 1944.

Ministry of Health, *Index to Ministry of Health Circulars*, London, HMSO, 1951–1963.

Ministry of Health, *Play with a Purpose*, London, HMSO, 1951.

Ministry of Health, *Memorandum on Maternal Care Under the Maternity Medical Services*, enclosure to E.C.N. 347 (E.C.L. 81/60), London, Ministry of Health, 1961.

Ministry of Health, Department of Health for Scotland, *Report of the Working Party on Social Workers in the Local Authority Health and Welfare Services*, London, HMSO, 1959.

National Health Service Bill. Summary of the proposed new service, London, HMSO, 1946, Cmd. 6761.

National Health Services Council, *Reports of the Central Health Services Council*, 1950–1959.

Onmi, *Raccolta delle Leggi dell'ONMI*, Roma, Colombo, 1967.

Report of the Committee on Children and Young Persons, London, HMSO, 1960, Cmd. 1191.

Report of the Committee of Enquiry into the Cost of the National Health System (Guillebaud Report), London, HMSO, 1956, Cmd. 9663.

Reports of the Ministry of Health, London, HMSO, 1950–1959.

Report by Sir Walter Monckton on the Circumstances which led to the boarding out of Terence and Dennis O'Neill at Bank Farm, Minsterley and the steps taken to supervise their welfare, London, HMSO, 1945, Cmd. 6636.

Report of the Care of Children Committee, London, HMSO, 1946, Cmd. 6922.

Report of the Committee on Homeless Children, Edinburgh, HMSO, 1946, Cmd. 6911.

Scottish Educational Department, *Ascertainment of Maladjusted Children*, Edinburgh, HMSO, 1964.

Social Insurance and Allied Services, London, HMSO, 1942, Cmd. 6404.

Parties and organisations' publications

Church of England

The Care of Children Lacking Normal Home Life, special number of the Bulletin of the Central Churches Group, which is a joint Committee of the Churches and the National Council of Social Service, November, 1947.

The Church of England and the Family, Recent Developments in the Moral Welfare Work of the Church of England (1947).

Moral Welfare in Christian Social Service, annual report of the Church of England Moral Welfare Council, 1948, London, The Church Assembly, (1948).

The Church of England and Family Planning, The Church of England, London (1949).

Moral Welfare Work Today, The Church of England, London (1950).

The Church, the Family, and the Welfare State. What the Moral Welfare Council is Doing, report prepared for presentation to the Church Assembly (1955).

Comment on the Wolfenden Report, 1957, by the Church of England Moral Welfare Council, The Church of England, London (1957).

The Family Today. The Report of Committee 5 of the Lambeth Conference 1958, together with the text of the relevant resolution passed by the Conference, SPCK (1958).

Edwards, Q., *What is Unlawful? Does Innocence Begin where Crime Ends? Afterthoughts to the Wolfenden Report*, CEMWC (1959).

Conservative party

A True Balance: in the Home, in Employment, as Citizens (1949).

The Right Road for Britain. The Conservative Party's Statement of Policy (1949).

This is the Road: the Conservative and Unionist Party's Policy (1950).

The Manifesto of the Conservative and Unionist Pay (1951).

Britain, Strong and Free: a statement of Conservative and Unionist Policy (1951).

The Young Marrieds (1956).

Conservative Political Centre (CPC), *Youth Astray. Being a Report on the Treatment of the Young Offenders* (1946).

——, *Conservatism, 1945–1950* (1950).

——, *The New Conservatism, an Anthology of Post-war Thought* (1955).

Christian democratic party

Democrazia cristiana. Spes Centrale. Annuario Politico (1953–1954).

La Dc di Fronte all'Avvenire (1954).

Sturzo, L., *La Prima Crisi del Dopoguerra*, Quaderni della DC 14, Roma (undated).

Labour party

Challenge to Britain: a Programme of Action for the next Labour Government (1953).

The national society of children's nurseries

Training in Child Welfare, Second Report of the Group Committee of the National Council for Maternity and Child Welfare, The National Society of Children's Nurseries, London, 1946.

Organisations' annual reports and periodicals

I Problemi dell'Assistenza Sociale (Magazine of the National Institute of Medical Assistance, INAM).

Maternità e Infanzia (ONMI's Magazine).

Nostro Figlio (ONMI's Magazine).

Children Society's Annual Report, Children's Society, Children's Society Annual Report, London, 1945–1970

Conferences and seminars

Italy

Atti del Primo Congresso Nazionale ONARMO, Roma, 16–17 Aprile, 1957.

I Convegno Nazionale di Studio della DC, San Pellegrino, Roma, 1962.

Convegno per Studi di Assistenza Sociale, UNRRA, Tramezzo (Como), 16 Settembre–6 Ottobre, 1946.

Mater et Magistra, Unione Cattolica Italiana Donne, Milano, 18 Novembre, 1961.

Matrimonio Fondamento della Famiglia, Atti del VII Convegno Nazionale di Studio dell'Unione Giuristi Cattolici Italiani, Roma, 3–5 November, 1955.

La Famiglia e le Trasformazioni della Società Italiana, Movimento Femminile della DC, Convegno di Studio, Roma, 10–11 Febbraio, 1963.

Questioni matrimoniali. I tre giorni di teologia morale, Facoltà di Teologia dei PP.Gesuiti, Torino, 6–8 Settembre, Torino, LICE, 1949.

Trasformazioni Sociali ed Economiche nel Mondo Contadino: Riflessi nella Vita della Donna, Movimento Femminile della DC, Convegno di Studio, Bari, 19–20 Gennaio, 1963.

Britain

Children without Homes, Proceedings of a Conference called by the Women's Group on Public Welfare, 8th and 9th February, 1945 in London.

Homes and Hostels of the Future, Report of a Conference arranged by The National Council for the Unmarried Mother and Her Child, London, 29 November, 1945.

Report of a Conference on Parentcraft and Homecraft, National Association of Maternity and Child Welfare Centres and for the Preventionof Infant Mortality, London, 30 January 1947.

Collections of speeches

Atti e Discorsi di S.S. Pio XII, Roma, Istituto Missionario Pia Società San Paolo, 1939–1955, 17 v.

Discorsi e Radiomessaggi di S.S. Pio XII, Città del Vaticano, Tipografia Poliglotta Vaticana, 1941–1958, 21 v.

Dossetti, G., Iotti, N. and Ruini, M., *Interventi alla Costituente*, Bologna, Analisi-Trend, 1986.

The Dignity and Happiness of Marriage. Selected Addresses of Pope Pius XII to Married Couples, London-Dublin, Campion Press, 1959.

Togliatti, P., *Discorsi alla Costituente*, Roma, Editori Riuniti, 1973.

——, *Discorsi Parlamentari*, Roma, Editori Riuniti, 1984.

——, *Opere*, Roma, Editori Riuniti, 1974–1984, 6 v.

Woman's Place in the World. Address by His Holiness Pope Pius XII, Catholic Truth Society of Ireland, 1946.

Dissertations and theses

Celotto, E., *L'ONMI 1925–75: il Caso Fiorentino*, Laurea thesis, Firenze, 1995–1996.

Cinatti, L., *Il Partito Comunista Italiano e la Famiglia: Ideologia, Modelli e Propaganda Fra il 1921 e il 1948*, Laurea Thesis, Firenze, 1998.

Incatasciato, F., *Ideologia Cattolica e Famiglia Cristiana negli anni '50*, Laurea Thesis, Firenze, 1997–1998.

Jones, H., *The Conservative Party and the Welfare State 1943–1955*, Ph.D., London, 1992.

Jarvis, M., *The Conservative Party and the Adaptation to Modernity 1957–1964*, Ph.D., London, 1998.

Quine, M. S., *From Malthus to Mussolini; The Italian Eugenics Movement and Fascist Population Policy, 1890–1938*, unpublished Ph.D. thesis, University of London, 1990, p. 79.

Books and articles

AA.VV., *La questione femminile in Italia dal '900 ad oggi*, Milano, Franco Angeli, 1977.

Accati, L., 'Il marito della santa. Ruolo paterno e ruolo materno e politica Italiana', *Meridiana*, 13 (1992).

Accornero, A. and Mannheimer, R., (a cura di), *L'identità comunista. I militanti, le strutture, la cultura del PCI*, Roma, Editori Riuniti, 1983.

Acerbi, A., *La chiesa nel tempo: sguardi sui progetti di relazione tra chiesa e società civile negli ultimi cento anni*, Milano, Vita e Pensiero, 1979.

——, 'Pio XII e l'ideologia dell'Occidente', in A. Riccardi, (a cura di), *Pio XII*, Roma-Bari, 1984

Agosti, A. (a cura di), 'Il militante Comunista Torinese (1945–55). Fabbrica, società e politica: una prima ricognizione', in *I muscoli della storia. Militanti e organizzazioni operaie a Torino 1945–1955*, Milano, Angeli, 1987.

Alasia, F. and Montaldi, D., *Milano, Corea. Inchiesta sugli immigrati*, Milano, Feltrinelli, 1960.

Allan, G. and Crow, G., *Home and Family. Creating a Domestic Sphere*, Basingstoke, Macmillan, 1989.

Allen, M., *Whose Children?*, London, The Favil Press, 1944.

Allen, M. and Nicholson, M., *Memoirs of an Uneducated Lady. Lady Allen of Hurtwood*, London, Thames and Hudson, 1975.

Almond, G. A., *The Appeals of Communism*, Princeton, Princeton University Press, 1954.

Almond, G. A. and Verba, S., *The Civic Culture. Political Attitudes and Democracy in Five Nations*, Princeton, Princeton University Press, 1963.

Macleod, I. and Maude, A.,*One Nation: a Tory Approach to Social Problems*, London, CPC, 1950.

Ambrosini, G. (a cura di), *La Costituzione Italiana*, Torino, Einaudi, 1975.

Ambrosini, M., 'Famiglia e stato assistenziale. In margine ad alcuni recenti contributi', in *Rassegna di Sociologia*, XVIII, 4, (1980).

Anderlini, F., *Terra rossa. Comunismo ideale e socialdemocrazia reale. Il PCI in Emilia Romagna*, Bologna, Istituto Gramsci, 1990.

Anderson, M., *Family Structure in Nineteenth-Century Lancashire*, Cambridge, Cambridge University Press, 1971.

——, 'Famiglia e rivoluzione industriale', in M. Barbagli (a cura di), *Famiglia e mutamento sociale*, Bologna, Il Mulino, 1977.

Angiulli, G., *L'infanzia, la famiglia, la scuola*, Napoli, Tipomeccanica, 1953.

Anshen, R. N., *The Family: Its Function and Destiny*, New York, Harper and Brothers, 1959 (first published, 1949).

Ardigò, A., 'La crescita dell'uomo nella società Industriale', in AA.VV., *Il problema della società Industriale*, Milano, Vita e Pensiero, 1979.

Aries, P., *Centuries of Childhood*, Harmondsworth, Penguin, 1962.

Ascoli, G., 'L'UDI fra emancipazione e liberazione (1943–1964)', in Ascoli, G., *La questione femminile in Italia*, Milano, Franco Angeli, 1977.

Aubert, R., 'Il mezzo secolo che ha preparato il vaticano II', in R. Aubert, J. Hajjar, J. Brulls and S. Tramontin, *La chiesa nel mondo moderno*, Vol. V di *Nuova Storia della Chiesa*, Torino, 1979.

Azzariti, G., *La indissolubilità del matrimonio nella nostra costituzione*, Roma, Iustitia, 1949.

Balbo, L., *Stato di famiglia*, Milano, ETAS, 1976.

——, 'Crazy Quilts: Rethinking the Welfare State Debate from a Woman's Point of View', in A. Showstack Sassoon (ed), *Women and the State*, London, Routledge, 1992 (first published, 1987).

Baldwin, P., *The Politics of Social Solidarity*, Cambridge, Cambridge University Press, 1990.

Banfield, E. C., *The Moral Basis of a Backward Society*, Glencoe, The Free Press, 1958.

——, *Una comunità del Mezzogiorno*, Bologna, Il Mulino, 1961.

——, *Le basi morali di una società arretrata*, Bologna, Il Mulino, 1976.

Baransky, Z. G. and Lumley, R., *Culture and Conflict in Post-War Italy. Essays of mass and popular culture*, Basingstoke, Macmillan, 1990.

Barbagli, M., *Sotto lo stesso tetto: mutamenti della famiglia in Italia dal XV al XX secolo*, Bologna, Il Mulino, 1984.

Barberi, M. and Tettamanzi, D., *Matrimonio e famiglia nel magistero della Chiesa. I documenti del Concilio di Firenze a Giovanni Paolo II*, Milano, Massimo, 1986.

Barker R., *Political Ideas in Modern Britain*, London, Routledge, 1997 (first published, 1978).

Barnes, J., 'Ideology and Factions', in Seldon, A. and Ball, S. (eds), *Conservative Century: the Conservative Party since 1900*, Oxford, Oxford University Press, 1994.

Bartocci, E., *Le politiche sociali nell'Italia liberale (1861–1919)*, Roma, Donzelli, 1999.

——, 'Alle origini del welfare state' in Cotesta, V., (a cura di), *Il Welfare Italiano*, Roma, Donzelli, 1995.

Becchi, E., *I bambini nella storia*, Roma-Bari, Laterza, 1994.

Bell, W., 'Familism and Suburbanisation: One test of the Social Choice Hypothesis', in *Rural Sociology*, 21 (1956).

Bentivoglio, G., 'Ancora troppi pregiudizi, troppi errori a danno dei bambini', *Maternità e Infanzia*, 20, 2 (1949).

Bertolissi, S. and Sestan, L. (a cura di), *Da Gramsci a Berlinguer*, Venezia, Edizioni del Calendario, 1985, Vol. II.

Bessone, M., Alpa, G., D'Angelo, A. and Ferrando, G., *La famiglia nel nuovo diritto*, Bologna Zanichelli, 1997 (prima ed. 1977).

Bianchi, A., *Matrimonio Cristiano. Istruzioni*, Bergamo, Editrice Sant'Alessandro, 1948.

Bigatello, S., *L'uomo, la donna e il matrimonio*, Milano, La Casa, 1951.

Bloch, M. N., 'Becoming Scientific and Professional: Historical Perspectives on the Aims and Effects of Early Education and child care', in Popkewitz, T. S. (ed.), *The Formation of School Subjects: the Struggle for Creating an American Institution*, New York, Philadelphia and London, Falmer Press, 2000.

Boarelli, M., 'Il mondo nuovo. Autobiografie di Comunisti Bolognesi, 1945–55', *Italia Contemporanea*, 182, (1991).

Bock, G., 'Povertà femminile, maternità e diritti della madre nell'ascesa dello stato assistenziale', in Duby, G. and Perrot, M. (a cura di), *Storia delle Donne. Il Novecento*, Roma-Bari, Laterza, 1992.

Bock, G. and Thane, P., *Maternity and Gender Policies. Women and the Rise of the European Welfare States 1880s–1950s*, London, Routledge, 1994 (first published, 1991).

Boele-Woelki, K. and Fichs, A. (eds), *Legal Recognition of Same Sex Couples in Europe*, Antwerp. Oxford, New York, Intersentia, 2003.

Bongiovanni, B. and Tranfaglia, N. (a cura di), *Dizionario storico dell'Italia unita*, Roma-Bari, Laterza, 1996.

Boschi, A., *Nuove questioni matrimoniali*, Torino, Marietti, 1952

Bott, E., *Family and Social Network*, London, Tavistock Publications, 1957.

Bourke, J., *Working Class Cultures in Britain 1890–1960. Gender, Class and Ethnicity*, London, Routledge, 1994.

Bowlby, J., *Maternal Care and Mental Health*, Geneve, WHO, 1951.

——, *Child Care and the Growth of Love*, Harmondsworth, Penguin, 1953.

——, *Child Care and the Growth of Love*, second edition, Harmondsworth, Penguin, 1965.

Bowlby, J., *Rediscovery of the Family and Other Lectures*, Sister Maria Hilda Memorial Lectures, 1945–1973, Aberdeen, Aberdeen University Press, 1981.

Boyd Carpenter, J., *The Conservative Case*, London, CPC, 1950.

Braghin, P. (a cura di), *Inchiesta sulla Miseria in Italia (1951–1952), Materiali della Commissione Parlamentare*, Torino, Einaudi, 1978.

Bravo, A. (a cura di), *Donne e uomini nelle guerre mondiali*, Roma-Bari, Laterza, 1991.

Bridgeland, M., *Pioneer Work with Maladjusted Children*, London, Staples Press, 1971.

Briggs, A., 'The Welfare State in Historical Perspective', *European Archives of Sociology*, 2, 2 (1961).

Buck, P. W. (ed.), *How Conservative Think*, Harmondsworth, Penguin, 1975.

Burgess, E. W. and Locke, H. J., *The Family: from Institution to Companionship*, New York, American Book Co., 1953 (second edn).

Burlingham, D. and Freud, A., *Young Children in War Time in a Residential War Nursery*, London, George Allen & Unwin, 1942.

——, *Infants Without Families, the Case For and Against Residential Nurseries*, London, George Allen & Unwin, 1943.

Butler, R. A., *The Conservatives. A History from Their Origins to 1965*, London, Allen and Unwin, 1977.

Butler, D. and Stokes, D., *Political Change in Britain*, London, Macmillan, 1969.

Calamandrei, P., *Uomini e città della Resistenza*, Milano, Linea d'Ombra, 1994.

Calder, A., *The People's War. Britain 1939–1945*, London, Pimlico, 1992 (first published, 1969).

Caldwell, L., *Italian Family Matters, Women, Politics and Legal Reform*, London, Macmillan, 1991.

Calogero, R., 'L'inchiesta sociologica', in ONARMO, Atti del Primo Congresso Nazionale, Rome 16–17 April, 1956.

Campanini, G., *Potere politico e immagine paterna*, Milano, Vita e Pensiero, 1985.

——, *Cattolici e società fra dopoguerra e post-Concilio*, Roma, AVE, 1990.

——, *Le stagioni della famiglia*, Milano, Ed. San Paolo, 1994.

Candeloro, G., *Storia dell'Italia moderna*, v. vi, *Lo sviluppo del capitalismo e il movimento operaio*, Milano, Feltrinelli, 1970.

Canfora, L.*Togliatti e i dilemmi della politica*, Bari, Laterza, 1989.

Capace Elisi, E., 'Sulla obbligatorietà del riconoscimento materno', in *Maternità e Infanzia*, 21, 4 (1949).

Capussotti, E., 'Scenarios of Modernity. Youth culture in 1950s Milan', in R. Lumley and J. Foot (eds), *Italian Cityscapes. Culture and Urban Change in Contemporary Italy*, Exeter, University of Exeter Press, 2004.

Cardia, *Il diritto di famiglia in Italia*, Roma, Editori riuniti, 1975.

Caredda, G., *Governo e opposizione nell'Italia del dopoguerra*, Roma-Bari, Laterza, 1995.

Carlebach, J., *Caring for Children in Trouble*, London, Routledge, Kegan Paul, 1970.

Caroli, D., 'Il bambino collettivo', in Niccoli, O. (a cura di), *Infanzie*, Firenze, 1993.

Casella, M., *L'Azione Cattolica*, Roma, Studium, 1984.

——, *Cattolici e Costituenti. Orientamenti e iniziative del Cattolicesimo organizzato (1945–47)*, Napoli, Edizioni Scientifiche Italiane, 1987.

Castelli Avolio, G., *I Democratici Cristiani. Chi sono e cosa vogliono*, Roma, Libertà e Rinascita, n. 2, 1945.

Castellina, L., 'Quali compromessi', in Sartogo, A. (a cura di), *Le donne al muro. L'immagine femminile nel manifesto politico italiano, 1947–1977*, Roma, Savelli, 1978.

Castronovo, V., 'Economia e classi sociali', in *L'Italia contemporanea*, Torino, Einaudi, 1976.

Cazzola, F., *Anatomia del potere democristiano*, Bari, De Donato, 1978.

Cecil, H., *Conservatism*, London, William & Norgate, 1912.

Centro Nazionale di Prevenzione e Difesa Sociale, *Relazione della Commissione Speciale per un'Indagine sulle Condizioni dell'Infanzia nella Provincia di Milano*, Milano, Giuffré, 1955.

Cerizza, A. (a cura di), *La Costituzione Italiana. Analisi degli emendamenti*, Milano, IBM, 1979.

Cervi, A. and Nicolai, R., *I miei sette figli*, Roma, Editori Riuniti, 1956.

Chabod, F., *L'Italia contemporanea (1918–1945)*, Torino, Einaudi, 1961.

Cheal, D., *Family and the State of Theory*, London, Harvester Wheatsheaf, 1991.

Cherubini, A., *Storia della previdenza sociale in Italia*, Roma, Editori Riuniti, 1977.

Chianese, G., *Storia sociale della donna in Italia*, Napoli, Guida, 1980.

Chinigo, M. (ed.), *The Teachings of the Pope Pius XII*, London, Methuen & Co., 1958.

Chittolini, G. and Miccoli, G., *Storia d'Italia. Annali 9, La Chiesa e il potere politico dal Medioevo all'Età Contemporanea*, Torino, Einaudi, 1986.

Civardi, L., *Cristianesimo e vita familiare*, Roma, AVE, 1946.

Clarke, D., *The Conservative Faith in a Modern Age*, London, CPC, 1947.

Clarke, J., Cochrane, A. and Smart, C., *Ideologies of Welfare*, London, Hurchinson, 1987.

Coleraine, R. K. L., *For Conservative Only*, London, Tom Stacey, 1970.

Cook, H., *The Long Sexual Revolution*, Oxford, Oxford University Press, 2004.

Cooper, C., 'The Illegitimate Child', in *The Practitioner*, 174, 1042 (1955).

Coopey, R., Fielding, S. and Tiratsoo, N. (eds), *The Wilson Government, 1964–1970*, London, Pinter, 1993.

Corr, H. and Jameson, L. (eds), *Politics of Everyday Life. Continuity and Change in Work and the Family*, London, Macmillan, 1990.

Corsanego, C., *L'educazione in famiglia*, Roma, Signorelli, 1952.

Costa, M., 'L'Italia non può lasciare che un solo fanciullo si perda', in *Maternità e Infanzia*, 25, 1, (1953).

Crainz, G. *Storia del miracolo Italiano*, Roma, Donzelli, 1997.

Creak, M., 'The Age of the Expert', in J. Bowlby et.al., *Rediscovery of the Family and Other Lectures*, Sister Maria Hilda Memorial Lectures, 1954–73, Aberdeen, Aberdeen University Press, 1981.

Cronin, J. E. and Schneer, *Social Conflict and the Political Order in Modern Britain*, London, Croom Helm, 1982.

Crosby, T. L., *The Impact of Civilian Evacuation in the Second World War*, London, Croom Helm, 1986.

Crosland, A., *The Future of Socialism*, London, Jonathan Cape, 1956.

Crossman, R., 'Towards a Philosophy of Socialism', in Crossman, R., (ed.), *New Fabian Essays*, London, Turnstile Press, London, 1952.

——, *Plato Today*, London, George Allen & Unwin, 1937.

Cunningham, H., *Children and Childhood in Western Societies since 1500*, London, Longman, 1995.

Da Castellanza, I., *Nuzialità e maternità*, Bergamo, SESA, 1946.

Daly, M., *The Gender Division of Welfare. The Impact of the British and German Welfare States*, Cambridge, Cambridge University Press, 2000.

Daly, M. and Rake, K., *Gender and the Welfare State, Care, Work and Welfare in Europe and the USA*, Cambridge, Polity, 2003.

D'Amelia, M., *Storia della maternità*, Roma-Bari, Laterza, 1997.

D'Attorre, P., *I Comunisti in Emilia Romagna. Documenti e materiali*, Bologna, Graficoop, 1981.

——, (a cura di), *Nemici per la pelle. Sogno Americano e mito Sovietico nell'Italia Contemporanea*, Milano, Angeli, 1991.

Dau Novelli, C. (a cura di), *Donne del nostro tempo. Il Centro Italiano Femminile (1945–1995)*, Roma, Studium, 1995.

——, 'La famiglia come soggetto della ricostruzione sociale', in De Rosa G., *Cattolici, Chiesa, Resistenza*, Bologna, Il Mulino, 1997.

Davidoff, L., Doolittle, M., Fink, J. and Holden, K., *The Family Story. Blood, Contract and Intimacy, 1830–1960*, London, Longman, 1999.

Davie, G., *Religion in Britain Since 1945, Believing without Belonging*, Oxford, Blackwell, 1994.

Davitti, L., *La protezione sociale della maternità nel mondo*, Roma, Istituto di Medicina Sociale, 1960.

Deacon, A., *From Welfare to Work: Lessons from America*, London, Institute of Economic Affairs, 1997.

De Felice, F., 'Doppia lealtà e doppio stato', *Studi Storici*, 30, 3 (1989)

De Gasperi, A., *Idee sulla DC*, Roma, 5 June, 1974.

De Grazia, V., *How Fascism Ruled Women. Italy 1922–1945*, Berkeley, University of California Press, 1992.

De Martino, E., 'Intorno a una storia del mondo popolare subalterno', *Società*, v, (1949).

De Masi, D., 'Arretratezza del mezzogiorno e analisi sociologica', in Banfield E. P. (ed.), *Le basi morali di una società arretrata*, Bologna, 1976.

De Swaan, A., *In Care of the State. Health Care, Education and Welfare in Europe, and the USA in the Modern Era*, Cambridge, Polity Press, 1988.

Del Bo Boffino, A., *Figli di mamma*, Milano, Rizzoli, 1986.

Della Valle, 'Nubi sul mondo sereno dei piccoli', *Maternità e Infanzia*, xiii, 7, (1951).

Delmati, V., 'Natura e scopi del servizio sociale', in ONARMO, *Atti del Primo Congresso Nazionale*, Rome 16–17 April, 1956.

Devine, F., *Affluent Workers Revisited*, Edinburgh, Edinburgh University Press, 1992.

——, 'Privatised Families and Their Homes', in Allan, G. and Crow, G. (eds), *Home and Family*, Basingstoke, Macmillan, 1989.

Diaz, F., *La stagione arida: riflessioni sulla vita civile in Italia dal Dopoguerra ad oggi*, Milano, Mondadori, 1992.

Di Francesco, A., *Makarenko e la pedagogia del collettivo*, Acireale, Tringale editore, 1985.

Digby, A., *British Welfare Policy: Workhouse to Workforce*, London, Faber and Faber, 1989.

Dobson, B., 'Children, Crime and the State', in Golson, B., Lavalette, M., McKechnie, J., *Children, Welfare and the State*, London, Sage, 2004 (first published 2002).

Doms, M. H., *The Meaning of Marriage*, London, Sheed & Ward, 1939.

Donati, P., *Famiglia e politiche sociali*, Milano, Franco Angeli, 1981.

Donati, P. and Saraceno, C., *Sociologia della famiglia*, Bologna, CLUEB, 1978.

Donolo, C., 'Social Change and Transformation of the State in Italy', in Scase, R. (ed.), *The State in Western Europe*, London, Croom Helm, 1980.

Donzelot, J., *The Policing of Families*, Baltimore and London, John Hopkins University Press, 1997 (first published, 1977).

Dossetti, G., *Scritti politici 1943–51*, Roma, Marietti, 1995.

Douglas, J. W. B., Bloomfield, J. M., *Children under Five*, London, Allen and Unwin, 1958.

Drucker, H. M., *Doctrine and Ethos in the Labour Party*, London, George Allen & Unwin, 1979.

Dunleavy, P., 'The United Kingdom. Paradoxes of an Ungrounded Statism', in Castles, F. G. (ed), *The Comparative History of Public Policy*, Cambridge, Polity Press, 1989.

Durbin, E., *The Politics of Democratic Socialism*, London, Routledge, 1940.

Durbin, E. and Catlin, G., *War and Democracy. Essays on the Causes and Prevention of War*, London, Kegan Paul, 1938.

Dwyer, P., *Welfare, Rights and Responsibilities: contesting social citizenship*, Bristol, the policy press, 2000.

Eccles, D., *What Do You Think? About a Property-Owning Democracy*, London, CPC, 1948.

Eccleshall, R., 'English Conservatism as Ideology', in *Political Studies*, 25, 1 (1977).

Eekelaar, J., Dingwall, R. and Murray, T., 'Victims or Threats? Children in Care Proceedings', *Journal of Social Welfare Law*, March (1982).

Ellwood, D. W., *Italy 1943–1945*, Leicester, Leicester University Press, 1985.

Elshtain, J. (ed.), *The Family in Political Thought*, Amherst, The University of Massachusets, 1982.

Epstein, B. L., *The Politics of Domesticity. Women, Evangelism, and Temperance in Nineteenth Century America*, Middletown, Wesleyan University Press, 1986 (first published, 1981).

Esping Andersen, G., *The Three Worlds of Welfare Capitalism*, Princeton, Princeton University Press, 1990.

Eve, M., 'Comparing Italy: The Case of Corruption', in Forgacs D. and Lumley, R. (eds), *Italian Cultural Studies*, Oxford, 1996.

Fabbri, S., *Direttive e schiarimenti intorno allo spirito informatore della legislazione riguardante l'ONMI e le sue pratiche applicazioni*, Roma, Colombo, 1933.

Falconi, C., *L'Assistenza Italiana sotto bandiera pontificia*, Milano, Feltrinelli, 1957.

Family Needs and the Social Services, London, Political and Economic Planning, 1961.

Fanfani, A., *Persona, beni, società in una rinnovata civiltà Cristiana*, Milano, Giuffré, 1945.

Fasolo, F., 'Il fanciullo e la città', *Maternità e Infanzia*, 25, 11 (1953).

Fausto, D., *Il sistema Italiano di sicurezza sociale*, Bologna, Il Mulino, 1978.

Fava, A., 'Alle origini di nuove immagini dell'infanzia: gli anni della Grande Guerra', in M. C. Giuntella, I. Nardi *Il bambino nella storia* (a cura di), Napoli, Editrice Scientifica Italiana, 1993.

Federici, N., *Procreazione, famiglia e lavoro della donna*, Torino, Loescher, 1984.

Ferrera, M., *Welfare state in Italia. Sviluppo e crisi in prospettiva comparata*, Bologna, Il Mulino, 1984.

Ferretti, A., *I Cervi. Le idee, l'azione*, Reggio Emilia, ANMPI, 1980.

Fielding, S., *The Labour Party, Socialism and Society since 1951*, Manchester, Manchester University Press, 1997.

Filippucci, P., 'Anthropological Perspectives on Culture in Italy', in Forgacs, D., Lumley, R., *Italian Cultural Studies*, Oxford, 1996.

Finch, J. and Grove, D., *A Labour of Love. Family, Work and Caring*, London, Routledge and Kegan Paul, 1983.

——, *Family Obligations and Social Change*, Cambridge, Polity, 1989.

Finch, J. and Mason, J., *Negotiating Family Responsibilities*, London, Routledge, 1993.

Finlayson, G., *Citizen, State and Social Welfare in Britain, 1830–1990*, Oxford, Clarendon Press, 1994.

Fletcher, R., *Britain in the Sixties. Family and Marriage. An Analysis and Moral Assessment*, Harmondsworth, Penguin, 1962.

Flora, P. (ed.), *Growth to Limits. The Western European Welfare States since World War II*, Vol. I, Berlin and New York, Walter de Gruyter, 1986.

Foot, J., 'The Family and the 'Economic Miracle': Social Transformation, Work, Leisure and Development at Bovisa and Comasina (Milan), 1950–1970', *Contemporary European History*, 4, 3 (1995).

Foote, G., *The Labour Party's Political Thought. A History*, Basingstoke, Macmillan, 1997 (first published, 1985).

Foucault, M., *Discipline and Punish. The Birth of the Prison*, London, Allen Lane, 1977 (first published, 1975).

Fox Harding, L., *Family, State and Social Policy*, Basingstoke, Macmillan, 1996.

——, *Perspectives in Child Care Policy*, London, Longman, 1997 (first published, 1991).

Francis, M., *Ideas and Policies Under Labour, 1945–1951*, Manchester, Manchester University Press, 1997.

——, ' "Set the People Free?" Conservatives and the State, 1920–1960', in M. Francis and Zweiniger-Bargielowska (eds), *The Conservative and British Society, 1880–1999*, Cardiff, University of Wales, 1996.

——, 'Labour and Gender', in Tanner, D., Thane, P. and Tiratsoo, N. (eds), *Labour's First Century*, Cambridge, 2000.

Frost, N. and Stein, M., *The Politics of Child Welfare. Inequality, Power and Change*, London, Harvester Wheatsheaf, 1989.

Freud, A., 'Why Children Go Wrong', in W. D. Wall and A. Freud (eds), *The Enrichment of Childhood*, London, The Nursery School Association of Great Britain, 1962.

Furedi, F., *Therapy Culture. Cultivating Vulnerability in an Uncertain Age*, London and New York, Routledge, 2004.

Gagliani, D., 'Welfare state come umanesimo e antipatronage. Un'eperienza delle donne nel secondo dopoguerra', in D. Gagliani and M. Salvati, *La sfera pubblica femminile. Percorsi di storia delle donne in età contemporanea*, Bologna, CLUEB, 1990.

Gaiotti De Biase, P., *La donna nella vita sociale e politica della Republica 1945–48*, Milano, Vangelista, 1978.

Gallerano, N. (a cura di), *L'altro Dopoguerra. Roma e il Sud*, Milano, Angeli, 1985.

Galli della Loggia, E., 'Una guerra al femminile? Ipotesi sul mutamento dell'ideologia e dell'immaginario Occidentale tra il 1939 e il 1945', in Bravo, A. (a cura di), *Donne e uomini nelle guerre mondiali*, Roma-Bari, Laterza, 1991.

Gamble, A., *The Conservative Nation*, London, Routledge and Kegan Paul, 1974.

Garbett, C., *In an Age of Revolution*, London, Hodder & Stoughton, 1952.

Garcia, J., Kilpatrick, R. and Richards, M. (eds), *The Politics of Maternity Care*, Clarendon, Oxford, 1990.

Gastaldi, E., 'Il giovane delinquente', *Maternità e Infanzia*, 25, 3 (1953).

Gatti, V., 'Dura lex, sed lex', *Maternità e Infanzia*, 19, 1, September–October, (1947).

Geiger, H. K., *The Family in Soviet Russia*, Cambridge Mass., Harvard University Press, 1968.

Giddens, A., *The Transformation of Intimacy: Sexuality, Love and Eroticism in Modern Societies*, Oxford, Polity Press, 1995.

Giles, J., 'Help for Housewives: Domestic Service and the Reconstruction of Domesticity in Britain, 1940–50, *Women's History Review*, 10, 2 (2001).

Gill, D., *Illegitimacy, Sexuality and the Status of Women*, Oxford, Basil Blackwell, 1977.

Gilmour, I., *Inside Right. A study of Conservatism*, London, Quarter Books, 1978 (first published, 1977).

——, *Whatever Happened to the Tories, The Conservatives since 1945*, London, Fourth Estate, 1997.

Ginantempo, N., (a cura di), *Donne del Sud. Il prisma femminile sulla questione meridionale*, Gelka, Palermo, 1993.

Ginsborg, P., *A History of Contemporary Italy. Society and Politics, 1943–1988*, Harmondsworth, Penguin, 1990.

——, 'Family Culture and Politics in Contemporary Italy', in Baransky, Z. G. and Lumley, R. (eds), *Culture and Conflict in Post-War Italy. Essays of Mass and Popular Culture*, Basingstoke, Macmillan, 1990.

——, 'Famiglia, società civile e stato nella storia contemporanea: alcune considerazioni metodologiche', *Meridiana*, VII, 2, (1993).

——, 'Familismo', in Ginsborg, P. (a cura di), *Stato dell'Italia*, Milano, Il Saggiatore, 1994.

——, *Il tempo di cambiare, Politica e potere della vita quotidiana*, Torino, Einaudi, 2004.

Giovagnoli, A., 'La Pontificia Commissione Assistenza e gli aiuti Americani (1943–1945)', *Storia contemporanea*, ix, 5–6, (1978).

——Chiesa, assistenza, e società a Roma tra il 1943 e il 1945', in Gallerano, N. (a cura di), *L'altro Dopoguerra. Roma e il Sud*, Milano, 1985.

Glass, D. V. (ed.), *Social Mobility in Britain*, London, Routledge & Kegan Paul, 1954.

Glennerster, H., *British Social Policy since 1945*, Oxford, Blackwell, 1995.

Godano, F., 'Per una migliore protezione dell'infanzia',*Maternità e Infanzia*, 20, 2, (1949).

Goldman, P., *Some Principles of Conservatism*, London, CPC, 1961 (first published, 1956).

Goldring, P., *Friend of the Family. The Work of Family Service Units*, Newton Abbott, David & Charles, 1973.Goldthorpe, J. E., *Family Life in Western Society: a Historical Analysis of Family Relationship in Britain and North America*, Cambridge, Cambridge University Press, 1987.

Goldthorpe, J. H., *The Affluent Worker. Industrial Attitudes and Behaviour*, Cambridge, Cambridge University Press, 1968.

Goode, W. J., *World Revolution and Family Patterns*, New York, Free Press of Glencoe, 1963.

——, *The Family*, Englewood Cliffs, N.J., Prentice Hall, 1964.

Gorer, G., *Sex and Marriage in England Today*, London, Nelson, 1971.

Goulbourne, H., *Race Relations in Britain since 1945*, Basingstoke, Macmillan, 1998.

Gozzini, G., Martinelli, R., *Storia del Partito Comunista Italiano. Dall'attentato a Togliatti all'VIII Congresso*, Torino, Einaudi, 1998.

Graham, H. 'Caring: a Labour of Love', in Finch, J. and Groves, D.(eds), *A Labour of Love: Women, Work and Caring*, London, 1983.

Gray, N. and Brazil, D., *Blackstone Guide to The Civil Partnership Act 2004*, Oxford and New York, Oxford University Press, 2005.

Green, S. J. D. and Whiting, R. C. (eds), *The Boundaries of the State in Modern Britain*, Cambridge, Cambridge University Press, 1996.

Gribaudi, G., 'Images of the South', in Forgacs, D. and Lumley, R. (eds), *Italian Cultural Studies*, Oxford, Oxford University Press, 1996.

Gronchi, G., *Per la storia della DC. Una politica sociale (1948–1954)*, Bologna, Il Mulino, 1962.

Gueli, I. and Pezzali, G., 'Ripresa', *Maternità e Infanzia*, 19, 1, September–October (1947).

Gundle, S., 'L'Americanizzazione del quotidiano. Televisione e consumismo nell'Italia degli anni Cinquanta', *Quaderni Storici*, 62 (1986).

Hajnal, J., Laslett, P., Wall, R., *Family Forms in Historic Europe*, Cambridge, Cambridge University Press, 1983.

Hajnal, J., 'European Marriage Patterns in Perspective', in Glass, D. V. and Eversley, D. E. C. (eds), *Population in History*, Chicago, Chicago University Press, 1965.

Hall, L. H., *Sex, Gender and Social Change in Britain since 1880*, Basingstoke, Macmillan, 2000.

Hareven, T. K., *Family Time and Industrial Time. The Relationship between the Family and Work in a New England Community*, Cambridge, Cambridge University Press, 1982.

——, 'The History of the Family and the Complexity of Social Change', *American Historical Review*, 96, 1 (1991).

Harris, J., 'Some Aspects of Social Policy in Britain during the Second World War', in Mommsen, W. J. (ed.), *The Emergence of the Welfare State in Britain and Germany 1850–1950*, London, Croom Helm, 1981.

——, 'Political Thought and the Welfare State, 1870–1940: An Intellectual Framework for British Social Policy', in *Past and Present*, 135 (1992).

Harris, R. and Webb, D., *Welfare, Power and Juvenile Justice. The Social Control of Delinquent Youth*, London, Tavistock Publications, 1987.

Hartley, S. F., *Illegitimacy*, Berkeley, University of California, 1975.

Hendrick, H., *Child Welfare in England, 1872–1989*, London, Routledge, 1994.

Heywood, J., *Children in Care. The Development of the Services for the Deprived Child*, London, Routledge & Kegan Paul, 1978 (first published, 1959).

Higgins, P., *Heterosexual Dictatorship: Male Homosexuality in Pos-war Britain*, London, Fourth Estate, 1996.

Hill, M., *The Welfare State in Britain. A Political History Since 1945*, Aldershot, Edward Elgar, 1993.

Hine, D., *Governing Italy*, Oxford, Clarendon, 1993.

Hogg, Q., *The Case for Conservatism*, Harmondsworth, Penguin, 1947.

Hoggart, R., *The Uses of Literacy*, Harmondsworth, Penguin, 1960 (First published, 1957).

Holman, B., *Putting Families First. Prevention and Child Care*, London, Macmillan, 1988.

Inglis, R., *The Children's War. Evacuation, 1939–1945*, London, Fontana, 1990 (first published 1989).

Ingram, E., 'Play and Leisure Time in the Children's Home', in Tod, R. J. N. (ed.), *Children in Care. Papers on Residential Work*, London, 1976.

ISTAT, *Sommario di statistiche storiche dell'Italia 1861–1975*, Roma, 1976.

Jedin, H., 'Popes Benedict XV, Pius XI, and Pius XII, Biography and Activity within the Church', in, H. Jedin, K. Repgen and J. Dolan (eds), *History of the Church*, Vol. X, London, Burns & Oates, 1981.

Jemma, R., 'Morbilità nell'infanzia nel dopoguerra', *Maternità e Infanzia*, 19, 1 (1947).

Jennings, H., *Societies in the Making. A Study of Development and Redevelopment Within a County Borough*, London, Routledge & Kegan Paul, 1962.

Jessop, B., 'The Transformation of the State in Post-war Britain', in Scase, R. (ed.), *The State in Western Europe*, London, 1980.

Johnson, P., 'Social Policy in the Twentieth Century', in *Contemporary European History*, 2, 2 (1993).

Jones, H., *Reluctant Rebels. Re-education and Group Process in a Residential Community*, London, Tavistock, 1960.

——, 'The Post-War Consensus in Britain: Thesis, Antithesis, Synthesis?', in Brivati, B., Buxton, J., Jones, H., and Kandiah, M. (eds), *The Myth of Consensus: New Views of British History 1945–1964*, London, Macmillan, 1996.

Jones, K., *The Making of Social Policy in Britain 1830–1990*, London, The Athlone Press, 1994.

Jordan, M. D., *Blessing Same-Sex Unions. The Perils of Queer Romance and the Confusions of Christian Marriage*, Chicago and London, The University of Chicago Press, 2005.

Kaelble, H., *Verso una società europea. Storia sociale dell'Europa, 1880–1980*, Bari, Laterza, 1990, (original title *Auf dem Weg zu einer europäischen Gesellschaft. Eine Sozialgeschichte Westeuropas. 1880–1980*, C. H. Beck'sche Verlagsbuchhandlung, Munich, 1987).

Keane, J., *Civil Society. Old Images, New Visions*, Cambridge, Polity, 1998.

Kertzer, D. I. and Hogan, D., *Family, Political Economy and Demographic Change: the transformation of life in Casalecchio, Italy, 1861–1921*, Madison, Wisconsin, University of Wisconsin Press, 1989.

King, M., 'Welfare and Justice', in King, M. (ed.), *Childhood, Welfare and Justice. A Critical Examination of Children in Legal and Childcare Systems*, London, Batsford Academic and Educational,1981.

Kingsley Kent, S., *Making Peace. The Reconstruction of Gender in Interwar Britain*, Princeton, Princeton University Press, 1993.

Kollontaj, A., *Comunismo, famiglia, morale sessuale*, Roma, Savelli, 1976.

Koven, S. and Michel, S. (eds), *Mothers of the New World. Maternalist Politics and the Origin of Welfare States*, London, Routledge, 1993.

Laing, R. D., *The Divided Self*, London, The Tavistock Institute of Human Relations, 1960.

Laing, R. D. and Esterson, A., *Sanity, Madness and the Family*, London, The Tavistock Institute of Human Relations, 1964.

Land, H., 'The Boundaries Between the State and the Family', in Harris, C. (ed.), *The Sociology of the Family. New Directions for Britain*, Keele, University of Keele, 1979.

La Palombara, J., 'Italy: Fragmentation, Isolation, Alienation', in Pye, L. N. and Verba, S. (eds), *Political Culture and Political Development*, Princeton, 1965.

——, *Democracy, Italian Style*, New Haven, Yale University Press, 1987.

La Rossa, R., *The Modernization of Fatherhood: A Social and Political History*, Chicago, University of Chicago Press, 1997.

Lasch, C., *Haven in a Heartless World. The Family Besieged*, New York, Basic Books, 1979.

Laslett, P., *The World We Have Lost*, London, Mathuen, 1965.

—— (ed.), *Household and Family in Past Time*, Cambridge, Cambridge University Press, 1972.

Law, I., *Racism, Ethnicity and Social Policy*, Hemel Hampstead, Prentice Hall, 1996.

Law, R., *Return from Utopia*, London, Faber, 1950.

Lawrence, J. and Taylor, M., *Party, State and Society. Electoral Behaviour in Britain since 1820*, Aldershot, Scolar Press, 1997.

Layton-Henry, Z. (ed), *Conservative Politics in Western Europe*, London, Macmillan, 1982.

Lewis, G., 'Coming Apart at the Seams: the Crises of the Welfare State', in, G. Hughes and G. Lewis (eds), *Unsettling Welfare: the Reconstruction of Social Policy*, London, Routledge, 1998.

Lewis, H., *Deprived Children. The Mersham Experiment. A Social and Clinical Study*, Oxford, The Nuffield Foundation/Oxford University Press, 1954.

Lewis, J., 'Anxiety about the Family and the Relationships Between Parents, Children and the State in Twentieth Century England', in Richards, M. and Light, P.

(eds), *Children of Social Worlds. Development in a Social Context*, Cambridge, Polity, 1986.

—— (ed.), *Women and Social Policies in Europe. Work, Family and the State*, Aldershot, Elgar, 1993.

——, *The End of Marriage? Individualism and Intimate Relationships*, Aldershot, Elgar, 2001.Lewis, J., Clark, D. and Morgan, D. H. J., 'Whom God had Joined together'. The Work of Marriage Guidance, London, Routledge, 1992.

Lewis, P. M., 'Mummy, Matron and the Maids. Feminine presence and absence in male institutions', in Roper, M., Tosh, J., *Manful Assertions, Masculinities in Britain since 1800*, London, Routledge, 1991.

Livi Bacci, M. and Breschi, M., 'La fecondità', in Barbagli, M. and Kertzer, D. I. (eds), *Storia della famiglia Italiana, 1750–1950*, Bologna, Il Mulino, 1992.

Lovenduski, J., Norris, P. and Burness, C., 'The Party and Women', in Seldon, A. and Ball, S. (eds), *Conservative Century: the Conservative Party Since 1900*, Oxford, Oxford University Press, 1994.

Lovenduski, J. and Hills, J. (eds), *The Politics of the Second Electorate*, London, Routledge & Kegan Paul, 1981.

Lowe, R., *The Welfare State in Britain since 1945*, Basingstoke, Macmillan, 1999 (first published, 1993).

——, 'The Second World War, Consensus and the Foundations of the Welfare State', *Twentieth Century British History*, 1, 2 (1990).

Lumley, R. and Morris, J., *The New History of the Italian South. The Mezzogiorno Revisited*, Exeter, Exeter University Press, 1997.

Luzzatto Fegiz, P., *Il volto sconosciuto dell'Italia, 10 anni di sondaggi Doxa*, Milano, Giuffré, 1956.

——, *Il volto sconosciuto dell'Italia. Seconda serie*, 1956–1965, Milano, Giuffré, 1966.

Mackenzie, N. (ed.), *Conviction*, London, MacGibbon, 1959.

Macleod, I. and Powell, E., *The Social Services – Needs and Means*, London, CPC, 1952.

Macnicol, J., 'The Effect of the Evacuation of School Children on Official Attitudes to State Intervention', in Smith, H. L. (ed.), *War and Social Change. British Society in the Second World War*, Manchester, 1986.

Makarenko, A. S., *Consigli ai genitori*, Roma, Tipografia dell'Orso, 1950.

——, *Bandiere sulle torri*, Roma, Cultura Sociale, 1955.

——, *La marcia dell'anno '30*, Roma, A. Amando, 1960.

——, *Poema pedagogico*, Roma, Rinascita, 1955.

——, *Selected Pedagogical Works*, Moscow, Progress Publishers, 1990.

Malinowski, B., 'Parenthood – the Basis of the Social Structure', in Calverton, V. F. and Schmalhausen (eds), *The New Generation. The Intimate Problems of Modern Parents and Children*, London, Oxford University Press, 1954.

Mancina, C., *La famiglia*, Roma, Editori Riuniti, 1981.

Marazziti, M., 'Cultura di massa e valori cattolici: il modello di Famiglia Cristiana', in Riccardi, A. (ed.), *Pio XII*, Roma-Bari, 1984.

Marshall, T. H.,*Citizenship and Social Class and Other Essays*, Cambridge, Cambridge University Press, 1950.

——, *Class, Citizenship and Social Development: Essays by T.H. Marshall*, Garden City, Doubleday, 1964.

Marsiglio, W., *Procreative Man*, New York and London, New York University Press, 1998.

Martin, X., 'The Paternal Role and the Napoleonic Code', in L. Spaas (ed.), *Paternity and Fatherhood, Myths and Realities*, Basingstoke and London, Macmillan, 1998.

Martina, G., *La Chiesa in Italia negli ultimi 30 anni*, Roma, Studium, 1977.

Martinelli, R., *Storia del Partito Comunista Italiano. Il 'Partito Nuovo' dalla Liberazione al 18 Aprile*, Torino, Einaudi, 1995.

Marxism and the Family, Selected Contributions from a Discussion in Marxism Today, London, Communist Party Pamphlet, 1974.

Mattai, G., 'La società familiare', in *Enciclopedia Sociale*, I, Torino, 1958.

Maxwell, A., *The Home Office, its Functions in relation to the treatment of Offenders. Second Annual Lecture in Criminal Science*, delivered at Cambridge on October 31, 1947, London, Stevens & Sons Ltd, 1948.

——, *The Institutional Treatment of Delinquents, The Ninth Clarke Hall Lecture*, London, The Clarke Hall Fellowship, 1950.

Mead, L., 'From Welfare to Work: lessons from America', in Deacon, A. (ed.), *From Welfare to Work: Lessons from America*, London, Institute of Economic Affairs, 1997.

Melchiorre, V., *Amore e matrimonio nel pensiero filosofico e teologico moderno*, Milano, Vita e Pensiero, 1976.

Melograni, P. and Scaraffia, L., *La famiglia Italiana dall'Ottocento a oggi*, Bari, Laterza, 1988.

Il messaggio sociale di Pio XII, Milano, Vita e Pensiero, 1942.

Mezzardi, L., 'Catholicism in Italy', in Jedin, Repgen, Dolan, *History of the Church*, Vol. x., London, 1980.

Middleton, N., *When Family Failed. The Treatment of Children in the Care of the Community During the First Half of the Twentieth Century*, London, Victor Gollancz, 1971.

Millham, S., Bullock, R. and Hosie, K., *Locking Up Children. Secure Provision Within the Child-Care System*, Westmead, Saxon House, 1978.

Minella, A., Spano, N. and Terranova, F. (a cura di), *Cari bambini vi aspettiamo con gioia. Il Movimento di Solidarietà Popolare per la Salvezza dell'Infanzia negli anni del Dopoguerra*, Milano, Teti Editore, 1980.

Mitterauer, M. and Sieber, R., *The European Family. Patriarchy to Partnership from the Middle Ages to the Present*, Oxford, Blackwell, 1982.

Montagnana, R., *La maternità e l'infanzia nell'URSS*, Soc, Ed. L'Unità, 1945.

——, *La famiglia, il divorzio, l'amore (nel pensiero delle donne comuniste)*, Roma, APE, 1945.

Montini, L., *Verso la Costituente. Relazione al Congresso della DC di Brescia il 30 Settembre 1945*, Brescia, Ed. Morcelliana, 1945.

Morgan, D. H. J., *The Family, Politics, and Social Theory*, London, Routledge and Kegan Paul, 1985.

——, *Family Connections. An Introduction to Family Studies*, Cambridge, Polity, 1996.

Morris, T., *Crime and Criminal Justice*, Oxford, Blackwell, 1989.

Mort, F., *Dangerous Sexualities. Medico-Moral Politics in England Since 1830*, London, Routledge & Jegan Paul, London, 1987.

Moscucci, O., *The Science of Woman. Gynaecology and Gender in England, 1800–1929*, Cambridge, Cambridge University Press, 1990.

Mosse, G. L., *The Image of Man. The Creation of Modern Masculinity*, New York-Oxford, Oxford University Press, 1996.

Mount, F., *The Subversive Family. An Alternative History of Love and Marriage*, London, Jonathan Cape, 1982.

Murray, C., *Losing Ground: American Social Policy, 1950–1980*, New York, Basic Books, 1984.

Myrdal, A. and Klein, V., *Women's Two Rules, Home and Work*, London, Routledge & Kegan Paul, 1956.

Nenni, P., *Una battaglia vinta*, Roma, edizioni Leonardo, 1946.

Niccoli, O. (a cura di), *Infanzie*, Firenze, Ponte alle Grazie, 1993.

Noce, T., *Rivoluzionaria professionale*, Milano Bompiani, 1977.

Nye, F. I. and Berardo, F. M., *The Family, Its Structure and Interaction*, New York-London, Macmillan, 1973.

Oakley, A., 'A Case of Maternity: Paradigms of Women as Maternity Cases', in *Signs, Journal of Women in Culture and Society*, 4, 4 (1979).

O'Gorman, F., *Conservative Thought from Burke to Thatcher*, London, Longman, 1986.

Orfei, R., *L'occupazione del potere. I Democristiani, '45/'75*, Milano, Longanesi, 1976.

Osgerby, B., *Youth in Britain since 1945*, Oxford, Blackwell, 1998.

Paci, M., *La struttura sociale italiana*, Bologna, Il Mulino, 1982.

——, *Pubblico e privato nei moderni sistemi di welfare*, Napoli, Liguori, 1989.

Packman, J., *The Child Generation. Child Care Policy in Britain*, Oxford, Blackwell and Robertson, 1981 (first published, 1975).

Page, R. M. and Silburn, R., *British Social Welfare in the Twentieth Century*, Basingstoke, Macmillan. 1999.

Pain Relief in Childbirth, The Family Planning Association, London, 1953.

Parker, R., 'The Gestation of Reform: the Children Act, 1948', in Bean, P. and MacPherson (eds), *Approaches to Welfare*, London, Routledge and Kegan and Paul, 1983.

Parsons, T., 'The Social Structure of the Family', in R. N. Anshen (ed.), *The Family: its Function and Destiny*, New York, 1959.

——, 'The American Family: Its Relations to Personalities and to the Social Structure', in Parsons, T. and Bales, R. F., *Family Socialisation and Interaction Process*, London, Routledge and Kegan Paul, 1956.

Pascall, G., *Social Policy: a New Feminist Analysis*, London, Routledge, 1997.

Pavone, C., *Una guerra civile. Saggio storico sulla moralità della Resistenza*, Torino, Bollati Boringhieri, 1991.

——, 'La continuità dello Stato. Istituzioni e uomini', *Italia, 1945–48,le Origini della Repubblica*, Torino, Giappichelli, 1974.

Pearson, G., *Hooligan. A History of Respectable Fears*, Basingstoke, Macmillan, 1983.

Pedersen, S., *Family, Dependence and the Origin of the Welfare State. Britain and France 1914-1945*, Cambridge, Cambridge University Press, 1993.

Peplar, M., *Family Matters. A History of Ideas about the Family since 1945*, London, Longman, 2002.

Petrone, I., 'Madri che lavorano nella societa moderna', *Maternità e Infanzia*, 22, 9, (1951).

Philp, A. F., *Family Failure. A Study of 129 Families with Multiple Problems*, London, Faber and Faber, 1963.

Philp, A. F. and Timms, N., *The Problem of the 'Problem Family'. A Critical Review of the Literature Concerning the 'Problem Family' and Its Treatment*, London, Family Service Units, 1957.

Piccone Stella, S. and Saraceno, C., *Genere. La costruzione sociale del fmminile e del maschile*, Bologna, Il Mulino, 1996.

Pini, I., 'Duecentomila bambini negli istituti Italiani per l'infanzia', *Maternità e Infanzia*, 2, March-April (1951).

Pinna, L., *La famiglia esclusiva. Parentela e cientelismo in Sardegna*, Bari, Laterza, 1971.

Piretti, M. S., 'La stampa democristiana; tra prospettiva personalista e preoccupazione garantista', in Ruffilli, R. (a cura di), *Costituente e lotta politica. La stampa e le scelte costituzionali*, Firenze, Vallecchi, 1978.

Piro, F., *Comunisti al potere: economia, società e sistema politico in Emilia Romagna,1945–1965*, Venezia, Marsilio, 1983.

Pizzorno, A., 'Familismo amorale e marginalità storica ovvero perché non c'è niente da fare a montegrano', in Banfield, E. P., *Le basi morali di una società arretrata*, Bologna, Il Mulino, 1976.

Poggi, G., *The State. Its Nature, Development and Prospects*, Cambridge, Polity Press, 1990.

Politi, M., 'I Diritti vengono da Dio, non dallo Stato', *La Repubblica*, 16 October, 2005.

Pombeni, P., *La Costituente*, Bologna, Il Mulino, 1995.

——, *Il Gruppo Dossettiano e la fondazione della Democrazia Cristiana (1943–1948)*, Bologna, Il Mulino, 1979.

——, Pombeni, P., 'Il Gruppo Dossettiano', in R. Ruffilli (a cura di), *Cultura politica e partiti nell'età della Costituente*, Bologna, 1979.

Powell, J. E., Maude, A., *Change is Our Ally*, London, CPC, 1954.

——, *The Welfare State*, London, CPC, 1961.

Preti, D., 'Uno stato sociale senza riforme', *Italia Contemporanea*, 176, (1992).

Prochaska, F., *Women and Philanthropy in Nineteenth Century England*, Oxford, Oxford University Press, 1980.

——, *The Voluntary Impulse. Philanthropy in Modern Britain*, London, Faber and Faber, 1988.

Pugh, M., *State and Society. A Social and Political History of Britain 1870–1997*, London, Arnold, 1999 (first ed. 1994).

——, *Women and the Women's Movement in Britain, 1914–1999*, Basingstoke, Macmillan, 2000.

Pugliaro, M. V., 'Essere madre', *Maternità e Infanzia*, 23, 1–3 (1959).

Putnam, R., *The Beliefs of Politicians. Ideology, Conflict and Democracy in Britain and Italy*, New Haven, Yale University Press, 1973.

——, *Making Democracy Work*, Princeton, Princeton University Press, 1993.

Pye, L. N. and Verba, S. (eds), *Political Culture and Political Development*, Princeton, Princeton University Press, 1965.

Quine, M. S., *Population Politics in Twentieth-Century Europe*, London, Routledge, 1996.

——, *Italy's Social Revolution. Charity and Welfare from Liberalism to Fascism*, Basingstoke, Palgrave, 2002.

Raison, T., *Tories and the Welfare State*, Basingstoke, Macmillan, 1990.

Ravaioli, C., *La questione femminile: intervista col PCI*, Milano, Bompiani, 1976.

Ravera, C., *Diario di trent'anni*, Roma, Editori Riuniti, 1973.

Reekie, G., *Measuring Immorality. Social Inquiry and the Problem of Illegitimacy*, Cambridge, Cambridge University press, 1998.

Rendel, L., 'The Administrative Framework', in *Children Without Homes*, Proceedings of a Conference called in London by the Women's Group on Public Welfare, 8–9 February, 1945, London, The National Council of Social Service, 1945.

Rhodes, R. A. W., 'A Squalid and Politically Corrupt process? Intergovernmental Relations in Post-war Period', *Local Government Studies*, 11, 6, November–December, (1985).

Riccardi, A., (a cura di), *Le Chiese di Pio XII*, Roma-Bari, Laterza, 1986.

——, 'Governo e profezia nel Pontificato di Pio XII, in A. Riccardi (a cura di), *Pio XII*, Bari, Laterza, 1984.

Riley, D., *War in the Nursery. Theories of the Child and Mother*, London, Virago, 1983.

Rose, J., *For the Sake of the Children: Inside Dr. Barnardo's: 120 Years of Caring for Children*, London, Hodder and Stoughton, 1987.

Rose, N., *Governing the Soul: the Shaping of the Private Self*, London, Routledge, 1990.

Rose, R. (ed.), *Studies in British Politics*, London, Macmillan, 1966.

——, 'England: a Traditionally Modern Political Culture', in Pye, L. N., Verba, S., *Political Culture and Political Development*, Princeton, 1965.

——, *Cultura politica e partiti nell'età della Costituente*, Bologna, Il Mulino, 1979.

Ruffini, E., 'Il matrimonio alla luce della teologia Cattolica' in Melchiorre, V., *Amore e matrimonio nel pensiero filosofico e teologico moderno*, Milano, 1976.

Russo, A. (a cura di), *La pedagogia del collettivo*, Torino, Paravia, 1976.

San Secondo, R., 'Bimbi senza nome', in *Maternità e Infanzia*, 19, 1, September–October, (1947).

Saraceno, C., 'La nuclearità della famiglia contemporanea, Un assioma problematico', in *Quaderni di Sociologia*, 2 (1973).

——, 'Women, Family and the Law 1750–1942', in *Journal of Family History*, XV, 4 (1990).

——, 'Le donne nella famiglia: una complessa costruzione giuridica", in Barbagli, M. and Kertzer, D. I., *Storia della famiglia Italiana 1750–1950*, Bologna, 1992.

——, 'The ambivalent familism of the Italian welfare state', in *Social Politics*, 1 (1994), 1.

——, *Mutamenti della famiglia e politiche sociali in Italia*, Bologna, Il Mulino, 1998.

Sartori, G., *Parties and Party System, a Framework for Analysis*, 2v., Cambridge, Cambridge University Press, 1976.

Sassoon, D., *The Strategy of the Italian Communist Party. From the Resistance to the Historic Compromise*, London, Frances Pinter, 1981.

——, *One Hundred Years of Socialism. The West European Left in the Twentieth Century*, London, Tauris, 1996.

——, *Contemporary Italy. Politics, Economy and Society Since 1945*, Harlow, Longman, 1997 (first published, 1986).

Savalli, G., 'Maternità e lavoro', *Maternità e Infanzia*, 19, 1, September–October (1947).

——, 'Struttura organizzativa e partecipazione di base nel PCI', in Savini, G. (a cura di), *Partiti e partecipazione politica in Italia. Studi e ricerche di sociologia politica*, Milano, Giuffré, 1972.

Scattigno, A., 'La figura materna tra emancipazionismo e femminismo', in D'Amelia, M., *Storia della maternità*, Roma-Bari, 1997.

Schmideberg, M. *Children in Need*, London, George Allen and Unwin, 1948.

Schmolke, M., 'Information and the Mass Media', in Jedin, Repgen and Dolan (eds), *History of the Church*, Vol. x, London, 1980.

Scoppola, P., *La proposta politica di De Gasperi*, Bologna, Il Mulino, 1977.

——, 'Chiesa e società negli anni della modernizzazione', in A. Riccardi, (a cura di), *Le Chiese di Pio XII*, Roma-Bari, Laterza, 1986.

Scott, J., *Gender and the Politics of History. Revised Edition*, New York, Columbia University Press, 1999.

Scroppo, E., *Donna, privato e politico. Storie personali di 21 Donne del PCI*, Milano, Mazzotta, 1979.

Sheridan, M. D., 'The Intelligence of 100 Neglectful Mothers', *British Medical Journal*, 14 January, (1956),

Shorter, E., *The Making of the Modern Family*, New York, Basic Books, 1975.

Showstack Sassoon, A., *Women and the State*, London, Routledge, 1992 (first published, 1987).

——, 'Women's New Social Role: Contradictions of the Welfare State', in Showstack Sassoon, A. (ed.), *Women and the State*, London, Routledge, 1992 (first published, 1987).

Signorelli, A., 'Il pragmatismo delle donne. La condizione femminile nella trasformazione delle campagne' in *Storia dell'agricoltura Italiana in età contemporanea*, 11, (1990).

——, 'Ancora sul pragmatismo femminile', in N. Ginantempo (a cura di), *Donne del Sud. Il prisma femminile sulla questione meridionale* , Palermo, 1993.

Small, R., 'Marxism and the Family', in *Marxism and the Family, Selected Contributions from a Discussion in Marxism Today*, London, Communist Party Pamphlet, 1974.

Smith, H. L. (ed.), *War and Social Change. British Society in the Second World War*, Manchester, Manchester University Press, 1986.

Spaas, L. (ed.), *Paternity and Fatherhood, Myths and Realities*, Basingstoke and London, Macmillan, 1998.

Spano, N. and Camarlinghi, F., *La questione femminile nella politica del PCI*, Roma, Edizioni Donne e Politica, 1972.

Spence, J. C., *The Purpose of the Family. A Guide to the Care of Children*, London, The Epworth Press, 1947 (first published, 1946).

——, *A Thousand Families in Newcastle-Upon-Tyne. An Approach to the Study of Health and Illness in Children*, London, Oxford University Press, 1954.

Spriano, P., *Storia del Partito Comunista Italiano*, Torino, Einaudi, 1976.

Starkey, P., *Families and Social Workers. The Work of Family Service Units, 1940–1985*, Liverpool, Liverpool University Press, 2000.

Stephens, T. (ed.), *Problem Families: an Experiment in Social Rehabilitation*, Pacifist Service Units, Liverpool, 1947.

Stevenson, O., 'Reception Into Care – Its Meaning for All Concerned', in Tod, R. J. N. (ed.), *Children in Care. Papers on Residential Work*, London, Longman, 1976 (first published, 1968).

Stroud, J., *An Introduction to the Child Care Service*, London, Longmans, 1965.

Sumner, W. G., *Folkways*, Boston, Ginn & Co./The Athenaeum Press, 1907.

Tamburrino, G., *La filiazione*, Torino, UTET, 1984.

Tanner, D., Thane, P. and Tiratsoo, N., *Labour's First Century*, Cambridge, Cambridge University Press, 2000.

Teichman, J., *Illegitimacy. A Philosophical Examination*, Oxford, Blackwell, 1982.

Temple, W., *Christianity and Social Order*, Harmondsworth, Penguin, 1942.

Terracini, U., *Come nacque la Costituzione*, Roma, Editori Riuniti, 1978.

Thane, P., *Foundations of the Welfare State*, London, Longman, 1996.

Therborn, G., *Between Sex and Power. Family in the World, 1900–2000*, London, Routledge, 2004.

Thomas, R., *Children Without Homes. How Can They Be Compensated for the Loss of Family Life?*, London, National Association for Mental Health, 1946.

Thomas, W. and Znaniecki, F., *The Polish Peasant in Europe and America. Monograph of an Immigrant Group*, 5 vv., Boston, Richard G. Badger, 1918–1920.

Thompson, P., 'Labour's "Gannex Conscience"? Politics and Popular Attitudes in the "Permissive Society"', in Coopey, R., Fielding, S. and Tiratsoo, N., *The Wilson Government, 1964–1970*, London, 1993.

Timmins, N., *The Five Giants. A Biography of the Welfares State*, London, Harper Collins, 1995.

Titmuss, R., *Essays on Welfare State*, London, George Allen and Unwin, 1958.

——, *Social Policy, an Introduction*, London, Allen and Unwin, 1974.

Tod, R. J. N. (ed.), *Children in Care. Papers on Residential Work*, London, Longman, 1976 (first published, 1968).

Townsend, P., *The Family Life of Old People*, London, Routledge and Kegan Paul, 1957.

——, 'A Society for People', in N. Mackenzie (ed.), *Conviction*, London, 1959.

Trabucchi, C., *Parole chiare di un medico agli sposi*, Milano, Istituto La Casa, 1955.

Travis, Alan, 'Blair Spells Out his Mmasterplan for a Safer, Fairer Society', *The Guardian*, 11 January, 2006.

Tucker, T. F., *Children Without Homes. The Problem of the Their Care and Protection*, London, The Bodley Head, 1952.

Tullio Altan, C., *La nostra Italia. Arretratezza socioculturale, clientelismo, trasformismo, e ribellismo dall'Unità a oggi*, Milano, Feltrinelli, 1986.

——, *Gli Italiani in Europa. Profilo storico comparato delle identità nazionali Europee*, Bologna, Il Mulino, 1999.

Turner, J., *Macmillan*, London, Macmillan, 1994.

——, 'A Land Fit for Tories to Live in: the Political Ecology of the British Conservative Party, 1944–94', *Contemporary European History*, 4, 2 (1995).

Ulivieri, S., 'Alfabetizzazione, processi di scolarizzazione femminile e percorsi professionali, tra tradizione e mutamento', in S. Ulivieri (a cura di), *Educazione e ruolo femminile. La condizione delle donne in Italia dal dopoguerra ad oggi*, Scandicci, La Nuova Italia, 1992.

Ungerson, C., *Policy is Personal: Sex, Gender and Informal Care*, London, Tavistock, 1987.

——, *Gender and Caring: work and the Welfare in Britain and Scandinavia*, Hemel Hampstead, Harvester Wheatsheaf, 1990.

Unione, *Per il bene dell'Italia, Programma di governo 2006–2011*, Roma, 2006.

Veronese, L. D., 'Per una maggiore tutela del lattante', *Maternità e Infanzia*, 17, 4–5 (1942).

——, 'Bambini mendicanti', *Maternità e Infanzia*, 22, 1, January–February (1950).

Vigorelli, A., 'Orfanotrofi', *Maternità e Infanzia*, 3, May–June (1948).

Vincent, C. E., *Unmarried Mothers*, New York, Free Press of Glencoe, 1961.

Violante, A., *I rapporti di filiazione e le azioni di stato*, Napoli, Jovene, 1983.

Wall, R. (ed.), *Family Forms in Historic Europe*, Cambridge, Cambridge University Press, 1983.

Wall, W. D. and Freud, A., *The Enrichment of Childhood*, London, The Nursery School Association of Great Britain, 1962.

Wand, J. W. C., *What the Church of England Stands For*, London, Mowbarry & Co., 1951.

——, *Seven Steps to Heaven*, London, Longman, 1956.

——, *The Church Today*, Harmondsworth, Penguin, 1960.

Weber, M., 'Italy', Lovenduski J. and Hills J. (eds), *The Politics of the Second Electorate*, London, 1981.

Webster, W., *Imagining Home, Gender, 'Race' and National Identity, 1945–1964*, London, UCL, 1998.

Wertz, R. W. and Wertz, D. C., *Lying-In. A History of Childbirth in America*, New Haven, Yale University Press, 1989 (originally published 1977).

White, R. J., *The Conservative Tradition*, London, Nicholas Kaye, 1950.

Williams, F., *Rethinking Families*, London, Calouste Gulbekian Foundation, 2004.

Williamson, P., *Stanley Baldwin. Conservative Leadership and National Values*, Cambridge, Cambridge University Press, 1999.

Wilson, E., *Women and the Welfare State*, London, Tavistock, 1977.

——, *Only Halfway to Paradise: Women in Post-war Britain, 1945–1968*, London, Tavistock, 1980.

Wimperis, V., *The Unmarried Mother and Her Child*, London, George Allen & Unwin, 1960.

Winch, R. F., 'Some Observations on Extended Familism in the United States' in Winch, R. F. and Goodman L. W. (eds), *Selected Studies in Marriage and the Family*, New York, Holt, Rinehart and Winston, 1968 (first published 1953).

Winnicott, D.W., *Getting to Know Your Baby*, London, Heinemann/The New Era, 1945.

——, *The Ordinary Devoted Mother and Her Baby. Nine Broadcast Talks (Autumn 1949)*, London, C. A. Brock &Co., 1949.

——, *The Child and the Family. First Relationships*, London, Tavistock Publications, 1957.

——, *The Child, the Family, and the Outside World*, Harmondsworth, Penguin, 1964.

Woman's Place in the World. Address by His Holiness Pope Pius XII, Dublin, Catholic Truth Society of Ireland, 1946.

Women's Group on Public Welfare,*The Neglected Child and His Family*, London, Oxford University Press, 1948.

Wood, K., *The Story of St. Mary's Cold Ash*, Child Care Study Paper n. 7, Church of England Children's Society, 1981.

Woodroofe, K., *From Charity to Social Work in England and the United States*, London, Routledge &Kegan Paul, 1962.

You and Your Children, BBC Talks by a Woman Medical Psychologist (Dr. Doris Odlum), Ministry of Health, London, HMSO, 1946.

Young, M. and Willmott, P., *Family and Kinship in East London*, London, Routledge and Kegan Paul, 1957.

——, *The Symmetrical Family*, London, Routledge and Kegan Paul, 1973.

Younghusband, E., *Social Work in Britain: 1950–1975*, 2 vol., London, 1978.

Zamagni, V., *Dalla periferia al centro, la seconda rinascita economica dell'Italia, 1961–1981*, Bologna, Il Mulino, 1990.

Zaretsky, E., 'The Place of the Family in the Origins of the Welfare State', in Thorne, R. and Yalom, M. (eds), *Rethinking the Family: Some Feminist Questions*, New York, Longman, 1982.

Zweig, F., *Labour, Life and Poverty*, London, Victor Gollancz, 1948.

——, *The British Worker. A Social and Psychological Study, Presenting the Problems, Difficulties and Struggles of the Ordinary Men at Home, Work, and His Leisure Hours*, Harmondsworth, Penguin, 1952.

Zweiniger-Bargielowska, I., 'Explaining the Gender Gap: the Conservative Party and the Women's Vote', in Francis, M. and Zweiniger-Bargielowska, I. (eds), *The Conservative and British Society*, Cardiff, 1996.

Index